WHITMAN AMONG THE BOHEMIANS

D1561682

THE IOWA WHITMAN SERIES

Ed Folsom, series editor

Whitman
among the Bohemians

EDITED BY JOANNA LEVIN & EDWARD WHITLEY

UNIVERSITY OF IOWA PRESS, IOWA CITY

University of Iowa Press, Iowa City 52242

Copyright © 2014 by the University of Iowa Press

www.uiowapress.org

Printed in the United States of America

Design by Richard Hendel

The University of Iowa Press is a member of Green Press Initiative and is committed to preserving natural resources.

Printed on acid-free paper

ISSN: 1556-5610

Library of Congress Cataloging-in-Publication Data

Whitman among the Bohemians / edited by Joanna Levin and Edward Whitley.

pages cm.—(The Iowa Whitman Series)

Includes bibliographical references and index.

ISBN 978-1-60938-272-8 (pbk)

ISBN 978-1-60938-293-3 (ebk)

1. Whitman, Walt, 1819–1892—Criticism and interpretation. 2. Bohemianism—United States—History—19th century. 3. Bohemianism in literature. I. Levin, Joanna, editor of compilation. II. Whitley, Edward Keyes, editor of compilation.

PS3238.W44 2014

811′.3—dc22   2014010201

CONTENTS

ACKNOWLEDGMENTS

We are very grateful for the many people, institutions, and organizations that have supported this project along the way, beginning with Eliza
Richards, whose first, enthusiastic "yes!" to the idea of a collection of
essays on Whitman and the bohemians let us know that we were on the
right track. Ed Folsom, the series editor for the Iowa Whitman Series, and
everyone associated with the University of Iowa Press—Charlotte Wright,
Elisabeth Chretien, Joseph Parsons, and the anonymous peer reviewer—
have been supportive and encouraging at every step of the process. We
also thank Alfred Bendixen and the American Literature Association for
giving us a venue to try out early versions of the material that appears
in this collection, as well as Leif Eckstrom for organizing a panel at the
annual conference of the Modern Language Association to do the same.
Other scholars to whom we are indebted for thoughtful suggestions, encouraging words, nods of approval at conference presentations, and other
forms of support include Gavin Jones, Virginia Jackson, Mark Lause,
Bryan Waterman, Renee Sentilles, Karen Sanchez-Eppler, Leon Jackson, Jerome Loving, Ezra Greenspan, Michael C. Cohen, Vivian Pollak,
Robert S. Levine, and Martha Nell Smith.

Whitman among the Bohemians would not exist without its digital
counterpart, The Vault at Pfaff's: An Archive of Art and Literature by the
Bohemians of Antebellum New York (http://lehigh.edu/pfaffs). Robert
Weidman and Julia Maserjian have provided continued support for The
Vault at Pfaff's since 2004. We are all tremendously indebted to them and
to everyone else who has contributed to this website over the course of the
past ten years. We are particularly grateful to Kurt Hoberg not only for in-
dexing every issue of the *New York Saturday Press* for The Vault at Pfaff's
as an undergraduate research assistant, but also for returning as a post-
graduate to help format and copyedit *Whitman among the Bohemians* for
publication. We also thank Ed Folsom and Ken Price for making the Walt
Whitman Archive the invaluable resource that it is.

We are grateful to the University of Iowa Press and the *Walt Whitman
Quarterly Review* for permission to reprint, in modified form, Amanda

Gailey's "Walt Whitman and the King of Bohemia: The Poet in the *Saturday Press*" and Robert J. Scholnick's "'An Unusually Active Market for Calamus': Whitman, *Vanity Fair*, and the Fate of Humor in a Time of War, 1860–1863." These essays appeared in issues 25.4 (2008) and 19 (2002), respectively. We are similarly grateful for permission to reprint the images that appear on the cover of this book and in chapters 8 and 11 by the New York Public Library, the Rare Book and Manuscript Library at the University of Illinois at Urbana-Champaign, and the Thomas Biggs Harned Collection at the Library of Congress.

ABBREVIATIONS

BDT   *Brooklyn Daily Times.* Brooklyn, NY: Bennett and Smith, 1855–1932.

Corr.   *Walt Whitman: The Correspondence.* 6 vols. Edited by Edwin Haviland Miller. New York: New York University Press, 1961–1977.

LG   Walt Whitman, *Leaves of Grass.* Philadelphia: David McKay, 1891–1892.

LG55   Walt Whitman, *Leaves of Grass.* Brooklyn, NY: n.p., 1855.

LG56   Walt Whitman, *Leaves of Grass.* New York: Fowler and Wells, 1856.

LG60   Walt Whitman, *Leaves of Grass.* Boston: Thayer and Eldridge, 1860.

NUPM   Walt Whitman, *Notebooks and Unpublished Prose Manuscripts.* 6 vols. Edited by Edward Grier. New York: New York University Press, 1984.

PW   Walt Whitman, *Walt Whitman Prose Works 1892.* 2 vols. Edited by Floyd Stovall. New York: New York University Press, 1963.

SP   *New York Saturday Press.* New York: Henry Clapp Jr., 1858–1860 and 1865–1866. Available at The Vault at Pfaff's, http://lehigh.edu/pfaffs.

VF   *Vanity Fair.* New York: Frank J. Thomson, 1859–1863. Available at Making of America, http://quod.lib.umich.edu/m/moagrp/.

WWA   The Walt Whitman Archive. Edited by Ed Folsom and Kenneth M. Price. http://www.whitmanarchive.org.

WWC   Horace Traubel, *With Walt Whitman in Camden.* 9 vols. Various publishers, 1906–1996.

Note: The following sources are available online at the Walt Whitman Archive: LG, LG55, LG56, LG60, and WWC.

INTRODUCTION

JOANNA LEVIN & EDWARD WHITLEY

At some point in 1861 or 1862, Walt Whitman pulled out the notebook that he had been using to jot down ideas and keep track of the names of new friends (and lovers) and wrote the beginnings of a poem that he titled "The Two Vaults." He never published the poem, and, given that he describes only one of the vaults promised in the title, we can assume that he never finished it either. As it stands, this poem fragment gives us a glimpse into Whitman's brief tenure with the self-styled bohemians of antebellum New York who gathered at Charles Pfaff's beer cellar to drink and talk.

> The vault at Pfaffs where the drinkers and laughers meet to eat and
>   drink and carouse
> While on the walk immediately overhead, pass the myriad feet of
>   Broadway
> As the dead in their graves, are underfoot hidden
> And the living pass over them, recking not of them,
> Laugh on laughters! [*sic*] Drink on drinkers!
> Bandy the jests! Toss the theme from one to another!
> Beam up—Brighten up, bright eyes of beautiful young men!
> Eat what you, haveing ordered, are pleased to see placed before you—
>   after the work of the day, now, with appetite eat,
> Drink wine—drink beer—raise your voice.
> Behold! your friend, as he arrives—Welcome him, when, from the
>   upper step, he looks down upon you with a cheerful look
> Overhead rolls Broadway—the myriad rushing
> The lamps are lit—the shops blaze in—the fabrics and jewelry are
>   seen through the plate glass windows
> The strong lights from above pour down upon them and are shed
>   outside
> The thick crowds, well-dressed—the continual crowds as if they
>   would never end

The curious appearance of the faces—the glimpses first caught of the
    eyes and expressions, as they flit along.
(You phantoms! oft I pause, yearning, to arrest some one of you!
Oft I doubt your reality—whether you are real—I suspect all is but a
    pageant.)
The lights beam in the first vault—but the other is entirely dark
In the first[1]

Whitman joined the "drinkers and laughers" at Pfaff's sometime around
1858. "I used to go to Pfaff's nearly every night," he wrote later in life, remi-
niscing that, as it grew dark, "Pfaff would politely invite everybody who
happened to be sitting in the cave he had under the sidewalk to some other
part of the restaurant" so that the group of writers, artists, and intellectuals who came to the underground bar at 647 Broadway could continue
with their efforts to transport a European-style bohemianism from Paris's
Latin Quarter to downtown Manhattan. Whitman continued, "There was
a long table extending the length of this cave; and as soon as the Bohemians put in an appearance . . . there was as good talk around that table as
took place anywhere in the world."[2]

Whitman found Pfaff's at a low point in his career: the first two editions of *Leaves of Grass* in 1855 and 1856 had received a modest amount
of critical praise, but the public acclaim that Whitman thought he deserved had never materialized. The bohemians at Pfaff's, as Whitman recounts in "The Two Vaults," lifted his spirits at a time when he desperately
needed it. They gave him friendship and laughter—in addition to wine
and beer. They introduced him to "beautiful young men." They engaged
with him both playfully ("Bandy the jests!") and intellectually ("Toss the
theme from one to another!"). If "The Two Vaults" is any indication, they
also commiserated with him on the financial pitfalls of a literary career:
the poem contrasts the struggling writers and artists in the dimly lit vault
with the "well-dressed" shoppers on Broadway who bask in the electric
glow of midcentury prosperity as "the shops blaze" with a light that the
bohemians experience only second-hand ("The strong lights from above
pour down upon them") in the same way that the workers in the antebellum culture industry—writers, artists, journalists, actors, musicians, all
of whom were represented at Pfaff's—got little more than the leftovers
from the feasts that adorned the tables of bourgeois New York. Perhaps it
is this feeling of being overlooked by the dominant culture of the city that

led Whitman to compare the bohemians to "the dead in their graves . . . underfoot hidden."

At the same time, though, by depicting the entombed bohemians in the double-vaulted ceiling of the basement beer cellar, the poem inaugurates the enduring trope of a countercultural "underground," quite literally dividing the emerging bohemian-bourgeois opposition into above-ground and below-ground locations. In their sepulchral "vault at Pfaffs," the bohemians provide a paradoxically vibrant antithesis to the "well-dressed," reified "phantoms" who haunt the sidewalk overhead, those whose "myriad feet" march to the relentless beat of "myriad rushing" Broadway and whose human vitality has been extinguished by blazing lights and the vivid fabric of the marketplace. But below ground, the bohemians speak in loud voices and spark witticisms and have bright eyes.

Fellow Pfaffian Fitz-James O'Brien posited a similar dichotomy between the bohemians and the bourgeoisie in his "Counter-Jumps. A Poemettina.—After Walt Whitman," one of the many Whitman parodies that the patrons of Pfaff's published at the time:

> I am the Counter-jumper, weak and effeminate.
> I love to loaf and lie about dry-goods.
> I loaf and invite the Buyer.
> I am the essence of retail. The sum and result of small profits and
>   quick returns.
>
> .   .   .   .   .   .
>
> I sound my feeble yelp over the woofs of the World.[3]

Absurdly reducing Whitman to petit bourgeois status, the parody would seem to operate ironically, highlighting everything that Whitman—that larger-than-life bohemian who would "loafe and invite his soul" and sound his "barbaric yawp"—was not.[4] And yet, much like the unfinished poem "The Two Vaults," O'Brien's parody unsettles the very bohemian-bourgeois division that it appears to support. The bohemians did rely on small profits and quick returns on their writing, and they did "lie" about their goods and "invite the Buyer" at a time when they often found themselves questioning whether there was in fact a market for literature "in a money-grubbing community like this."[5] But just as Whitman relished his distance from the bourgeois marketplace in his retreat at Pfaff's, so too did he long to "arrest" the passersby, to promote his 1860 edition of *Leaves of Grass* (which he did with the help of bohemian compatriots like O'Brien), and to forge a wider community.

That community thrived in physical locations like Pfaff's bar and the West Forty-second Street apartment of Ada Clare, a writer, actress, and journalist who was universally regarded as the "Queen of Bohemia." (The same notebook in which Whitman wrote "The Two Vaults" also contains Clare's name and address.) In addition to these physical locations, the bohemian community came to life in the pages of *Vanity Fair* and the *New York Saturday Press*, literary weeklies that prominently featured work by the Pfaff's crowd and that, throughout 1860, threw their collective support behind promoting the third edition of *Leaves of Grass*. Whitman was, by no means, the "King of Bohemia"—that title went to Henry Clapp Jr., the founding editor of the *Saturday Press*—but the bohemians embraced and supported him at a crucial moment in his career. Scholars have known for years that the Pfaff's bohemians were instrumental in elevating Whitman and his poetry at a time when he most needed it, but to a large degree that has been the extent of the bohemians' presence in Whitman scholarship: they are little more than background characters who swelled a scene or two before Whitman left New York for the more noble work of tending to the wounded and dying in the hospitals of Civil War Washington.

But there is more to the story of Whitman's sojourn among the bohemians than that. Like "The Two Vaults" itself, scholarship on Whitman and the bohemians is unfinished—in some cases unpublished—and largely unread.[6] Albert Parry's *Garrets and Pretenders: A History of Bohemianism in America*, published in 1933, was the first real attempt to place Whitman among the bohemians. Parry was generous enough to dedicate a handful of chapters of his historical survey of American bohemianism to the Pfaff's scene—which was more than the token chapter that Van Wyck Brooks gave them in *The Times of Melville and Whitman* in 1947—but by the time of the centennial celebration of *Leaves of Grass* in 1955 Malcolm Cowley could still refer to Whitman's bohemian years as "a curious period in Whitman's life that . . . has never been properly interpreted."[7]

Despite Cowley's call to action, scholarship on the Pfaff's bohemians only trickled in over the next forty years. In 1967 Emily Hahn updated Parry's *Garrets and Pretenders* with her *Romantic Rebels: An Informal History of Bohemianism in America*, and in 1979 Gene Lalor published the first scholarly article on Whitman and the Pfaff's bohemians.[8] None of the major Whitman biographies from the twentieth century gave more than a few pages to the bohemians, so in 1993, at Ed Folsom's behest, historian Christine Stansell wrote an article for the *Walt Whitman Quarterly Review* that attempted to fill in the gaps left by these biographies with further information about the antebellum bohemians and the cultural contexts within which they operated.[9] Nevertheless, by 1998 the entry on "Pfaff's Restaurant" in *Walt Whitman: An Encyclopedia* would lament that "the depth and importance of [the bohemians'] influence on [Whitman] remain uncertain, principally because of scanty and contradictory evidence."[10]

Within the past decade, however, scholars have unearthed a wealth of new evidence and opened up new interpretive possibilities not only for understanding Whitman's relationship to bohemianism (and the bohemians' relationships with Whitman), but also for exploring the national and transnational role of "bohemia" as a mobile and cosmopolitan territory of aspiring artists, writers, and rebel souls who gravitate toward, in Ada Clare's words, "all things above and beyond convention."[11] Robert J. Scholnick, Amanda Gailey, and Stephanie M. Blalock each published articles in the *Walt Whitman Quarterly Review* on the bohemians' involvement in periodicals such as *Vanity Fair* (Scholnick) and the *Saturday Press* (Gailey) and the homosocial gatherings of men that presaged the emergence of New York's gay counterculture generations later (Blalock).[12] Karen Karbiener has given perhaps the most detailed account of Whitman's time at Pfaff's in an essay that puts the 1860 *Leaves of Grass* within the context of the activities of the antebellum bohemians.[13] Joanna Levin's survey of U.S. bohemianism, *Bohemia in America, 1858–1920*, begins with an analysis of how Whitman and the Pfaffians first "transplanted" *la vie bohème* from the "mother asphalt of Paris" and reconfigured bohemian-bourgeois opposition—a fluid and ever-shifting opposition that, in the antebellum context, highlighted tensions between the national and the cosmopolitan, the democratic and the elite, and the public and the private. In his 2009 microbiography *Walt Whitman and the Civil War: America's Poet during the Lost Years of 1860–1862*, Ted Genoways provided many new insights about Whitman and the bohemians—including the revelation that Ellen Eyre, a mysterious "woman" in Whitman's life who frequented Pfaff's, was actually a cross-dressing man who attempted (with little success) to scandalize Whitman by revealing his true gender after several nights of intense flirtation. Historian Mark A. Lause's *The Antebellum Crisis and America's First Bohemians*, published around the same time, was the first study to take seriously the Pfaffians' relationship to radical political movements, and Daniel Cottom's *International Bohemia: Scenes of Nineteenth-Century Life* situates Whitman and the bohemians in a broad, transatlantic network of bohemian movements in England, Italy, Spain, Germany, and of course France. Similarly, Virginia Jackson's forthcoming *Before Modernism: Nineteenth-Century American Poetry in Public* reconsiders Whitman's relationship to the idea of a national reading public by examining the reception of his poetry in the bohemian *Saturday Press*. In addition to all of this published scholarship, Lehigh University's digital archive The Vault at Pfaff's has, since 2006, made widely accessible every issue of the bohemians' primary literary organ, the *Saturday Press*, along with detailed information about more than 150 figures associated in one way or another with the Pfaff's scene.

Whitman among the Bohemians contributes to this growing body of scholarship with twelve essays that follow Whitman's experiences with the antebellum bohemians from his initial discovery of the counterculture scene at Pfaff's to his relationships with individual bohemians and beyond. In "Bridging Brooklyn and Bohemia: How the *Brooklyn Daily Times* Brought Whitman Closer to Pfaff's," Karen Karbiener asks why Whitman inconvenienced himself with lengthy ferry and omnibus rides to get to Pfaff's when so much of his personal and professional life was centered in Brooklyn and finds the answer in the poet's editorial work for the *Brooklyn Daily Times*. As the editor of the *Times*, Whitman not only had regular opportunities to travel to neighboring Manhattan to report on cultural and political events, but he also had sufficient income to pay for both the commute and the rounds of lager beer that he had developed a taste for at German taverns in Williamsburg. The political temper of the *Brooklyn Daily Times*—which Karbiener says "was in tandem with bohemian politics"—also facilitated Whitman's transition from Brooklynite to Manhattan bohemian, which in turn provided opportunities for him to leave his post at the *Times* and pursue his poetry more actively.

Perhaps the greatest opportunity that opened up for Whitman during his time at Pfaff's was the active support that he received from Henry Clapp Jr., the "King of Bohemia" and the editor of the literary weekly the *New York Saturday Press*. As Amanda Gailey demonstrates in "Walt Whitman and the King of Bohemia: The Poet in the *Saturday Press*," Clapp published more than forty-five poems, parodies, reviews, and notices by or about the poet (not counting advertisements) from the end of 1859 and into 1861. Gailey reveals that not only did Clapp's support prove instrumental in ensuring the success of the 1860 edition of *Leaves of Grass*, but the *Saturday Press* also ended up presenting Whitman as "a factional poet of the North." Biographers such as David Reynolds have held that the antebellum bohemians were "without political direction" and that they did "virtually nothing" to address "the intensifying slavery crisis."[14] Gailey, in contrast, presents a much more complicated picture of the bohemians' political commitments and Whitman's role in furthering their cause.

Henry Clapp and the publishing practices of the *Saturday Press* are also the focus of Ingrid Satelmajer's essay "Publishing Pfaff's: Henry Clapp and Poetry in the *Saturday Press*." Complementing Gailey's profile of Clapp as the principal architect behind Whitman's revived career in 1860, Satelmajer looks beyond the Whitman-related material in the *Saturday Press* and finds that Clapp published poetry according to a philosophy of literary composition that "aligned poetry with a social environment [that is, Pfaff's bar] that valued collaborative entertainment . . . over solitary genius." Scholars have known for years that the *Saturday Press* played a key role in promoting Whitman's poetry at a vulnerable time in the poet's career; what we have not fully appreciated is that the paper also had a life outside of Whitman, a life centered on creating poetry that was playful and collaborative (even to the point of being derivative) rather than one that was entirely focused on canonizing the great works of a major poet.

Leif Eckstrom's essay "On Puffing: *The Saturday Press* and the Circulation of Symbolic Capital" similarly reconsiders the bohemians' support of Whitman in the *Saturday Press* from within the context of Henry Clapp's editorial policies. Eckstrom takes Clapp to task for his professed disdain of "puffing," the common practice among newspaper editors to run positive reviews of recently published books in exchange for advertising dollars from the books' publishers. Clapp repeatedly claimed that the *Saturday Press* was opposed to "the whole system of Puffing," a claim that gave increased credibility to his efforts to promote Whitman and his poetry.[15] It was also a claim that was not borne out by the facts: throughout 1860 the *Saturday Press* was "financially dependent upon Thayer and Eldridge's publishing house," the firm responsible for the third edition of *Leaves of Grass*. Eckstrom demonstrates that Clapp's compromise on the issue of puffing was part of a larger "set of conflicted exchanges that wrestled with the possibility of autonomy in the literary marketplace and underscored the stakes of symbolic capital production in late-antebellum New York."

Joanna Levin's "'Freedom for Women from Conventional Lies': The

'Queen of Bohemia' and the Feminist Feuilleton" demonstrates that Ada Clare, the undisputed "Queen of Bohemia," connected her own refusal to "puff" in the *Saturday Press* to her feminist commitments. Though her characterization of Augusta Evans's *Beulah* as "sentimentalism of the blabbiest sort" apparently led its publishers to pull their ads from the periodical, Clare insisted that she would never compromise her "honest convictions." Many of the convictions that she articulates most strongly in her trenchant, witty, and passionate weekly column "Thoughts and Things" concern representations of women in literature, on the stage, and in salacious gossip. Just as she yoked her dismissal of *Beulah* to gender politics, so did she link her praise of Whitman—and of bohemia at large—to the cause of female emancipation from "conventional lies."

Similar to Levin's demonstration of "how [Ada] Clare's support of Whitman fit into *her* larger bohemian agenda" rather than the other way around, Edward Whitley's essay "Whitman, the Antebellum Theater, and the Cultural Authority of the Bohemian Critic" considers how a group of bohemian theater critics used Whitman's burgeoning reputation as both a poet and a public figure to bolster their own cultural authority. These critics—Fitz-James O'Brien, Edward G. P. "Ned" Wilkins, and William Winter—regularly retreated to Pfaff's to talk about the current offerings in the New York theater and dish on the city's most popular actors, actresses, and stage managers. O'Brien, Wilkins, and Winter almost always found themselves disagreeing with the consensus of the majority of theatergoers, which left them more than a little anxious over their presumed authority as cultural tastemakers. On a number of occasions in the theater criticism that they published in the *Saturday Press*, they turn to the poetry and public persona of Walt Whitman in an effort to anchor their cultural authority, revealing that the bohemians were as likely to enlist Whitman's support for their own agendas as they were to leverage whatever cultural capital they had at their disposal to support the third edition of *Leaves of Grass* in 1860.

Beyond the *Saturday Press*, Robert J. Scholnick shows that the bohemians also played a central role in the creation of the comic weekly *Vanity Fair* in 1859. The bohemians similarly used this new periodical to foreground Whitman's work through playful parodies and, more generally, to feature humorous commentary and illustrations as a means of deflating bourgeois "pomposity, hypocrisy, and the cant of politicians, preachers, and literary highbrows." In "'An Unusually Active Market for Calamus:'

Whitman and *Vanity Fair*," Scholnick analyzes the references to Whitman that appeared in the periodical between 1860 and 1862, all of which highlighted varying aspects of Whitman's persona and poetic style as part of the bohemian effort to prime the market for "the grass school of poetry" and forge a sense of collective identity, both through the bohemian-bourgeois opposition and teasing, self-referential in-jokes.

Vanity Fair and the *Saturday Press* were close cousins, both in their shared origins around the tables at Pfaff's and in their common project to imagine new forms of countercultural identity. The artists and illustrators associated with *Vanity Fair* that Ruth Bohan profiles in her essay "Whitman and the 'Picture-Makers'" include well-known figures such as political cartoonist Thomas Nast and Dickens illustrator Sol Eytinge, as well as lesser-known artists like Ned Mullen, whom Whitman regarded as a close personal friend. Bohan's essay expands on a line of argument from her 2006 book *Looking into Walt Whitman: American Art, 1850–1920* that Whitman's "association with the artists and writers at Pfaff's gave renewed impetus to his concerns with matters of identity and its pictorial manifestations." Specifically, Bohan details the regular interactions between Whitman and these bohemian artists over issues of identity formation, visual representation, and the management of one's public persona. As she writes, "the question of bohemian identity and its pictorial manifestations was a recurring focus of the nightly discussions at Pfaff's."

Logan Esdale's close reading of the 1860 *Leaves of Grass* from within the context of its reception by both the Pfaff's bohemians and the public at large reveals that, while the bohemians were among Whitman's most ardent supporters, they were not his most careful readers. In "Adorning Myself to Bestow Myself: Reading *Leaves of Grass* in 1860," Esdale argues that in their eagerness to embrace Whitman as a poet who had stripped naked both poetry and the human body, the Pfaff's bohemians missed a crucial element in Whitman's evolving poetic theory: the notion of *adornment* as a concept that mediates between *nakedness* as a raw and unmediated state of purity, and the *ornamentation* of both conventional poetry, with its overly formalized versification, and of overly repressed human beings ashamed of their unclothed bodies. In contrast, Esdale posits that *adornment* fuses the natural and the expressive while at the same time "nam[ing] the body's extensions" into spiritual, literary, and erotic embraces.

One such extension of Whitman's poetic project was the Fred Gray Association. In "'Tell what I meant by *Calamus*': Walt Whitman's Vision

of Comradeship from Fred Vaughan to the Fred Gray Association,"
Stephanie M. Blalock provides the most detailed account to date of this
group of young middle-class and upper-class bachelors who began to
socialize with Whitman at Pfaff's in late 1861 or early 1862. Though the
"Calamus" poems were published in 1860, Whitman later suggested to
Horace Traubel that the story of this group of men was essential for conveying the meaning of his poems of "manly attachment." It is this narrative
that Blalock reconstructs, demonstrating that Whitman became close to
the men of the Fred Gray Association in the wake of his relationship with
the stage driver Fred Vaughan. While Vaughan shied away from the label
"Sincere Friend," the Fred Gray Association, Blalock argues, "represented
both the extension of 'adhesiveness' to a larger group of men and a step
toward the 'City of Friends' he imagined in the 'Calamus' poems."

The desire to express and "adorn" the self through intersubjective bonds
was one that Whitman shared with fellow bohemian Adah Isaacs Menken.
In "Whitman and Menken, Loosing and Losing Voices," Eliza Richards explores Menken's deeply conflicted attempts to adopt Whitman's style and
poetic agenda, alongside her quest to find a community of readers that
would allow her meaning to crystallize and be understood. Famous for
her scandalous relationships and racy performances (she achieved international notoriety in a theatrical adaptation of *Mazzepa* by appearing in
a nude body stocking, lashed to the back of a horse), "the Menken" was
best known for one of the principal qualities that the bohemians revered
in Whitman: a transgressive nakedness. Yet, just as Whitman recognized
that nakedness could be tantamount to dangerous exposure, so Menken
discovered that her status as what Richards calls "a hyperembodied
actress" paradoxically inhibited poetic self-expression, preventing her
from emulating Whitman's representative selfhood. Whereas Ada Clare
celebrated both Whitman and female performers as conduits to liberatory
inner depths, Menken found her effort to "loose" her own voice stymied
by Whitman's example and her status as an objectified performing self.

In 1885, another onetime Pfaffian, the poet, critic, and stockbroker
Edmund Clarence Stedman, initiated a major step in the canonization
of Whitman by including a chapter on the poet in his anthology *Poets of
America*. Mary Loeffelholz's "Stedman, Whitman, and the Transatlantic
Canonization of American Poetry" analyzes "Stedman's pioneering consideration of Whitman's place in American poetry," noting that his account was also "a retrospective investigation of bohemia by one of its

own former habitués." Cognizant of the extent to which the marketing of bohemia—and of Whitman as a bohemian—depended upon the staging of bohemian-bourgeois opposition, Stedman cast a somewhat jaundiced eye on the phenomenon; perhaps recalling Clapp's own marketing strategies, Stedman addressed the subsequent "transatlantic poetic network of friendship, backbiting, and patronage that William Michael Rossetti enlisted in Whitman's support in 1876," a network that once again used claims of Whitman's supposed rejection by American readers as the occasion to rally the poet's supporters and to help sell his latest edition of *Leaves of Grass*, in this case, the *Centennial Edition*. Sharing the Pfaffians' marketing strategies, this transatlantic circuit nonetheless highlighted a different Whitman: not the naked poet stripped free of the cumbersome layers of civilization, but the polar opposite—an "over-refined," even decadent poet who, in Stedman's words, "utters the cry of culture for escape from over-culture" and opposes "rough conventionalism" to the "conventionalism of culture."

The essays in this collection tell a story about Whitman's experiences among the bohemians that begins with Whitman finding his way from Brooklyn to Pfaff's (Karbiener), and from there into the pages of the *Saturday Press* (Gailey), a publication that experimented with modes of poetic composition (Satelmajer) as it struggled to navigate the competitive publishing market of antebellum New York (Eckstrom). While at Pfaff's, Whitman rubbed shoulders with artists (Bohan), theater people (Whitley), women writers (Levin and Richards), and the contributors to yet another bohemian periodical, *Vanity Fair* (Scholnick). He was adored by some of the Pfaffians (Blalock), misunderstood by others (Esdale), and left a lasting impression on at least one erstwhile bohemian who later emerged as a tastemaker of American poetry (Loeffelholz).

The narrative arc that we have traced out over the course of these essays is but one of many that could be told about the bohemians of antebellum New York. Much could still be said about the drug and alcohol use (and abuse) among the "drinkers and laughers" whom Whitman wrote about. Pfaff's regular Fitz Hugh Ludlow, for example, published *The Hasheesh Eater* (an American take on Thomas De Quincey's infamous 1821 book *Confessions of an English Opium Eater*) in 1857, and the inaugural issue of the *Saturday Press* in 1858 featured William North's short story "The Living Corpse," which tells of an addict who inadvertently kills his wife and embalms himself through a noxious combination of legal and illegal drugs.[16] The bohemians' influence on the antebellum theater also has yet to be fully chronicled—dozens of actors, playwrights, stage managers, and other theater folk regularly gathered at Pfaff's—as does their effect on the U.S. publishing industry at precisely the moment when the center of gravity in American literary culture was shifting from Boston to New York. And although we have focused on the *Saturday Press* and *Vanity Fair* in these essays because of Whitman's looming presence in their pages, other New York periodicals—such as the *Leader*, the *Tribune*, the *Times*, the *Illustrated News*, and *Harper's*—featured works by Pfaffians who remained in the city after Whitman took up residence in Washington, D.C. These periodicals were interconnected via relationships nurtured in underground beer halls and makeshift living-room salons in ways that we have yet to fully comprehend.

And of course the story of Whitman among the bohemians continues to this day, as subsequent generations once again discover that the poet remains both tantalizingly present and elusive, "somewhere waiting" for us to catch up with him.[17] From the hobohemians to contemporary hipsters, Whitman still commands center stage, providing an ever-magnetic focal point for countercultural self-fashionings. Even though in the years immediately following the bohemia at Pfaff's several genteel bohemians defined themselves against Whitman's more earthy version (Bret Harte, for instance, characterized bohemia as a "fairy land, full of flowers" and distanced himself from those who "don't like flowers . . . [and] want Leaves of Grass, dirt and all"), later bohemians, much like their antebellum counterparts, recognized in Whitman and his poems the quintessence of the bohemian spirit. In "Bohemia as It Is Not" (1903), Mary Heaton Vorse observed that bohemia "was a kingdom that existed more between the covers of books than anywhere else," and for many a would-be bohemian the most vivid evocation of what they hoped to find and create in bohemia already existed between the covers of *Leaves of Grass*.[18]

Consider, for instance, Floyd Dell, one of the editors of the *Masses*, the latter-day bohemian periodical that helped to shape the Greenwich Village of the 1910s, who claimed that Whitman had "renovated the modern soul, and made us see, without any obscene blurring by Puritan spectacles, the goodness of the whole body"—adding, in a statement that Ada Clare may well have endorsed, "This is as much a part of the women's movement as the demand for a vote." And Max Eastman, another editor of the *Masses*, who echoed Whitman's declaration that "amativeness is just as divine as spirituality," affirming that this was Whitman's "chief contribution to human culture—or to those humans who can raise themselves to it." Here again was the "savage," antibourgeois (or anti-Puritan, in the parlance of the 1910s) Whitman that the *Saturday Press* trumpeted, the poet who defied prudery and united soul and body.[19]

This too was the Whitman that a young Jack Kerouac hailed in an essay written for Alfred Kazin's literature course in 1948 that he titled "Whitman: A Prophet of the Sexual Revolution." By reading Whitman, Kerouac glimpsed "a world where it is finally admitted that we want to mate and love, and eat and sleep, and bask in the days and nights of our true, fundamental life."[20] And through emulating Whitman's poetic style, Kerouac hoped to find and express the self that might achieve such "fundamental life": "Tap from yourself the song of yourself, *blow!—now!—your* way is your only way—'good'—or 'bad'—always honest, ('ludicrous'), spontaneous, 'confessional' interesting, because not 'crafted.'"[21] Malcolm Cowley described Kerouac as a "jived up Whitman," and *Time Magazine* insisted that Kerouac's friend Allen Ginsberg was the "discount-house Whitman of the Beat Generation"; but whatever the modifier, commentators were convinced that Whitman's spirit lived on in the Beats.[22] And despite *Time*'s dig about his lesser status, Ginsberg no doubt welcomed the link to Whitman, an association he reinforced in his poetry and prose again and again, perhaps most explicitly in his 1980 series of recorded observations "Allen Ginsberg on Walt Whitman: Composed on the Tongue."

Here, the famous poet laureate of the Beat Generation reflects on his predecessor, and returns him to his bohemian roots: "Pfaff's was a bar he used to go to, a Bohemian hang-out, a downstairs beer hall, sort of like a German *bierstuben*. Bohemian friends used to meet there, probably like a gay gang, plus a newspaper gang, plus a theatrical gang, and the opera singers, and some of the dancers, a Broadway crowd sort of, way down, downtown though. And that was his hang-out."[23]

Ginsberg sensed that these "gangs," and this downtown location, mattered a great deal to Whitman and that they were somehow integral to his poetic and personal development. *Whitman among the Bohemians* tells the story of these intersecting social and professional groupings that converged on the basement beer cellar in the late 1850s and early 1860s. The essays in this collection fill out the vague notions that Ginsberg had about Whitman's bohemian days, opening multiple avenues of scholarly inquiry as we travel "way down" through the layers of history and print to rediscover what animated both the vault at Pfaff's and the subsequent generations of bohemians who have continued to recognize Whitman as their comrade.

NOTES

1. *NUPM* 1:454–55.

2. "A Visit to Walt Whitman," *Brooklyn Eagle*, July 11, 1886. Brooklyn Daily Eagle Online. http://eagle.brooklynpubliclibrary.org.

3. Fitz-James O'Brien, "Counter Jumps," *VF*, Mar. 17, 1860.

4. *LG60*, 23, 104.

5. "Bohemian Walks and Talks," *Harper's Weekly* (1858), quoted in Parry, *Garrets and Pretenders*, 58.

6. We are aware of a handful of unpublished scholarly works on the antebellum bohemians, including a biography of Ada Clare by Gloria Goldblatt and a dissertation by Eugene T. Lalor titled "The Literary Bohemians of New York City in the Mid-Nineteenth Century" (Ph.D. diss., St. John's University, 1977). A colleague has also shared with us his experience reviewing an unpublished book-length manuscript arguing that Whitman's poetry was influenced by drug use (specifically opium), with one chapter devoted to drug use at Pfaff's.

7. Cowley, Introduction, vii.

8. Lalor, "Whitman among the New York Literary Bohemians."

9. Stansell, "Whitman at Pfaff's."

10. Yannella, "Pfaff's Restaurant," 515.

11. Clare, "Thoughts and Things," *SP*, Feb. 11, 1860.

12. Gailey, "Walt Whitman"; Scholnick, "'Unusually Active Market'"; Blalock, "My Dear Comrade." Gailey's and Scholnick's articles are reprinted in modified form in the present volume, along with a new essay by Blalock.

13. Karbiener, "Whitman at Pfaff's."

14. Reynolds, *Walt Whitman's America*, 377.

15. "Characteristics of *The New York Saturday Press*," *SP*, Dec. 11, 1858.

16. See Auclair, "Language of Drug Use."

17. *LG60*, 104.

18. Harte, "The Bohemian Concerning," *Golden Era*, Nov. 11, 1860; Vorse, "Bohemia as It Is Not," *Critic* 43, no. 2 (1903): 177–78.

19. Dell, *Women as World Builders*, 48; Eastman, *Enjoyment*, 293.

20. Kerouac quoted in Maher, *Kerouac*, 174.

21. Kerouac, "Essentials of Spontaneous Prose," in Charters, *Portable Beat Reader*, 58.

22. Cowley and *Time Magazine* quoted in Theado, *Beats*, 162, 84.

23. Ginsberg, "Allen Ginsberg on Walt Whitman: Composed on the Tongue" (1980), in Perlman, Folsom, and Campion, eds., *Walt Whitman*, 332.

WHITMAN AMONG THE BOHEMIANS

Bridging Brooklyn and Bohemia

How the *Brooklyn Daily Times* Brought Whitman Closer to Pfaff's

KAREN KARBIENER

The stretch of years between the second and third editions of *Leaves of Grass* remains a particularly quiet moment in the unfolding story of Walt Whitman's life and work. Even so, little attention has been given to his association with the *Brooklyn Daily Times* between 1856 and 1860 and the ways in which these experiences may have helped transform the self-proclaimed "Brooklyn Boy" into a regular at Pfaff's Cellar Saloon, the hip hub of Manhattan's literary culture. This essay attempts to bridge these two as yet disconnected, relatively obscure moments in Whitman's life to bring light to his most significant and interesting decade as an artist.

Whitman's association with the *Brooklyn Daily Times* became a standard inclusion in Whitman chronologies after the publication of Emory Holloway's and Vernolian Schwarz's 1932 study *I Sit and Look Out: Editorials from the Brooklyn Daily Times*. Holloway's claim that Whitman edited the paper from May 1857 through June 1859 was supported by Gay Wilson Allen in *The Solitary Singer: A Critical Biography of Walt Whitman* (1955); in *Walt Whitman: An Encyclopedia* (1998), Dennis Renner notes that Whitman as editor wrote "more than 900 *Times* items," though scholarly examination of this work remains "incomplete."[1] Indeed, despite the long history of the critical acceptance of Whitman's *Times* editorship, scholarship on this period remains thin—much thinner than on Whitman's work for the *Brooklyn Daily Eagle*, though this editorial sit there was shorter and produced fewer journalistic writings.

{1}

The lack of a follow-up study to *I Sit and Look Out* helps explain why Whitman's experiences at Pfaff's have not been seen in light of his employment immediately preceding (and perhaps even coinciding with) them. But the incomplete scholarship is also an indicator of the lingering doubts regarding Whitman's *Times* editorship. In his 1999 biography *Walt Whitman: The Song of Himself*, Jerome Loving makes a strong argument against Whitman as editor based on two points: Holloway's lack of empirical evidence and the conservative slant of many of the editorials attributed to Whitman, written "at a time when Whitman was radicalizing American poetry in theme as well as manner."[2] Indeed, inconsistent editorial practices in *I Sit and Look Out*, as well as the surprisingly divergent opinions professed in *Times* editorials on subjects such as women's rights and the death penalty, call into question Holloway's claims.

Whitman himself claimed to have worked as an "editorial writer" for the *Brooklyn Daily Times* "in 1856, or just before," and to have had editorial sway over the paper on the subject of the Brooklyn Water Works, completed on December 12, 1858.[3] A prose draft on "Important Questions in Brooklyn" regarding the newly completed Water Works lies on the verso of a "Calamus" manuscript; according to Fredson Bowers and Gay Wilson Allen, it is the basis for a *Times* editorial published on or around March 16, 1859.[4] Whether or not Whitman was the sole editor of the newspaper, the case for his regular and extended employment at the *Times* is further substantiated on both biographical and political grounds by his unusual decision to patronize Pfaff's in the late 1850s. Whitman was not the type to become a regular at a bar; he had not been one before and would not drink regularly again elsewhere. Frequenting Pfaff's required a considerable investment of Whitman's limited funds and time, as it was a six-mile round trip from his Brooklyn home. The saloon's location at 647 Broadway was at the center of the "most intense cultural commerce" in the United States and convenient for artists and writers who worked for or reported on the attractions of the immediate neighborhood, but certainly not for Whitman.[5] And the scene there was not really his: Whitman never felt entirely comfortable with or accepted by the bohemians with whom he kept company at Pfaff's. He was not considered a radical by the rest of the group; he was never a socialite; he was not even a "Manhattanese," though he gave himself this title in several poems. Whitman had lived and worked in Manhattan for brief periods and was a lifelong spectator of its cultural offerings and street life, but he did not participate in Manhattan life as a native New Yorker.[6] Though he had drawn inspiration from Manhattan, Whitman and his *Leaves* were rooted in the quieter, greener streets of Brooklyn. And yet by mid-1859, he began spending most evenings in Manhattan's fashionable bohemian enclave and did so for more than three years. What inspired Whitman to find and then stay in this place, so far from his experience in so many ways?

Whitman encountered many closed doors during these trying first years as a poet; working at the *Times* would have kept some of them open and might have helped open up new ones—including the entry to Pfaff's cellar. His employment at the newspaper would have stabilized his precarious economic situation until mid-1859 and might even have supplied him with a supply of scrap paper, the blue defunct "City of Williamsburgh" tax forms upon which many "Calamus" poems were drafted. He thus had the funds, for at least a short period, needed to commute to and drink at Pfaff's—even with the physical means to compose freely and at his leisure. The *Times*'s Republican-leaning but independent political stance was in tandem with bohemian politics, whereas most Pfaffians would have been considerably less welcoming to an editor of a Democratic organ such as the *Brooklyn Daily Eagle*. Additionally, the *Times*'s changing demographics would have tested Whitman's ability to adapt his voice to different audiences, readying him for the bigger challenge of fitting in at Pfaff's. The *Times* would have brought him physically closer to the saloon by way of the Grand Street Ferry, and its Williamsburg location might have introduced him to German culture and to the lager and gemütlichkeit he would so enjoy at Pfaff's. He would have met another Brooklynite who managed the leap over the East River and found success in the cultural whirl of downtown New York City. Most importantly, the *Times* editorship would have kept him writing, reading, and in contact with urban culture even as his lack of success as a poet might have taken him off his literary course.

If Whitman did indeed write for the *Times* within or around this time span, he and the newspaper at large would have been a likely team with much in common. They had both become ambitious contenders in the local publishing industry in the late 1840s; they welcomed the challenge of an expanded, diversified readership; they were independent and free thinking in their political and social views, though the excitement around the new Republican Party in the mid-1850s had encouraged their cautious support of John Frémont, the party's first presidential candidate. And they seem to have been mutually supportive: as the *Times* prospered through this period, the first three editions of *Leaves of Grass* all received positive notice on the paper's editorial page.[7]

If Whitman began working for the newspaper in or after 1856, he would have known it as a well-regarded four-page daily that vied with the *Eagle* for Brooklyn's widest circulation. Started in 1848 by George Bennett, Aaron Smith, and Egbert Guernsey, the *Williamsburgh Daily Times* fought to establish a readership in the independent city of Williamsburg, where four papers already competed for the public's attention.[8] Its politically independent status and the "uncommon energy and ambition" of twenty-three-year-old Bennett helped the *Times* flourish.[9] It moved from a "one story shanty" to a three-story brick building in 1850 and in 1852 congratulated itself that "we have a circulation larger than that of any other paper in town."[10] When Williamsburg consolidated with Brooklyn in 1855, the paper's potential readership grew and Bennett changed its name to the *Brooklyn Daily Times* to cater to the new market. Bennett became sole proprietor in 1856 and sold out his shares of the *Times* to Bernard Peters in 1868.[11]

Though the *Times* was at its humble beginnings when Whitman was fired from his *Eagle* position, records indicate that the younger paper needed only two years to catch up to the well-established daily. *The Catalogue of Newspapers and Periodicals Published in the United States* lists the *Eagle* as a Democratic daily with a circulation of eighteen hundred, while the *Williamsburgh Times* was a daily "neutral" paper with a circulation of two thousand.[12] These numbers must have increased dramatically for both papers over the next ten years, particularly because of the annexation of Williamsburg and Bushwick to Brooklyn in 1855. *The American Newspaper Directory and Record of the Press for 1860* records a population increase in Brooklyn from 96,836 in 1850 to 273,425 in 1860, making Brooklyn the third largest city behind New York and Philadelphia.[13] Despite its growing size, only three dailies supported Brooklyn's population in 1860: the *Eagle*, the *Times*, and the *Long Island Star*—with only the *Eagle* and the *Times* still publishing in 1865.[14] Bennett's ambition and success, along with his hiring the former *Eagle* editor, may explain why the *Eagle* often targeted the *Times* in its abusive campaigns.[15]

The Brooklyn historian Henry Reed Stiles describes the *Brooklyn Daily Times* as "a prosperous local newspaper" that was a "success from the start"; in his *History of the City of Brooklyn*, it is the "*sine qua non* to the inhabitants of the 'Burgh."[16] And yet, Stiles notes, "The *Brooklyn*

Eagle, by primogeniture, circulation, and influence, deservedly claims the first place among its contemporaries."[17] Indeed, the *Eagle* grew bigger, lived longer, and has been more lovingly memorialized than its old rival. Just as Whitman was beginning his affiliation with the *Times*, the political situation in the United States solidified the *Eagle*'s stance as the Democratic organ of the Democratic city of Brooklyn.

"In 1841 the Democrats of the county received representation in a new newspaper, the *Brooklyn Eagle and Kings County Democrat*," announces Stephen Ostrander in his *History of the City of Brooklyn and Kings County*.[18] One of its founders, Isaac Van Anden, remained at the helm until 1872. A member of the conservative faction of the Democratic Party known as the Hunkers, Van Anden steered the paper toward a "strong pro-slavery position" and thus represented public opinion for the city of Brooklyn.[19] The seriousness with which Van Anden took his politics is demonstrated by his termination of Whitman's employment in 1848, a year when tensions among Democrats had reached a fever pitch, with both the radical Barnburners and the more moderate Free Soilers (favored by Whitman at this time) abandoning the Democratic Party.

Like the majority of Brooklynites and most other Brooklyn newspapers, the *Eagle* did not favor Lincoln in the 1860 election.[20] In fact, the *Eagle*'s lukewarm support of the war and the administration inspired a hostile mob of several hundred to gather in April 1861. "Show us your colors, hang out your flag," they demanded; when a night watchman did so, the mob moved on to other "less than patriotic" newspapers, the *Brooklyn City News*, the weekly *Brooklyn Standard*, and the *Star*.[21] Despite such altercations, or because of them, the *Eagle* prospered during the Civil War, when "it enlarged its news service and gained in political influence as well as in material prosperity."[22] Visiting Brooklyn from Washington in 1864, Whitman was overwhelmed by the size and energy of the political rallies against the current administration.[23] "I do not know what move I shall make, but something soon, as it is not satisfactory any more in New York & Brooklyn," he complained to William O'Connor, chagrined by the number of people he saw wearing buttons supporting George B. McClellan's run against Abraham Lincoln in the 1864 election. "I should think nine-tenths, of all classes, are copperheads here."[24]

While the *Eagle* "had become a lusty leader of public opinion" in Brooklyn during the war, the *Brooklyn Daily Times*, "on the other side of the city was making for itself a creditable name."[25] Ostrander's description of the paper referred to its location across the old Williamsburg/Brooklyn divide, as well as its politics. A "Historical Sketch" in a commemorative *Times* publication relates its move to the "other side" with great drama:

> In the beginning, the *Williamsburgh Times* was without political inclination, but the anti-slavery movement made a strong appeal to the quick intelligence of its founder, and, in 1856, he swung his newspaper into line for Frémont. With pen and tongue Bennett supported "the pathfinder," and four years later he entered the battle for the election of Abraham Lincoln with a burning enthusiasm and a fiery eloquence that brought his publication to the front rank of those who were supporting the cause of a free people living in an indissoluble United States.[26]

The *Times*'s change from political independence to Republicanism was not quite as direct as this propagandistic piece suggests. Though the paper did support Frémont in the 1856 presidential election and came to favor the Republican Lincoln in the 1860s, it maintained its nonpartisanship through the intermittent period. In its relatively thin coverage of the Lincoln-Douglas debates of 1858, the *Times* cautiously supported Stephen A. Douglas for his status as an "independent Representative" who might now organize "a great middle conservative party, neither proscribing slavery, like Seward, nor fostering it, like Buchanan."[27] In local elections of the time, too, the *Times* urged readers to vote for "principle over party."[28]

The *Times*'s strong independent streak and simmering Republican inclinations through the late 1850s ran concurrently with Whitman's politics of the time. It should be noted that critical opinions vary widely on his politics during this period, and Whitman complicated matters by claiming that he did not support any single party.[29] But for the 1856 election at least, the former editor of Brooklyn's Democratic organ took interest in the charismatic Republican nominee Frémont and included a positive notice (if not direct support) of him in the political tract "The Eighteenth Presidency!"[30] Whitman did not publish the essay, and there is no evidence of his intention to write another political tract for the 1860 presidential election; perhaps his engagement in Republican politics flagged when Frémont could not answer his call for a "Redeemer President of These States." But on February 19, 1861, Lincoln's appearance in New York left an impression on Whitman that lasted for decades. Though he did not count himself among the few supporters of Lincoln in the crowd, that day marked the beginning of his worshipful allegiance to the man he would later call America's "first great Martyr Chief," "precious to this Union—precious to Democracy—unspeakably and forever precious."[31]

Did the *Times* help steer Whitman toward Republicanism? Certainly Bennett would have been an active political guide as an employer. The *Times*'s proprietor, who "devoted much of his time to politics" even while "he still managed to take the leadership of the editorial staff,"[32] would later run for commissioner of public works and city assemblyman on the Republican ticket himself.[33] Working alongside of him undoubtedly would have been a political education for Whitman, particularly in the newly emerging Republican Party. But even reading the *Times* might have influenced his politics, and there are signs that Whitman was doing so at the time—further, that the *Times* was reading Whitman. Whitman's self-review of *Leaves of Grass* (and one of the earliest reviews of the first edition) appeared in the *Times* on September 29, 1855; on December 17, 1856, one of the very few reviews of the second edition was published. The *Times* supported his work and possibly his family; it provided a fresh alternative to the messy Democratic politics Whitman had become embroiled in at the *Eagle*; it was young and independent but also critical and engaged. It hardly seems coincidental that the politics of Whitman and the *Times* ran parallel to each other.

The bohemian movement emerged from the same political crisis that created the new Republican Party. In *The Antebellum Crisis and America's First Bohemians*, Mark Lause notes that "most radicals embraced the Republican campaigns," particularly during the party's inaugural years, taking places "among the officers and speakers at the large Republican campaign rallies in New York." Their activities revolved around the new "Mechanics and Workmen's Central Republican Union," launched in September 1856 to welcome "all workingmen favorable to the cause of Free Labor, Free Soil and Frémont and Dayton."[34] The rhetoric and aims of the union activists are similar to those found in "The Eighteenth Presidency!," which may well have been written with such an audience in mind.

Indeed, Whitman's interest in the emergence of the Republican Party—and the zeitgeist that led him to the *Brooklyn Daily Times*—also might have brought the bohemians to his attention. American bohemianism and the Republican Party were both rooted in the dissatisfactions Whitman expressed in his essay: in the rampantly corrupt U.S. political landscape, in the factionalism and disunity created by petty rivalries among "old politicians." In 1856, Whitman, Republicans, and bohemians were united in their belief that a new political era was necessary and imminent, and that Frémont might turn out to be the "Redeemer President." After the energy around the 1856 election disintegrated, bohemians quickly became disillusioned by what looked like old party politics among Republicans; by the time Whitman arrived at Pfaff's, most of the revelers (including Clapp) had become ambivalent to Republicanism.[35] So, too, had Whitman and the *Times*, at least until the next presidential election. As Whitman's connection with the *Times* had made him more sympathetic to and engaged by Pfaffian politics, so had he become more credible and interesting as a participant in their scene.

His association with the *Times* also may have prepared Whitman for the physical and psychological leap he would have to make to become a fixture in the Manhattan hotspot. From his *Brooklyn Daily Eagle* editorship (1846–1848) up to his publication of the first edition of *Leaves*, Whitman had invested himself in Brooklyn in various ways: he wrote about local politics, people, and events; bought Brooklyn property; built Brooklyn houses; and "toured" its neighborhoods by moving frequently through the city for almost two decades.[36] Brooklyn did not have a thriving arts scene, nor did it have a community of intellectuals like that at Pfaff's; but it could be a supportive and neighborly place, as Whitman found out when he was in search of a publisher for his unusual poems. The Brooklyn heritage of the first two editions of *Leaves of Grass* was announced on its title page, and Whitman himself helped boost this image with the publication of his self-review "Walt Whitman, A Brooklyn Boy" in the *Brooklyn Daily Times* of September 1855. There were distinct advantages to being a local hero, of course, though flagging sales for *Leaves* may have prompted him to broaden his audience and appeal. A first step was his run of articles for Fowler and Wells's *Life Illustrated* between April and August 1856; these show the "Brooklyn boy" enjoying an opera at Manhattan's Academy of Music, critiquing a service at Grace Church on Broadway, and warning tourists about city scams. A second and more definitive indicator that he was reaching beyond the borders of his own "old Brooklyn" was his acceptance of a position at the Williamsburg-based *Brooklyn Daily Times*.

Though the *Times* was a ferry crossing away from Manhattan, as was the rest of Brooklyn, the location of its offices actually did bring Whitman physically closer to Pfaff's neighborhood in the heart of Manhattan. The paper moved from 145 Grand Street to 12–14 South Seventh Street in

Williamsburg during Whitman's tenure; both sites were located near Williamsburg's two ferry landings on the East River, which Bennett apparently saw as a business advantage.[37] Whitman's well-known "passion for ferries" inspired editorials throughout his years at the paper;[38] it is easy to imagine Whitman crossing on a boat when the landings offered such convenient after-work divergences. In fact, an editorial of January 16, 1858, demonstrates Whitman's eager engagement in the "late contest between the rival ferries" of Williamsburg. Ostrander so closely associated Whitman with these ferries that he named Whitman's poem as "Crossing the Williamsburgh Ferry" rather than "Crossing Brooklyn Ferry" in his *History of the City of Brooklyn and Kings County.*[39]

The Grand Street Ferry, located a few blocks west of the 145 Grand Street offices and seven blocks north of the South Seventh Street location, offered an exciting new point of entry to Manhattan: Houston Street on the Lower East Side. From there it was a short walk or omnibus ride west on Houston and through the Bowery to Broadway, then up one block to Bleecker—and to Pfaff's. This was a considerably shorter trip to the cellar than from the Fulton Ferry landing, from which Whitman would have had to walk west on Fulton to Broadway and take a 1.3-mile omnibus ride along Broadway's busiest stretch from lower Manhattan to Greenwich Village. If Whitman did begin to frequent Pfaff's during his *Times* tenure, the very location of the job would have encouraged him to leave Brooklyn.

Whitman probably lived in his family's Classon Avenue residence for the duration of his *Times* years. The walk from home to work was not a long one, but it did take Whitman over an old boundary: the divide between the cities of Brooklyn and Williamsburg. The prospect of a newly expanded readership probably made a job at the *Times* more attractive to him after the 1855 consolidation of the cities. Yet the rapid geographic and demographic shift in its audience would have challenged any editor, especially one getting his start only a year or two after the cities merged. Williamsburg had changed from a modestly sized city to a neighborhood in the country's third largest city, and its predominantly Whig population had been absorbed into Democratic Brooklyn. For three days in early January 1855, the paper ran the masthead *East Brooklyn Daily Times* as a nod to Williamsburg's new identity as Brooklyn's Eastern District. Significantly, Bennett altered the masthead again on January 5 to the *Brooklyn Daily Times*. His ambition to publish a paper of record for the third largest city in the United States, after catering to the growing but still modestly sized city of Williamsburg, presented obvious difficulties to his staff.

Though Williamsburg legally became part of Brooklyn in 1855, the newly named *Brooklyn Daily Times* and its readership were facing their own identity crises. According to Brooklyn historians who lived through this era, the consolidation "reduced Williamsburgh to the position of an insignificant suburb of a comparatively distant city, which was in no way identified with, or informed of the needs, economies, or real interests of its new adjunct."[40] The *Times* editor sensed this disconnection. Through 1857, editorials struggle to define common ground for readers. "Consolidated Brooklyn is an immense city, or rather union of cities," writes the editor on March 14. "We are not some little country village; we form one of the great cities of the earth. In our limits are included a great variety of nativities; settlements, regions, interests, and tastes. These need not necessarily interfere with each other; a little toleration will allow every one in perfect good-nature to pursue its own path, without prejudice to the other."[41]

Who is "we"? Though the reference is ostensibly to consolidated Brooklynites, the editor seems to be speaking as a Williamsburgh resident to his neighbors, particularly those who remember living in the Village of Williamsburgh before 1840. If Whitman was behind these personalized editorials, writing for the *Times* succeeded not only in taking the boy out of old Brooklyn, but Brooklyn out of the boy. Whitman often shape-shifted in his poetry ("I am the mashed fireman . . ."), but these *Times* editorials called for recurring, consistent, and extended identification with a peculiar audience that did not include himself. Perhaps these experiments made it easier for him to consider mingling with the artsy Manhattanese at Pfaff's—a greater challenge because doing so required the establishment of common ground with uncommon types often exoticized by the press.[42] Whitman the loner, the walker, the man on the street left his comfort zone to take a seat among the bohemians at Pfaff's; becoming a Williamsburgher may well have been the first step toward leaving old Brooklyn.

While greater Brooklyn bustled with diversity, Williamsburg itself—the mainstay of the *Times*'s readership—still preserved much of its small-town character and communal spirit. Advertisements and editorials in the paper made clear that "the German element . . . is very large" in its "Dutchtown."[43] Thousands of German immigrants settled into the eastern end of Williamsburg as refugees from 1840 to 1860, bringing with them a strong interest in preserving their culture.[44] They set up community organizations such as gymnastic societies, popular for their emphasis on both physical culture and social outlets.[45] They were politically active and strongly supported the union. And the Germans brought with them a love of drinking beer as well as the expertise to make it. Because of an alternate fermentation process, German lager was lighter and easier to drink than traditional English and American ales and thus "irrevocably changed the nation's drinking habits."[46] Lager beer was first produced in small operations in Brooklyn neighborhoods with large numbers of German immigrants: Williamsburg, Bushwick, and Greenpoint. Its popularity made Brooklyn a major beer-producing and beer-drinking area, with more than one hundred saloons listed in the 1860 city directory.[47]

Whitman's home on Classon Avenue was within walking distance of "Dutchtown," and yet he seems to have been first introduced to German Americans and their culture while working at the *Times*. He developed a friendship with Frederick Huene, a printer at the *Times* who had fled the revolution in Germany (and was hence known as an *Acht-und-vierziger* or "48er"). Whitman and Huene traded books of poetry, and Whitman asked Huene whether he would consider translating *Leaves of Grass* into German.[48] Huene may have served as guide for the explorations of the sixteenth ward that appeared on the *Times* editorial page: "the innumerable lager bier shops, the promenading groups, the harmonious strains issuing from latticed gardens and curtained halls, the 'sweet German accent'—all bear witness to this locality. Our present stringent license law has no apparent effect on Dutchtown; there you encounter no difficulty in getting whatever you wish to assuage your thirst."[49] It was likely in Williamsburg, then, and not at Pfaff's, that Whitman developed his long-lived fondness for lager beer. Further, it was here that he first enjoyed the down-to-earth, communal ambience that he later so relished at the cellar. In the *Times* of December 6, 1858, a tour of Williamsburg "bier saloons" welcomed readers into interiors Whitman seemed to know well:

> These houses are much the same, so far as externals go. A few round and square tables, round which the customers sit, perhaps a billiard table or two, a bar behind which stands the inevitable bier keg, a few pictures and prints which are not usually art treasures, and in every

place of any pretensions a piano, which is nightly fingered by some aspiring amateur—all Germans are amateurs—and the establishment is complete. The burly landlord is civil and attentive, his wife efficiently aids and abets him in the exhibition of those qualities, and in the background there are glimpses of the small-fry and indubitable evidence of infantile life. Dominoes, cards, newspapers, lager, and tobacco, make the evening pass pleasantly for the frequenters, and there are rarely any disturbances.[50]

In the mid-nineteenth century, German immigrants introduced the United States to an alternative social culture that defied Puritan dictates, discouraged lower-class rowdyism, and ignored New York elitism. Homey and unpretentious, a German beer saloon was an extended kitchen or living room for friendly gatherings. Men, women, and children were all welcome; a guest could sit alone to drink and read or engage in a group activity. Thus even if Pfaff's clientele was not comfortably familiar to Whitman, the gemütlichkeit of the cellar certainly was. Even better for him, Charles Pfaff extended the idea of "family" to his patrons and to non-traditional variations on that theme. Whitman described Pfaff as a benign paternal figure known for his open-mindedness and generosity. The obliging restaurateur welcomed the brotherhood of the Fred Gray Association[51] and even the unwed mother and Free Love supporter Ada Clare, "paying no attention to the shocked gossip on the street" and causing his patrons to remark that "the Germans are not shocked when a woman enters a restaurant."[52]

Years spent in service of the *Times* would have provided Whitman with material rewards that would enhance his experience at Pfaff's. A stable income through the Panic of 1857 and its aftermath may have been one of the reasons Whitman stayed on the job as long as he did; the money helped his whole family through the crisis and also enabled his explorations of Pfaff's. "One of the coterie of writers and actors which used to squander its much wit and little wealth at Pfaff's tells me that of the whole party, Whitman was the only one who was never tipsy and never 'broke,'" notes Charles M. Skinner in his article "Walt Whitman as an Editor."[53] Whitman also may have accumulated a supply of favored scrap paper while working at the *Times*: blue "City of Williamsburgh" tax forms, probably printed at the *Times* offices and stored there after Williamsburg consolidated with Brooklyn in 1855, rendering them obsolete. Whitman used the versos of these highly identifiable forms for everything from debt notices to drafts of poems from 1857 through 1860.[54]

If Whitman needed a precedent for a career leap, the *Times* would have provided an excellent and immediately relevant example in Charles W. Gaylor. Generations of artists have regarded the trip from Brooklyn to Manhattan as a life-changing journey, from Whitman to Alfred Kazin to Woody Allen. But before all these, Gaylor was transformed from Brooklyn editor to New York playwright and the toast of Pfaff's. Gaylor was a Brooklyn resident from Whitman's neighborhood who according to the *Times* was Whitman's predecessor at the paper's editorial desk, remaining "some months only, as he refused to read proofs which came down occasionally from the job office."[55] Gay Wilson Allen claims that Gaylor "had never forgiven Walt for having succeeded him on the *Times*," thus explaining Gaylor's vicious attack on *Leaves of Grass* (1860) in the short-lived daily comic newspaper *Momus*.[56] But a list of Gaylor's accomplishments after leaving the *Times* makes it difficult to believe he maintained any hard feelings: his plays *Taking Chances, or, Our Cousin from the Country* (1855), *The Son of the Night from the Porte St. Martin, Paris* (1856), *The Love of a Prince* (1857), and *Olympiana, or, a Night with Mitchell* (1857) debuted on the New York stages in succession.[57] A member of the pre-Pfaffian Ornithorhyncus Club, Gaylor and his long white beard were a fixture at Pfaff's long before Whitman arrived on the scene.[58] Whitman may have been in awe of the more famous bohemians in residence such as Ada Clare and Adah Isaacs Menken, but here was a Pfaffian he knew from home who had also used his *Times* editorship as a stepping-stone.

The *Brooklyn Daily Times* likely provided Whitman with an important segue to Pfaff's. As editor of a paper with a staff of three (including himself),[59] he would have been responsible for much more than the editorial column: he would have reviewed new books and the content of magazines, including the writings of Bayard Taylor, William Curtis, and other Pfaffians;[60] he would have sifted through current sensational fiction for the front page, encountering Fitz Hugh Ludlow and Fitz-James O'Brien if he was not already familiar with their popular stories. The advertisements and feature articles he would edit or compose served as reminders that Manhattan, not consolidated Brooklyn, was the center of New York's cutting-edge literary culture. And the epicenter of that world was Pfaff's, where he could meet and converse with the unconventional artists he so admired and gain insight on how to propel his own literary project to their level of success. Thanks to the position afforded by the *Brooklyn Daily Times*, that world would have been closer—politically, psychologically, and physically—than it had ever been before.

Editing the paper also may have reminded Whitman that he needed to do more than edit a paper. In late 1858, the *Times* published "The Life of an Editor," containing a "true sketch of an Editor's life": "There are no strains upon the mind, no trials upon the temper, like those which beset writers for the press. Their work is never done. There is no 'covered walk of acacias'—no 'lake'—no 'mountains'—no 'Serene sky'—no 'silver orb of the moon'—no 'year of jubilee'—no period of rest to the Editor. His work never ends. He has no time to mature great works—to fashion out poems—to meditate stately histories."[61] A manuscript drafted by Whitman between 1857 and 1859 demonstrates his own struggle with the same dilemma faced in "The Life of an Editor": on one side writhes the heavily corrected scrawl of what would soon become "Calamus 2"; on the other is a messy sketch titled "Important Questions of Brooklyn," which Bowers and Allen recognize as the basis for at least one *Brooklyn Daily Times* editorial published in March 1859.[62] Dividing his energies between two such divergent writing tasks must have been both mentally and emotionally exhausting for Whitman, and it appears that writing for the *Times* had become a labor-intensive distraction. But working for the *Times* had also kept Whitman on track to Pfaff's, where he would find the time and the inspiration that would help him complete his most socially progressive and artistically innovative edition of *Leaves*.

NOTES

1. Allen, *Solitary Singer*, 208–16; Renner, "Brooklyn *Daily Times*," 82.

2. Loving, *Walt Whitman*, 227.

3. In a letter of January 19, 1885, to Charles M. Skinner, Whitman includes these dates and writes of how he "bent the whole weight of the [*Brooklyn Daily Times*] steadily in favor of the McAlpine plan" for Brooklyn's new water works. Skinner, who edited the *Times* from 1881 to 1885, wrote to Whitman to inquire about his editorial work for the paper. See *Corr.* 3:385–86.

4. Bowers, *Whitman's Manuscripts*, xxviii, xxix. See the manuscript for "Scented Herbage of My Breast" (MSS 3829) in the Papers of Walt Whitman at the Clifton Waller Barrett Library of American Literature, University of Virginia. The first four of the manuscript's five pages have notes for an editorial on the Brooklyn Water Works on their versos.

5. See Stansell, "Whitman at Pfaff's," 115. For more on the role of geography and place in Whitman's patronage of Pfaff's, see Karbiener, "Whitman at Pfaff's." Whitman's lists of addresses for other Pfaffian regulars indicate they lived much closer to Pfaff's: Ada Clare lived at "86 42nd St," William Swinton at "154 West 26th St bet. 7th & 8th av"; and Fred Gray Association member Charles Chauncey at "23 Lafayette Place" (*NUPM* 1:432, 453; 2:494).

6. Whitman lived in Manhattan from 1835 to 1836 and again from 1841 to 1845; his Brooklyn years span from 1823 to 1835 and from 1845 to 1862. See Krieg, *Whitman Chronology*.

7. The *Brooklyn Daily Times* is the only newspaper that published positive notices of each of the first three editions of *Leaves of Grass*. Whitman's self-review of the first edition appeared on September 29, 1855, and the second edition was reviewed on December 17, 1856. Though Whitman had solicited for the promotional blurb for "A Child's Reminiscence" that appeared in the *Times* on December 24, 1859, the published notice contains edits to his draft indicating a knowledge of and appreciation for his poetry. See Amanda Gailey's essay in this volume.

8. The town of Williamsburgh became the city of Williamsburg in 1852, when its spelling was changed.

9. "Sixty Years of Newspaper Making," *BDT*, Feb. 28, 1908.

10. *The Brooklyn Daily Times is Sixty-Eight Years Old* (Brooklyn, NY: *Brooklyn Daily Times*, 1916); untitled editorial, *BDT*, Feb. 28, 1852.

11. *The Brooklyn Daily Times is Sixty-Eight Years Old.*

12. Kennedy, *Catalogue*, 28. These figures are the only records available for the decade of 1850–1860, though they are unreliable. S. N. D. North commented in 1884 on "the well-known tendency of newspaper publishers to exaggerate circulation" as one of the difficulties in "securing accurate figures" concerning newspaper circulation (North, *History*, 74–75).

13. Kenny, *American Newspaper Directory*, 121.

14. Ibid., 42; see Hough, *Census*, 584–85. As Stiles clarifies, "Quite a number of periodicals, daily, weekly, and monthly, were started in Brooklyn, but most of them had such a short-lived existence that they scarcely impressed themselves on the public mind." These include the *Brooklyn City News* (1859–1863), mentioned later in this essay. Stiles, *Civil*, 1171.

15. Holloway elaborates on his point, that "both the *Eagle* and the *Star* subjected Bennett to a vast amount of scurrilous abuse," in Whitman, *I Sit and Look Out*, 17–18.

16. Stiles, *Civil*, 1177; Stiles, *History*, 938.

17. Stiles, *Civil*, 1181.

18. Ostrander, *History*, 88.

19. Mott, *American Journalism*, 354–55.

20. Livingston, *Brooklyn and the Civil War*, 50; Schroth, *Eagle and Brooklyn*, 11.

21. Livingston, *Brooklyn and the Civil War*, 50–51; Schroth, *Eagle and Brooklyn*, 64. See also the report of the event in the *Brooklyn Eagle* of April 13, 1861.

22. Mott, *American Journalism*, 355.

23. See Whitman's letter to Charles Eldridge of October 8, 1864, in *Corr.* 1:243.

24. "Copperheads" opposed President Lincoln's wartime politics and called for peace at any price. See Whitman's letter to William Douglas O'Connor of September 11, 1864, in *Corr.* 1:242.

25. Ostrander, *History*, 128.

26. *The Brooklyn Daily Times is Sixty-Eight Years Old*.

27. "Senator Douglas' Success," *BDT*, Nov. 5, 1858.

28. Untitled editorial, *BDT*, Nov. 1, 1858.

29. David Reynolds, for example, notes that Whitman supported Frémont in the election of November 4, 1856, while Edward Grier is satisfied with "certain evidence that he did not vote the Republican ticket." See Reynolds, *Walt Whitman's America*, 153; and Whitman, *"The Eighteenth Presidency!,"* ed. Grier, 9. There is no evidence that Whitman voted for Frémont, or Lincoln, or voted at all. What is clear is that the 1856 election turned Whitman's attention to the Republicans.

30. Whitman, *"The Eighteenth Presidency!,"* ed. Grier, 33, 39.

31. Whitman, "Death of Abraham Lincoln," *PW* 1:307–8.

32. "Sixty Years of Newspaper Making," *BDT*, Feb. 28, 1908.

33. "George C. Bennett (obituary)," *Brooklyn Daily Eagle*, Jan. 4, 1885.

34. Lause, *Antebellum Crisis*, vii, 86, 70, 71.

35. Ibid., 65, 84.

36. Through the 1850s, the Whitmans moved farther from developed downtown Brooklyn and "out of Brooklyn, nearly," as Moncure Conway wrote after trying to find Whitman at Ryerson Street in 1855. The next year, Conway visited the Whitmans four blocks east on Classon Avenue and spotted Whitman "at the top of a hill near by lying on his back and gazing at the sky" (Conway, *Autobiography*, 215, 218). Being a "Brooklyn boy" from Ryerson Street or Classon Avenue really meant that Whitman was a rural New Yorker. He seems to have cultivated this image in his dress and manners through his days at Pfaff's: one witness described his clothing as "very countrified" and "somewhat unsophisticated," while another wrote that it "seemed to belong to a farmer or miner rather than to an editor." See Chandos-Fulton's "A Walk Up Fulton Street," reprinted in Whitman, *New York Dissected*, ed. Holloway and Adimari, 228; and Skinner, "Walt Whitman as an Editor," 679.

37. "Sixty Years of Newspaper Making," *BDT*, Feb. 28, 1908.

38. Whitman wrote "My Passion for Ferries" in *Specimen Days*, among other works (*PW* 1:16). Editorials on ferry matters were frequently found in the *Times*

during Whitman's tenure; a notable run occurs almost daily from January into February 1859.

39. Ostrander, *History*, 89.

40. Stiles and Stearns, *History*, 36.

41. "Street Car Service," *BDT*, Mar. 14, 1857. This piece is signed "W.W."

42. Media hype on the bohemians at this time included the serial "Bohemian Walks and Talks" (*Harper's Weekly*, Nov. 14, 1857, to Mar. 3, 1858) and much of the content of Henry Clapp's *Saturday Press*, "on sale at all the Brooklyn news depots" when it began weekly publication in October 1858. Whitman notes the paper's availability in a draft advertisement referenced by Amanda Gailey in her essay in this volume.

43. "Street Car Service," *BDT*, Mar. 14, 1857.

44. Livingston, *Brooklyn and the Civil War*, 19.

45. See reports on "the German Turners of Williamsburgh" in the *Times* of March 16 and 19, 1857, and September 10 and 13, 1858.

46. Batterberry and Batterberry, *On the Town*, 125–26.

47. Livingston, *Brooklyn and the Civil War*, 21.

48. This may be the first sign of Whitman's interest in an international readership for *Leaves of Grass*. For more on Huene, see "Days' Past in the Times Office" and "Sixty Years of Newspaper Making," *Brooklyn Daily Times Sixtieth Anniversary Number*, Feb. 28, 1908, 5 and 3.

49. "Sunday in the Sixteenth Ward," *BDT*, June 27, 1857.

50. "Saturday Night—'Items' Makes a Tour," *BDT*, Dec. 6, 1858.

51. Whitman recalls in an 1863 letter how Pfaff's welcomed the Fred Gray Association: "I thought over our meetings together, our drinks and groups so friendly, our suppers with Fred and Charley Russell &c. off by ourselves at some table, at Pfaff's off the other end—O how charming those early times, adjusting our friendship" (*Corr.* 1:124).

52. Parry, *Garrets and Pretenders*, 21.

53. Skinner, "Walt Whitman as an Editor," 680.

54. Under the masthead of the *Williamsburgh Daily Times*, Bennett advertised for "Printing of Every Description." The *Times* printed official documents for the City of Brooklyn such as the *Manual of the Common Council of the City of Brooklyn* for 1856, 1858–1859, and 1859–1860, and the *Charter for the City of Brooklyn* in 1857. See "Check List of General Serial Municipal Documents of Brooklyn in the New York Public Library, 31 December 1901," *Bulletin of the New York Public Library*, vol. 6 (Jan.–Dec. 1902), 13, 15. For Whitman's use of the tax forms, see Bowers, *Whitman's Manuscripts*, xli–xliii. Bowers notes "the probability that [Whitman] secured [the tax forms] only when he came to edit the *Brooklyn Daily Times*," but does not suggest that the forms were actually printed in the *Times* offices (xliii).

55. See "Sixty Years of Newspaper Making," *BDT*, Feb. 28, 1908. Holloway notes that Gaylor lived on Myrtle while the Whitmans were close by on Portland Avenue; see Whitman, *New York Dissected*, 182.

56. Allen, *Solitary Singer*, 242. Whitman may have held a grudge against Gaylor because of the nasty review: in 1870, he described Gaylor's play "Fritz, Our German Cousin" as a "miserable, sickish piece" (Stovall, *Foreground*, 3).

57. All these plays receive mention in George Clinton Odell's *Annals of the New York Stage*, Vol. 6 (1850–1857) and Vol. 7 (1857–1865) (New York: Columbia University Press, 1931).

58. See "Gayler, Charles (1820–1892)" (an alternate spelling) at the Vault at Pfaff's, http://lehigh.edu/pfaffs.

59. According to D. J. McAuslan, the *Times*'s compositor in 1856, the staff that year was composed of a "business manager, an editor, and a reporter." See "Sixty Years of Newspaper Making," *BDT*, Feb. 28, 1908.

60. For example, Taylor is critiqued in "Wonders Will Never Cease," *BDT*, Mar. 22, 1859; Curtis appears in "Lectures and Lecturers," *BDT*, Jan. 19, 1859.

61. "Life of an Editor," *BDT*, Sept. 18, 1858.

62. Bowers, *Whitman's Manuscripts*, xxviii–xxix. For images of both sides of the manuscript, see WWA, "Guide to the Walt Whitman Poetry Manuscripts at the Clifton Waller Barrett Library of American Literature at the University of Virginia," item 34.

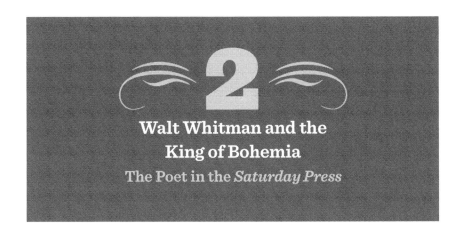

Walt Whitman and the King of Bohemia

The Poet in the *Saturday Press*

AMANDA GAILEY

After the disappointing reception of the second edition of *Leaves of Grass* in 1856, Walt Whitman deepened his connections with the New York art crowd and became a regular at Pfaff's beer cellar, notorious for its unconventional clientele. Because Whitman kept relatively little record of 1856–1860, the years between the publications of the second and third editions of *Leaves*, they have lent themselves to both speculation and neglect. These years were important ones, though: Whitman added almost 150 new poems to the third edition, increasing the number of poems in *Leaves* by more than fivefold. It was during this period that a commercial publisher first agreed to publish the book at no cost to Whitman. This milestone in Whitman's career—his entrance into the world of professional authorship—was enabled by Whitman's complex, symbiotic relationship with a New York newspaper editor, Henry Clapp Jr., whose interest in Whitman attracted the attention of the abolitionist Boston publishing firm Thayer and Eldridge. In turn, Whitman's association with these publishers on the eve of the Civil War transformed him, in the eyes of the reading public, into a distinctly factional, Northern poet.

By tracing the events that led to the 1860 publication of *Leaves of Grass*, we discover that Whitman's national reputation was first shaped by a series of barters. To secure his place in the pages of a prominent New York newspaper, Whitman agreed to weather whatever commentary—from abuse to praise—its editor sent in his direction. To leverage this exposure into a published book, this inclusive poet of "Yankee, Georgian, native, immigrant, sailors, squatters, old States, new States" was publicly cast as a keenly factional, Northern voice.[1] As the nation approached war, Whitman, because of his relationships with Clapp and Thayer and Eldridge, found himself cast not as the poet of a diverse yet cohesive union, but as the public symbol of the most radical aspects of Yankee politics and aesthetics.

AN ALLIANCE WITH THE "KING OF BOHEMIA"

In 1858 Whitman met Henry Clapp Jr., who, like the poet, was a former temperance writer turned carousing bohemian. It was Clapp, in fact, who imported "bohemianism" from Paris, earning him the moniker "King of Bohemia." The men had much in common: they were older than most of the other bohemians who frequented Pfaff's; they were interested in exploring alternatives to male-female monogamy; they both had Quaker roots but unorthodox religious beliefs; and they both felt trepidation about the looming war. As David Reynolds has noted, the late 1850s was a critical time for New York bohemians as they sought to evade real engagement with the national crisis by hiding behind a contrived and nihilistic individualism that "had sunk toward anarchic decadence."[2] War was only getting closer, and the bohemians would soon learn that any movement that neglected this somber fact would find itself irrelevant.

On the eve of national disaster, Clapp founded the ill-fated *Saturday Press*, which, though underfunded and short-lived, achieved prestige among Northern literary circles.[3] The sheer quantity of poems, parodies, homages, reviews, and essays concerning Whitman that were either first published or reprinted in the *Saturday Press* is astounding: in the single year between Whitman's first publication in the *Press* and the paper's closure in December 1860, Clapp printed or reprinted no fewer than forty-six items—excluding advertisements—by or about Walt Whitman. Virtually all of these Whitman-related pieces illuminate the making of a literary career and how the reading public responded to Whitman's controversial poems as he transitioned into the role of vocational poet.[4] Indeed, throughout his life, Whitman was cognizant of how this exposure influenced his early career, and decades later he said to Horace Traubel, "I've always told you it is essential for you to know about Henry Clapp if you want to really know me: he was one of the earlier fellows: he was literary but he was not shackled (except by debts): he gave me more than one lift: contended for me against odds."[5] The *Saturday Press* is a complex testimony to Clapp's dedication to Whitman. This essay focuses on those pieces in the *Press* that were most significant to molding Whitman, just before the Civil War, into a factional poet of the North.

In the December 24, 1859, issue of the *Saturday Press*, Whitman published "A Child's Reminiscence" (later "Out of the Cradle Endlessly Rocking"). In this first venture between Whitman and Clapp—also Whitman's first poetic publication since the 1856 edition—the poet and publisher set a pattern for their dealings over the next year. Clapp was a staunch supporter of Whitman and viewed the relationship between the paper and the poet as symbiotic: he would attract attention of any variety to Whitman, which would in turn attract readers to the paper that so frequently spotlighted the poet. Clapp's active participation in Whitman's public image began with the publication of "A Child's Reminiscence," not just through his acceptance of the poem, but also through a note in the same issue, encouraging readers to thoughtfully consider the poem:

WALT WHITMAN'S POEM.

Our readers may, if they choose, consider as our Christmas or New Year's present to them, the curious warble, by Walt Whitman, of "A Child's Reminiscence," on our First Page. Like the *"Leaves of Grass,"* the purport of this wild and plaintive song, well-enveloped, and eluding definition, is positive and unquestionable, like the effect of music.

The poem will bear reading many times—perhaps, indeed, only comes forth, as from recesses, by many repetitions.

Although the note appears to readers to have been written by Clapp, it was drafted by Whitman, as a manuscript in his hand at the New York Public Library shows, and was printed wholesale by Clapp on the editorial page.

Whitman wrote advertisements for "A Child's Reminiscence" to be sent to several newspapers. One that he sent to the *New York Times*, the *New York Sun*, the *New York Tribune*, and the *New York Evening Post* simply contained the text he wanted the papers to include. The *Times* omitted Whitman's wording, substituting its own text in its "Literary and Art Items": "Walt Whitman, the author of *Leaves of Grass* who shot up to the literary heavens so suddenly three years ago, and sent 'his barbaric yawp over the roofs of the world,' seems to be once more rousing himself to speech, and 'shoots his voice high and clear over the waves' in the *Saturday Press* of to-day with a new and characteristic poem entitled 'A Child's Reminiscence.'"[6]

Whitman's draft of a notice for a different paper, the *Brooklyn Eagle*, included directions to the printer for how to display the text. Similarly, his draft of the notice for Clapp specifies that it should appear "under notices—under editorial head."[7] These instructions indicate that Whitman knew his personal connections to these papers would mean that the advertisements would run as he wished. However, the advertisement that he sent to the *Times* lacked such instructions because he knew that the notice would be published at the paper's discretion, and that it would not follow specifications from him. He was, with Clapp's cooperation, guiding his publicity in the newspapers that he could influence while at the same time seeding newspapers beyond his control. Clapp clearly would have supported this media orchestration since he sought readers for the *Press*. The *Times*'s notice shows that the Clapp/Whitman alliance worked from the outset: as soon as Whitman began his association with the *Press*, both poet and editor were attracting attention.

The complement of Whitman's poem on the first page of the *Press* with the enthusiastic "editorial" comment on the inside of the paper set the pattern for the paper's dealings with Whitman over the next year, when the poet's own writing was frequently set against responses from or implied endorsements by others. Two weeks later, on January 7, 1860, Clapp included on the front page a damning review of the poem from the *Cincinnati Commercial*, which inadvertently praised the *Press* even as it condemned the poet who "soil[ed] the spotless white of its fair columns with lines of stupid and meaningless twaddle." To counter the *Commercial*'s criticism, Clapp printed an anonymous review, "All About a Mocking-Bird," which was, unsurprisingly, authored by Whitman. Even a public unaware of Whitman's and Clapp's marketing tactics probably could have deduced that Whitman was behind the effusive review. Not only did it contain several characteristic exclamations, it also imparted an insider's knowledge of Whitman's plans: "We are able to declare that there will also soon crop out the true 'LEAVES OF GRASS,' the fuller-grown work of which the former two issues were the inchoates—this forthcoming one, far, very far ahead of them in quality, quantity, and in supple lyric exuberance." Whitman further explains that the first two "issues" were "little pittance-editions, on trial" and that the nation needs to be supplied with "copious thousands of copies." This optimism is particularly striking given that, in January 1860, Whitman did not even have the support of publishers willing to back the book financially. It seems that Whitman was gambling on this very venue, the *Saturday Press*, to help him bring these claims to fruition.

THAYER AND ELDRIDGE AND FACTIONALISM

Accounts of the poet's dealings with Thayer and Eldridge usually speculate that the firm contacted Whitman in February of 1860 because it had just learned that Fowler and Wells had abandoned him. This seems unlikely, though, given that Fowler and Wells—who did not even pay to publish the 1856 edition of *Leaves*—had found Whitman too risky a client to sustain. However, Thayer and Eldridge were actively cultivating authors who would appeal to bohemians.[8] In the two months before the publishers contacted Whitman, he had published four poems in the *Saturday Press*—a fact that would have made publishers who courted a bohemian audience take notice. Furthermore, the frequency of these new poems likely signaled to Thayer and Eldridge that Whitman was on the verge of publishing a new book.

On March 15, 1860, Whitman arrived in Boston to oversee the production of *Leaves of Grass*.[9] Ezra Greenspan has noted the complex relationship among Whitman, Clapp, and Thayer and Eldridge, in which Whitman played the unfortunate go-between, trying to broker advertising revenue from the publishing firm for the increasingly desperate editor.[10] Eventually the arrangement fell apart, perhaps contributing to Clapp's and Whitman's ultimate estrangement, but for some time Clapp's paper was actively promoting Whitman's book for many reasons: friendship, a desire to boost readership, and advertising revenue, though the net effect was to position Whitman as a distinctly Northern poet.

In March, while Whitman was in Boston preparing the third edition, Clapp wrote reminding him to "let me know about when the book is to be ready. I can do a great deal for it."[11] He then suggests to Whitman that if Thayer and Eldridge move quickly they should be able to cash in on the publicity Whitman had gained through his recent publication of "Bardic Symbols" in the *Atlantic Monthly*. Coyly, he hints to Whitman that the *Saturday Press* may be the right venue for a full-fledged advertising campaign just before he frankly admits that he is in dire straits:

. . . The papers all over the land have noticed your poem in the Atlantic and have generally pitched into it strong; which I take to be good for you and your new publishers, who if they move rapidly and concentrate their forces will make a Napoleonic thing of it.

It just occurs to me that you might get Messrs. T. & E. to do a good thing for me: to wit, *advance me say one hundred dollars on advertising account*—that is if they mean to advertise with me. Or if they don't to let me act for them here as a kind of N.Y. agent to push the book, and advance me the money on that score.

I must have one hundred dollars before Saturday night or be in a scrape the horror of which keeps me awake o' nights. I could if necessary give my note at three mos. for the amount and it is a good note since we have never been protested.[12]

Clapp's plea for help from the publishing house was successful. Between April 21 and December 8, 1860, Thayer and Eldridge ran sixteen different advertisements in the *Saturday Press*, each appearing anywhere from one to ten times. Nine of these advertised *Leaves of Grass* alone, one advertised *Leaves of Grass* along with other Thayer and Eldridge publications, and six advertised other Thayer and Eldridge publications not including *Leaves of Grass*. Altogether, there were twenty-nine appearances of advertisements for *Leaves of Grass* alone; six for Thayer and Eldridge publications including *Leaves of Grass*, and ten for Thayer and Eldridge publications other than *Leaves of Grass*. All told, then, Thayer and Eldridge advertised *Leaves of Grass* in Henry Clapp's paper thirty-five times over the course of thirty-three weeks.

The advertising campaign was a mutually beneficial collaboration among Clapp, the publishing firm, and Whitman, and it served to significantly boost the poet's already considerable visibility in the newspaper. In the fifty-one weeks from the publication of "A Child's Reminiscence," his first appearance in the prewar run of the *Press*, to "A Portrait," his last, there were—counting advertisements—no fewer than seventy-two Whitman-related items in the newspaper.

Thayer and Eldridge's almost constant presence in the *Press* for these eight months far exceeded its advertising efforts in other publications. The *Boston Daily Evening Transcript* published small Thayer and Eldridge ads fairly frequently during this time but ran only two ads for *Leaves*, and these fewer than a dozen times. Neither ad compared to the stunning elaborateness of such appearances in the *Press* as one beginning with a quotation from "A Woman" (actually Juliette Beach) that packed endorsements of the book into a column that ran approximately twenty inches long. Thayer and Eldridge was much more visible within the pages of the *Liberator*, William Lloyd Garrison's weekly abolitionist paper also published in Boston. Here, though, where the firm clearly found one of its target audiences, its ads focused almost entirely on its overtly abolitionist texts. Its advertisements for James Redpath's *Life of Captain John Brown* even appealed to readers by announcing that a portion of the book's profits would go to Brown's family. Most of the firm's ads in the *Liberator* do not even mention Whitman; the one that does, which ran in October and November of 1860, gives Whitman only the bottom three lines of a sixty-three-line advertisement.

On March 24, 1860, the *Press* began running short notices of the forthcoming *Leaves of Grass*, but the first Thayer and Eldridge ad that ran in the *Press* included no mention of Whitman. Instead, it publicized four staunchly abolitionist works: Redpath's *Echoes of Harper's Ferry*, *Life of Captain John Brown*, and *Talks with the Slaves in the Southern States*, along with a pamphlet, "The Thrilling Narrative of Dr. John Doy, of Kansas; Or, Slavery as it Is—Inside and Out." The ad was highly political and helped establish a political context for Whitman's new edition of *Leaves* by forcefully declaring the publisher's abolitionist mission within the newspaper that it would use as the primary venue to advertise Whitman's book. The next week the firm ran its first *Leaves of Grass* ad and, just two weeks later, was again advertising *Echoes of Harper's Ferry*. Thayer and Eldridge's long campaign of interspersing publicity for Whitman's poetry among publicity for often militant abolitionist writings would have built, in the eyes of readers, a strong association between Whitman's new edition and the publishers' cause.

This first ad that Thayer and Eldridge placed in the *Saturday Press* (April 21, 1860) also began an exploitation of Ralph Waldo Emerson that rivaled Whitman's brazen use of Emerson's private comment, "I greet you at the beginning of a great career," on the spine of the 1856 edition. The ad begins, "IN PRESS! AND TO BE ISSUED IMMEDIATELY: Echoes of Harper's Ferry," and is followed by a quotation from Emerson's 1836 "Concord Hymn," appropriated by the publishers to cast abolitionism with the patriotism of the Revolution.

In an advertisement from July 21, Thayer and Eldridge again put Emerson to work for them, this time by quoting his famous letter to Whitman. The very next week, Emerson was yet again prominently positioned in a *Leaves of Grass* ad, this time through his quotation "Incomparable things, said incomparably well." The use of this statement, which appeared in the *Press* eleven times, was in especially bad form, given that Emerson had repeatedly urged Whitman to cut the scandalous "Enfans d'Adam" poems from the 1860 edition. Nevertheless, beneath the Emerson quotation are listed the contents of the new *Leaves*, including, of course, "Enfans d'Adam," thus making the well-worked blurb look like an endorsement for the very poems that Emerson wanted expunged. On the eve of the Civil War, these *Saturday Press* ads, mingling the names of Emerson, Whitman, and Thayer and Eldridge, serve as an unlikely intersection of Boston Brahmanism, New York bohemianism, and die-hard abolitionism. Though Emerson's approval was poached, it would nevertheless confirm Southern suspicions about Whitman's status as a factional, "representative man of the North."

REVIEWS OF THE 1860 *LEAVES* IN THE *SATURDAY PRESS*

On May 19, shortly after the advertising campaign was launched and as Whitman's new edition was just being released, the *Saturday Press* published one of the most adulatory reviews of *Leaves of Grass*—so adulatory, in fact, that scholars have disagreed about whether Clapp or Whitman authored it. Indeed, both Whitman and Clapp had such vested interests in the book at this point that the effusiveness could be attributed to either one of them. The review, one of the most well-known documentations of the contemporary reception of *Leaves*, begins: "We announce a great Philosopher—perhaps a great Poet—in every way an original man. It is Walt Whitman. The proof of his greatness is in his book; and there is proof enough." As testament to the collaboration that had evolved among Whitman, Clapp, and Thayer and Eldridge, the editorial concludes: "We should not conclude our notice of the Leaves of Grass without expressing our very great delight at the sumptuous elegance of the style in which Messrs. Thayer & Eldridge have published Walt Whitman's poetry. The volume presents one of the richest specimens of taste and skill in book-making, that has ever been afforded to the public by either an English or an American publisher."

Even this review, supposedly the straightforward opinion of the editor or a contributor, was really a result of the complex, symbiotic alliance of poet, periodical, and publisher that was working to forge Whitman's place in American letters. While critics have seldom assigned definitive authorship of the review to either Whitman or Clapp, Clapp was almost certainly its author. Just one week earlier, Clapp wrote to Whitman renewing his commitment to help Whitman's career: "The publishers and printers deserve high praise for the superb manner in which they have done their work. For the poet, he shall hear from me next week."[13] The review in question appeared the next week. To confirm matters further, Clapp even echoed in the review his letter's praise of the publishers' workmanship.

Clapp prided himself on his objectivity and made his refusal to "puff" a recurring theme in the *Saturday Press* by repeatedly stressing his impartiality in his own editorials. Of course, as his treatment of Whitman demonstrates, his personal tastes in poetry and politics were apparent all over the pages of the *Press*; and Clapp, a master of public relations if not of business management, knew that printing a healthy dose of condemnation of his pet causes greatly helped bolster the presumed "objectivity" of his editing. He believed not only that any publicity was good publicity, but also that bad publicity served the dual purpose of additional exposure and the appearance of neutrality. So, two weeks after printing his adulatory review, Clapp printed two negative reviews of *Leaves of Grass*, one of which was perhaps the most scathingly cruel review Whitman would receive in his life.

The tamer of the two reviews, which appeared in the June 2, 1860, *Saturday Press*, was an untitled, anonymous reprint from the May 1860 issues of the *Albion* and was composed primarily of parodic "excerpts" from *Leaves of Grass*. Echoing many other reviews of Whitman's work, this one concluded that Whitman drew "a slender thread of truth and purity" through "a confused mass of folly, fecundity, and falsehood." The review is notable, though, for the ways in which its parodies characterize Whitman's views of African Americans and women. Foreshadowing how Southern papers would soon characterize Whitman as the poet of abolition, the *Albion* review mocked Whitman's sense of aesthetics for finding beauty in Africans: "Of beauty. / Of excellence, of purity, of honesty, of truth. / Of the beauty of flat-nosed, pock-marked, pied Congo niggers!"

While the *Albion* review mocked Whitman, the other review in the June 2 *Press* was simply brutal. The piece, which the *Press* unfortunately misattributed to journalist and poet Juliette Beach, who was actually fond of Whitman's writing, recommended that Whitman kill himself:

> If Walt has left within him any charity, will he not now rid the taught and disgusted world of himself? Not by poison, or the rope, or pistol, or by any of the common modes of suicide, because some full man, to whom life has become a grievous burden, may at a later day be compelled to choose between death by the same means and a hateful life, and with the pride of noble manhood turn shuddering to live on, rather than admit so much of oneness as would be implied by going to death as did Walt Whitman. But let him search the coast of his island home until he finds some cove where the waves are accustomed to cast up the carrion committed to them, and where their bloated bodies ride lazily upon the waters which humanity never disturbs, and casting himself therein find at last the companionship for which, in death as in life, he is best fitted.

The next week, among many other Whitman-related items, the *Press* published a correction, properly attributing the nasty review to Calvin Beach, Juliette's husband. Later that month, on June 23, Mrs. Beach would herself publish an adulatory review. However, she signed it simply "A Woman," though whether this was to offer a general, feminine defense of Whitman or to simply keep the peace at home—as she intimated later to Clapp—is unclear.

SOUTHERN RESPONSES AND THE FOLDING OF THE *SATURDAY PRESS*

Controversy about Whitman had been brewing in the *Press* since his first appearance in its pages, and certainly the first Thayer and Eldridge advertisement to feature Whitman marked him as a factional poet. However, the June 9, 1860, issue of the *Press* proved pivotal in securing Whitman's reputation as a distinctively Northern poet. The issue included five Whitman-related items, not counting advertisements. On the first page was Whitman's "Manahatta," the title of which, as will be explained later, was tellingly misspelled—in the *Press* it is given only one "n," whereas in the 1860 *Leaves* it has two ("Mannahatta"). In addition to an enigmatic parody titled "The Song of Dandelions (After Walt Whitman)" by the pseudonymous Babbaga Thabab,[14] a correction explaining that Calvin Beach, not his wife, wrote the condemnatory article on Whitman in the previous week's issue, and an adulatory review by Mary Chilton, the *Press* also published an excerpt from *Leaves* titled "Longings from Home," in which Whitman adopts a Southern persona, pines for his homeland, and passingly mentions a "fugitive slave" in a "concealed hut." "Longings for Home" (eventually titled "O Magnet-South") has not been viewed as one of Whitman's great poems and has today settled into the background of Whitman scholarship. However, in 1860, the Northern newspaper's decision to print a poem by a Northern "bawd" claiming to be Southern was perhaps as controversial as any of its other Whitman-related articles. Surely this was aggravated by Whitman—the seeming abolitionist—dropping a reference to runaway slaves. The following month, the *Southern Literary Messenger*—a fiercely regionalist publication that had, in these months before war, turned more and more to ideological content—included an editorial rant against Whitman that highlighted the *Saturday Press*'s range of influence.

By this point, the *Press* had for several months been depicting Whitman as a Northern and distinctly partisan poet through its Thayer and Eldridge advertisements. M. Wynn Thomas has recently characterized "Longings for Home" as an example of Whitman's "conciliatory discourse" toward the South, the "poetical equivalent . . . of his states' rights philosophy."[15] If, however, Whitman intended the poem to assuage Southern readers, as Thomas convincingly argues, it failed. The editors of the *Southern Literary Messenger*, who apparently had followed Whitman's development in the *Press*, found this "conciliatory discourse" an unbearable insult. In the June 1860 "Editor's Table," the editors reprinted "Longings for Home" with these comments preceding it:

> The pantheism of Theodore Parker and Ralph Waldo Emerson, pervades and pollutes the entire literature of the North . . . It culminates in the spasmodic idiocy of Walt Whitman. The smart scribblers who compose the better part of the Northern literati, are all becoming infected with the new leprosy—Whitmancy. This latest "representative man" of the North has his imitators by the hundred, admirers by the thousand, and an organ—the slang-whanging paper called *The Saturday Press*. A specimen of the twangling-jack style of Whitman is given below. Take a pair of frog-legs, put a tongue to every toe of both legs, and place the legs under a galvanic battery—and you have the utterings of Whitman. In the following slosh, Whitman says he "grew up" in Virginia. We

should feel mean if this statement were anything else than a Whitma-niacal license, accent on the first vowel in license. Here is the sample of his obnubilate, incoherent, convulsive flub-drub.

Evidence of the *Press*'s power in forging Whitman's reputation is scattered throughout this editorial—in its placing him alongside Parker and Emerson, just as the *Press* advertising does (though just how many of the Emerson ads, running that month, already made their way South is unclear), in its acknowledgement of his imitators and admirers, and in its explicit recognition that the *Saturday Press* is an "organ" for Whitman.[16]

The *Press*'s influence on Southern opinions of Whitman is strikingly documented in one paper, the *New Orleans Sunday Delta*. In one year, 1860, the *Delta* published four pieces by or about Whitman, all on the front page. The first, titled simply "Walt Whitman," included editorial commentary along with a reprinted Whitman poem ("Poemet") and an untitled parody. The article begins:

> There is an unkempt, uncouth poet of New York, or rather of Brooklyn, whose name on earth, in common parlance, is Walt Whitman. The Cincinnati Commercial calls him the "Yahoo of American literature." Judging from specimens of his poetry, which we have seen, (his publishers have not sent the lately published volume of his "Leaves of Grass" to the South,) we think the Commercial scarcely does justice to his peculiar merits in calling him a Yahoo. We think rather that he can claim a comparison with the gorilla, one of the peculiarities of which is to pile up chunks of wood, in rude imitation of the house-building of his Ethiopian neighbors, but without having the slightest idea of making a house or any other rational object in view.[17]

Besides adding "gorilla" to the list of insults cast at Whitman, the review is striking in its passing factionalizing of him. Later in the review, before reprinting "Poemet," the editors write, "That we may not be suspected of exaggerating Walt Whitman's oddities as a poet, we give the least rhapsodic and ragged, and least unintelligible of his compositions which we have seen. It appeared some time ago in the *New York Saturday Press*." This review shows that Whitman was known to many Southern readers not through his book, but through the *Press*, in which his name and poems were framed by the factionalizing contexts of New York bohemianism and abolitionism.

The following week (June 24), the *Delta* ran an article titled "A Specimen from Walt Whitman," which claimed that "an alligator floundering in a slough, a hog wallowing in the mire, a buzzard plunging its beak into carrion . . . may all be lusty and natural, but not particularly sublime, beautiful, captivating, or even pleasant." The editors then offered their readers a selection "From Walt Whitman's 'Leaves of Grass,'" "Manahatta," with the same telltale typo—only one "n"—as the title had when it was printed in the *Saturday Press* two weeks earlier. The editors were still deriving their knowledge of Whitman from Clapp's paper.

A month later, on July 15, the *Delta* reprinted the parody "The Torch-Bearers" from, they claimed, *Vanity Fair*, though by that point it had already run in the *Saturday Press*, which may have been the *Delta*'s true source. At about this time, the *Delta*'s derivations from the *Press* became reciprocated as the two papers began a dizzying swap of Whitman materials. On July 14, the *Press* excerpted the parody from the first (June 24) Whitman review in the *Delta*, which had itself derived from a poem published in the *Press*. Later, on November 11, the *Delta* published an original parody, "The City," that mockingly applied Whitman's style to a description of New Orleans, and this parody was in turn reprinted in the November 24 *Saturday Press*. Even as Southern editors were formulating a heavily partisan image of Whitman that was derived from his relationship with the *Saturday Press*, the *Press* was cannibalizing these formulations back into its own relentless and increasingly factional spotlighting of Whitman.

After the flurry of Whitman pieces in the June 9 issue that provoked such hostile Southern responses, the *Press* continued to feature pieces on Whitman, but with much less frequency after the end of the summer. "Walt Whitman and American Art" appeared in the June 30 issue and is almost certainly Clapp's work. The essay was printed, unsigned, on the editorial page, among other unsigned miscellaneous pieces seemingly written by Clapp, and, in fact, loosely appear under his name, which is printed on the editorial column. Further, the style is effusively adulatory, as is so much of Clapp's writings on Whitman: "Into the company of poetasters, with their 'questionable, infirm paste-pots,' paint-pots, varnish-pots, their putty, plaster, rouge, buckram—a miscellaneous theatrical property—walks, naked and stalwart, Walt Whitman, and all this trumpery seems to shrivel and melt away before his eyes." Clapp would write only one more article about Whitman for the *Press* before its closure in December, and that review would not appear for five more months. Clapp likely felt that the *Press* had accomplished its mission regarding Whitman and that his participation was no longer needed. From December 24, 1859, when Whitman's first poem appeared in the paper, through the end of June 1860, when Clapp published this article, more than three-fourths of the essays and reviews published about Whitman in the *Press* were written specifically for that paper; afterward, only one-fifth were. So many other newspapers around the country and the world were printing articles on—and parodies of—the poet that Clapp merely had to reprint them: parodies from *Vanity Fair* and the *New Orleans Delta* along with reviews from the *Portland Transcript* and *London Leader* in July; a review from the *London Saturday Review*, William Dean Howells's essay from the *Ashtabula Sentinel*, and a parody from the *San Francisco Golden Era* in August; and a review from the *National Quarterly Review* in September.

Clapp's last editorial about Whitman before the *Press*'s closure in December commented, appropriately, on Whitman's supposed reception (the whole thing was actually a hoax) within the culture that had made Clapp a bohemian.[18] The article, published on November 17, is composed mostly of extracts from the preface to a nonexistent French translation of *Leaves* and of sample translations, making the editorial also the first published French translation of Whitman.[19]

The same issue of the *Press* was abuzz with the news that Clapp's paper was about to go under. In typical form, Clapp reprinted mentions of his failure from other newspapers, even those that delighted in its closure. The *Sunday Atlas* blamed the paper's demise partially on its support of Whitman: "All the world does not admire bad imitations of the French journalists and feuilletonists; nor appreciate continual puffs of Walt Whitman's dirty 'Leaves of Grass' . . . [W]hen the epitaph of the SATURDAY PRESS comes to be written. . . . That epitaph will read: 'Died of too much Bohemian twaddle.'"

Whitman's last appearance in this first run of the *Saturday Press* is nestled at the bottom of the last page of the last issue. Titled simply "A Portrait," the poem is an excerpt of what was "Enfans d'Adam" no. 3 in 1860, which would eventually become part of "I Sing the Body Electric." Its periodical context lent it a resonance that gets lost in the longer work. On the eve of war, with the paper of his friend and supporter in its last throes, Whitman's final lines impart a message of camaraderie and hope:

I have perceived that to be with those I like is enough,
To stop in company with the rest at evening is enough,
To be surrounded by beautiful, curious, breathing, laughing flesh is
    enough,
To pass among them, or touch any one, or rest my arm ever so lightly
    round his or her neck for a moment—what is this, then?
I do not ask any more delight—I swim in it, as in a sea.

There is something in staying close to men and women, and looking
    on them, and in the contact and odor of them, that pleases the soul
    well;
All things please the soul—but these please the soul well.

A POSTWAR RESURRECTION

Five years later, in August 1865, Clapp published the first issue of the new series of the *Press*, though this second incarnation was doomed from the start. Clapp, who had pieced together a living as a writer during the war, was still an inept businessman, and now the momentum behind antebellum bohemianism had petered out. Some of the most renowned New York bohemians had died; others had moved on, including Whitman, whose war experiences irrevocably shifted the course of his life. Clapp had lost the community needed for his paper to endure.

    In the intervening years Whitman and Clapp had become somewhat estranged. The reasons are not entirely clear—Whitman thought fondly of Clapp until the end of his life, and the appearance of some Whitman materials in the second run indicate that Clapp had not altogether soured on Whitman. Likely the sheer enormity of the war and the men's contrasting responses to it distanced them. Indeed, it is difficult to imagine the war nurse who moved to Washington and threw himself into his work for the injured finding much common ground with the New Yorker who maintained his geographic remove and biting sarcasm through the tragedy. Nonetheless, the men again collaborated, however briefly, in bringing attention to Whitman's poetry. In the ten months of the *Press*'s second run, Clapp published two pieces by or about Whitman: first "O Captain! My Captain!" and then a review of *Drum-Taps*.

    When read within *Leaves of Grass*, the conventional aesthetics of

"O Captain!" strike many contemporary readers as a blemish on the aesthetic of the rest of the book. Whitman did not originally publish "O Captain!" in *Leaves of Grass*, though, but instead published it in the *Press* just as he was releasing *Drum-Taps* and *Sequel to Drum-Taps*, which contained the poem. In keeping with Whitman's history of clever public relations maneuvers, the poem essentially functioned as a "teaser," however misleading, for *Drum-Taps*.

By 1865, Whitman's readership was overshadowed by his notoriety, gained through numerous public accusations and refutations of obscenity, including his recent dismissal from the Bureau of Indian Affairs on such charges. A few months later, when Whitman published "O Captain!" in the *Saturday Press*, it was possibly his business sense more than his poetics that inspired him to give a Northern, mourning audience—skeptical of him but eager to make sense of the tumult around them—a poem that they would find ideologically and aesthetically satisfactory. As with Whitman's and Clapp's earlier dealings, the publication of "O Captain!" was mutually beneficial: the inclusion of a poem by a famous and controversial poet attracted readers to the *Press*; their finding that the poem was conventional attracted them to Whitman's book.

Whitman's intentions to redeem his reputation with "O Captain!" are apparent in a manuscript draft held in the Library of Congress.[20] Ed Folsom has pointed out that Whitman sometimes turned to conventional poetics during times of political upheaval,[21] but it seems that this turn was not at all automatic, and in this case Whitman seemed to deliberately concoct a salve for his ailing country and, more practically, for his ailing finances. This early draft, written sometime between Abraham Lincoln's assassination in April and the publication of "O Captain!" in October, shows Whitman's intention to write the poem in unrhymed verse. He drafted the poem in ink, with no end-rhymes. Later, he revised this draft in pencil, sketching out the rhyme scheme that he would fully implement in the published version.

If Whitman intended to redeem his reputation and drum up a wider audience for his poetry through the publication of the conventional "O Captain!," his plan worked. Three months after its appearance in the *Press*, a reviewer for the *Boston Commonwealth* wrote on February 24, 1866, "this displaced and slighted poet has written the most touching dirge for Abraham Lincoln of all that have appeared" before quoting it in its entirety. "O Captain! My Captain!" soon became Whitman's most anthologized poem and perhaps his most famous poem, much to Whitman's chagrin. In 1889, he told Traubel, "It's My Captain again: always My Captain: the school readers have got along as far as that! My God! When will they listen to me for whole and good?"[22] The difference in the reception of Whitman's prewar offering of conciliatory imagination, "Longings for Home," and the postwar publication of "O Captain!" is striking. Both were enabled by Clapp in the *Saturday Press*, but "O Captain!"—for all its aesthetic deficiencies—shows how the intervening years matured Whitman's understanding of his role as a public poet.

The *Press* closed permanently in June 1866, the conclusion of a career that Whitman later summarized as "Henry's heroic struggle."[23] Clapp died in 1875 after years of alcoholic decline. Decades after Whitman's last appearance in the *Press*, he reflected on his lifelong dealings with editors: "The truth is, what for editorial hard blows, I haven't got a whole bone left in my body. . . . I think I have finally escaped the hounds and can go the rest of the way in comparative peace."[24] As Whitman knew, it was in fact an editor who helped him escape those hounds, even if he had set them on Whitman to begin with. Months later, Whitman told Traubel, "Henry was my friend: he would have done anything for me: . . . first of all he said he wished me to have a fair show: 'With half a fair show, Walt,' he used to say, 'I know you can take care of yourself.'"[25]

NOTES

This essay originally appeared in longer form and with illustrations as "Walt Whitman and the King of Bohemia: The Poet in the Saturday Press," *Walt Whitman Quarterly Review* 25, no. 4 (2008): 143–66. I thank Kenneth M. Price, Susan Belasco, Leo Iacono, and the anonymous reviewers for the *Walt Whitman Quarterly Review* for their very helpful comments on this article.

1. *LG56*, 194.

2. Reynolds, *Walt Whitman's America*, 378.

3. The *Press*, constantly plagued by financial instability, had two incarnations: the first ran from October 23, 1858, to December 15, 1860; the second from August 5, 1865, to June 2, 1866.

4. A complete list and the transcriptions of poems that Whitman published in the *Saturday Press* are available at WWA and additional materials are available at The Vault at Pfaff's.

5. *WWC* 4:195.

6. *New York Times, Dec. 24, 1859.*

7. Draft advertisement for the *Brooklyn Eagle*. The Henry W. and Albert A. Berg Collection of English and American Literature, New York Public Library.

8. Von Frank, "Secret World."

9. *Leaves* as a text was very much still in flux at this time. Just a month earlier Whitman published a single poem titled "Leaves" in the *Saturday Press*, which he divided and distributed into "Calamus" no. 21, "Calamus" no. 37, and "Enfans d'Adam" no. 15 in the new edition.

10. Greenspan, *Walt Whitman*, 210–12.

11. *WWC* 1:236.

12. Ibid., 1:237.

13. Ibid., 4:195.

14. No plausible theory for Babbaga Thabab's identity has been put forward.

15. Thomas, *Transatlantic Connections*, 101.

16. Interestingly, the page that contains this editorial also includes two pieces mocking African Americans and Native Americans, illustrating how on the eve of the Civil War, Whitman was viewed by some in the South as an "other." This provides an excellent example of how some nineteenth-century critics, as Kenneth M. Price has put it, "made [Whitman], as it were, black" and "an outsider in his own land" (*To Walt Whitman*, 10).

17. "Walt Whitman," *New Orleans Sunday Delta, June 17, 1860.*

18. Whether Clapp was the orchestrator of the hoax or an unwitting pawn in someone's practical joke is a matter of critical debate. See Greenspan, "Earliest French Review" and "More Light"; and Asselineau, "Earliest French Review."

19. The first review of Whitman in France was by Louis Etienne and was published in November 1861.

20. I thank Andrew Jewell for calling my attention to this manuscript.

21. Folsom, "Lucifer and Ethiopia," 54.

22. *WWC* 4:393.

23. Ibid., 4:196.

24. Ibid., 1:264.

25. Ibid., 4:196.

Publishing Pfaff's

Henry Clapp and Poetry
in the *Saturday Press*

INGRID SATELMAJER

On December 3, 1859, the *Saturday Press* reprinted "Pfaff's," an unsigned essay celebrating Charles Pfaff's beer cellar off Broadway. Describing the place frequented by the writers known as the New York bohemians, the essay was one of several pieces that month in which the periodical laid claim to its associated social spaces. In other issues from December 1859, the *Press* published Getty Gay's essay "The Royal Bohemian Supper" on bohemian "Queen" Ada Clare's private parties (December 31) and a reprint of Thomas Bailey Aldrich's poem "At the Cafe" (December 24); promotional notices for *Vanity Fair* additionally communicate the literary activities of Pfaffians at that time, as the newly formed comic journal similarly was "born in Pfaff's cellar" and shared many of the same writers.[1] But it is "Pfaff's" that most delineates a process important to the making of the journal—namely, how texts of any value emerge from the chaos of the lauded social environment. In Pfaff's, the anonymous essay claims of the beer cellar's literary environment, "the text of the moment is announced, and the mouths open all about the table for hap-hazard emissions of quip, and quirk, and queer conceit, of melancholy mirth and laughing madness"; the result, the essay claims, is "clay . . . turned to gold."[2] And in publishing the essay, the *Press* thus further aligns itself with a compelling philosophy of literary production that highlights community, collaboration, and the alliance between improvisation and the production practices of the journal in a developing print culture market.

That philosophy of literary production has existed in the shadows of one of the periodical's most canonically significant publications: Walt Whitman's "A Child's Reminiscence," presented that same month as a gift to the paper's readers (December 24). Whitman's poem, and the subsequent poems and critical articles surrounding Whitman, have served as preservative forces where the periodical is concerned, and Henry Clapp Jr., the paper's editor, emerges as a marketing genius in related accounts. Such accounts, however, while offering important readings of Whitman's career, rewrite the paper and its editor's function in a way that elides the larger community of writers at hand.[3] Rather than focus on Clapp's significant role in the promotion of Whitman, I highlight the paper's position as a collaborative performance space and draw attention to how it aligned its community of poets with the "emissions of quip, and quirk, and queer conceit" that were central to Clapp's philosophy of literary production. Clapp's philosophy, I argue, is rooted in his long-held ideas about free speech, which date back to his early work as an abolitionist and protemperance reformer. He created the *Saturday Press* as a dynamic, time-specific event and highlighted improvisation in its pages. Clapp set out poetry as generative and productive, and although largely a "silent" contributor to editorial departments during the December 1859 issues, he not only was the "King of Bohemia," the widely reputed head of the paper's associated social group; he also was a writer, and he often led the table, as it were, in verse: his unsigned poem "The Shadow on the Wall" is the opening text of the *Press*'s inaugural issue, and he frequently occupies the important lead spot in the paper's early years.

Although often highlighted by that position, Clapp's poetry also might readily be called "space-filler": even the inaugural poem, "The Shadow on the Wall," is derivative, and Clapp often reprinted his own poems without proper acknowledgement, a practice that, when followed by other magazines, the *Press* criticized harshly. One nineteenth-century critic, who dismissively refers to magazine poetry as "verselets," describes "magazine literature" as "light, fanciful, airy,—just such as a young man with a fair amount of training could throw off by the ream 'between the sleep and wake.'"[4] Given that Clapp was the time-pressed head of a cash-strapped enterprise, such writing seems valuable in part because it helped meet the unceasing demand for content. But a culture of derivation also supports a particular philosophy of production in the *Press*. In their respective scholarship on reprinting in antebellum America, Meredith McGill and Melissa Homestead have charted paths of autonomy and agency for writers in a system that traditionally was seen only as exclusionary toward such concerns.[5] Long-accepted characterizations of nineteenth-century poetry as derivative and imitative have been rewritten as strategies of communication, with Eliza Richards making the compelling argument that female poets imitating Edgar Allan Poe were part of a spiritualist network in which they "built a lyric telegraph whereby they could communicate with the dead poet and with others in his name."[6] And traditional formal devices—of the kind that Whitman overturned with his own verse—emerge in such valuations, at least metaphorically, as a technological basis for creating and disseminating such texts.[7] The culture of poetry in the *Saturday Press* aligned poetry with a social environment that valued collaborative entertainment to some degree over solitary genius and espoused a crossover between labor and leisure so highly valued by the bohemians. Derivative productions—both Clapp's and others'—become important components of the editor's view of communication in a social space and technological environment that valued a group's immediate response.

PFAFF'S AS A METAPHOR

In Pfaff's, the beer cellar that provided a convenient gathering site for writers and print culture workers in mid-nineteenth-century New York City, and in the *Saturday Press*, poetry was part of a generative, performative, and collaborative process. At Pfaff's, Whitman "read a draft" of "Beat! Beat! Drums," as well as "Out of the Cradle Endlessly Rocking."[8] And bohemian Fitz-James O'Brien, we are told, once followed a Broadway sidewalk brawl by entering Pfaff's and performing "a poem that he said he had that evening written."[9] O'Brien reportedly delivered the poem with a black eye on which he "applied" "a leech"; in Pfaffian William Winter's description of this memorable event, the "vial with a leech in it" came from one pocket, "the manuscript of a poem" from the other. Winter offers no direct lines from the poem in his account, but he emphatically recalls O'Brien's performance: "I have heard many readings: I have never heard one in which afflicting reality, hysterical excitement, shuddering dread, and tremulous pathos were so strangely blended as they were in O'Brien's reading of his 'Lost Steamship.'"[10] Although Winter highlights the emotional registers covered by O'Brien's poem, his account most emphasizes the degree to which the effect of the poem rests on its performance and on its context—on the role that it played in the sociable environment that was Pfaff's.[11] In her recent essay on Pfaff's, Karen Karbiener credits the space for its influence on Whitman's poetry, noting, in addition to structural changes in *Leaves of Grass*, that Whitman likely "opened his memorandum books in" Pfaff's, using them to record others' addresses and sketches, as well as to engage in the Pfaffian act of playing games.[12] If we recover the larger body of *Press* poetry in the context of Pfaff's, we follow Clapp's own efforts to align the periodical with its associated social spaces, and we recover a sense of dynamism and audience interest even where derivative "verselets" are concerned.

However, in connecting the poetry of the *Press* to the sense of community and play that dominate descriptions of the beer hall, the gaps between the social space and the periodical recall the degree to which Pfaff's was a metaphor. As a physical space, Pfaff's attracted a wide group of writers involved in a variety of publications, including *Harper's*, *Home Journal*, and *Vanity Fair*. And New York's general literary sociability also resided in other social spaces: bohemian Fitz-James O'Brien participated in parody contests with the group of budding New York genteel poets, and Ada Clare's West Forty-second Street apartment was a complementary site of bohemian activity that featured Clapp's "rattl[ing]" tongue.[13] Nor were there exclusive claims on contributors. Although Jerome Loving links the *Press* publication of "A Child's Reminiscence" to Whitman's earlier reading of "Out of the Cradle," O'Brien's "Lost Steamship" originally was published in *Harper's Monthly*, and the *Press* reprint reveals nothing of its original thrilling recitation in Pfaff's, as the poem appears in a back section near the advertisements, with *Harper's* getting publication credit at the top.[14]

In addition, although most descriptions of Pfaff's as a literary environment emphasize Henry Clapp Jr.'s interest in importing French bohemianism after his recent trip to Paris, Clapp also brought to his communal social spaces the influence of his early work as an editor and writer in New England during the 1840s. Joanna Levin connects Clapp's seemingly disparate worlds of early reform work and later bohemianism, highlighting his interest in transportation and his early critique of certain bourgeois social codes and laws; matters of media, I would argue, similarly bridge Clapp's early reform work and his later efforts in the increasingly vibrant print culture of 1850s New York City.[15] In particular, Clapp's early advocacy of free speech in the *Pioneer*, the protemperance, antislavery weekly he edited in Lynn, Massachusetts, before moving to France and, later, New

York, offers a template for understanding the literary network he later upheld as editor of the *Press*.

Associated with various reform movements through his editorial work
and speaking engagements, Clapp's early editorial work in the *Pioneer* repeatedly advocates the value of far-reaching communication networks
with language that later might characterize the *Press*.[16] In an essay on
"Free Speech," for example, Clapp memorably equates his subject with a
tree filled with birds:

> Now and then, one of the most musical of them would send forth a
> clear note, which would go flying abroad on its silver wings to all the
> surrounding woods, until every leaf seemed to tremble with joy at the
> thrilling strain,—and then it would be caught up by one after another
> of the vernal choir, until the whole heavens were made vocal with the
> great chorus, and the very winds held their breath to catch its divine
> inspiration.[17]

Clapp's description of "these beautiful songsters" anticipates the later
celebration of literary improvisation in the anonymous December 1859
article "Pfaff's," as well as Whitman's unpublished description of the beer
hall in "The Two Vaults": "Bandy the jests! Toss the theme from one to
another!"[18] Collaboration is key in such creative efforts: the "songsters"
together create a "chorus," and the value of an original idea thus rests in
part on its ability to transmit a "thrilling strain." In an early related essay
on "Reform Instrumentalities," Clapp says of a "spontaneous gathering"
that "it was truly inspiring to see how a new thought, uttered by one of the
men or women, would fly round the magic circle like electricity, waking
every one into new life with its pleasant shock, and leaving a bright spark
in every eye."[19] Clapp, who "engaged in the candle and oil business in Boston and New Orleans before new forms of energy made this trade obsolete,"[20] presumably had an especially close acquaintance with the ability
such a power source had to change things. The original "clear note," "new
thought," and "the text of the moment" all serve as generative forces, and
their very movement traces the path of—and enlivens—a network.

Clapp connects this model and the editorial philosophy behind the
Saturday Press with such texts as his sonnet "Adelina Patti," published in
the December 3, 1859, issue, his only signed poem published during that
landmark month. Celebrating the opera singer's recent debut, the poem
describes Patti's voice transported over "waters" and "hills." Her singing

recalls the "clear note" in "Free Speech" and is conveyed in much the same way that "a new thought" travels in Clapp's "Reform Instrumentalities"; it is delivered instantly, and it leaves, throughout the network, a trail of thrilling effect. Clapp's early interest in media as technology thus offers a compelling model for producing and conveying literature, and he brought to Pfaff's an ideology of transfer and collaboration that the *Press* would embody.

To Clapp, communication networks were flexible and powerful technologies that transcended individual conflict or disagreement, and his treatment of poetry in the *Press* employs a complementary model of call and response. Although illustrated most famously by the paper's handling of Whitman, this model existed in advance and independent of the many Whitman parodies, homages, and related articles, and it reveals that transmission was also always a process of transmutation.[21] From the earliest issues, poetry is marked as sociable and improvisatory, with the *Press* publishing parodies of famous poems by Henry Wadsworth Longfellow and G. P. Morris; after reprinting, with highly critical commentary, Alfred Lord Tennyson's "The War" (June 11, 1859), the *Press* printed parodies and other responses for several weeks, including Clapp's own "War" in the same issue and another poem the paper printed twice and underscored as a favorable contrast to Tennyson.[22] Similarly, reprinting David Marker's stirring "The Under Dog in the Fight" (April 16, 1859) led to the publication of several responses.[23] Swinging wildly between serious reflection and silly improvisation, the responses to Tennyson, Marker, and Whitman all highlight the "quip, and quirk, and queer conceit" celebrated in "Pfaff's." And the often-careful efforts on the *Press*'s part to guide readers through the larger conversation—tracing reiteration or lines of influence among the network of texts—repeatedly highlight further the fact of that conversation.

That other models were available becomes apparent with a brief comparison between Clapp's editorial practices and the policy stated in *Harper's Monthly*'s "Editor's Drawer," the popular humor department that likewise linked itself to a physical space—the editor's drawer—and to similarly impromptu texts. The department, intended to manifest "a drawer of the table whereon they [jotted-down thoughts] were written," advocated a certain level of collaboration, praising people for sending in contributions rather than "selfishly shut[ting] up these things between the covers of a private manuscript-volume."[24] What the *Harper's* model lacks, however, is cognizance of the conditions whereby the printed page could be generative and individual texts could be self-multiplying, strategic knowledge that Clapp would employ repeatedly in publishing his and others' poetry and in cementing the connection between performance of the lyric and the production of the journal.

CLAPP AS POET-EDITOR

Clapp's homage to Adelina Patti not only aligns his editorial work in the *Press* with his earlier reform efforts; the image of the opera singer also recalls, as does Clapp's first bird in "Free Speech," the especially intimate relationship between the lyric form and nineteenth-century literary networks. Nineteenth-century American poetry, as Eliza Richards argues, stands out as "an active medium of social exchange," and McGill points to conventional stylistic features by which poems "ma[de] themselves available for copying."[25] Clapp's own writing experience would have demonstrated to the editor the affinity between the lyric form and such a network.[26] Although Clapp did not set himself out primarily as a poet, he repeatedly turned to poetry over the course of his career, publishing poems that ranged from serious to comic to sentimental, all veins he continued to explore after he came to New York and saw his writing in such places as the *Knickerbocker* and *Harper's Weekly*. Clapp edited the *Press* during a period of compelling strength for the poet-editor mold, with James Russell Lowell editing the *Atlantic Monthly*, with New York–based examples of Nathaniel Parker Willis and William Cullen Bryant close at hand, and with editorial assistance at the *Press* from verse-writing Pfaffians Thomas Bailey Aldrich and William Winter. The reprinting of Clapp's own poetry in various periodicals and books, and the association Clapp had with reform movements, had placed his writing in a network that disseminated it beyond any original source of publication.[27] He thus would have been keenly aware of the lyric form's ability to travel when in contact with a communications network.

In further establishing that network as collaborative and performative, Clapp highlighted the "First Page" of the *Press* as a space of notable value but flexible properties. Although the *Press* generally opened with poetry, the space more significantly was wed to strategic ends: when, for example, Clapp famously presented Whitman as a gift to readers "on our First Page," he removed a recently standard department—"The Saturday Press Book-List"—as well as the listing of the *Press*'s address, terms, and editor(s) so that Whitman's poem would dominate the page.[28] The lead poetry spot, as well as the paper itself, included writers closely connected to the bohemians—Thomas Bailey Aldrich, George Arnold, Charles D. Gardette, Fitz-James O'Brien, N. G. Shepherd, and William Winter—as well as more loosely associated genteel writers such as Edmund C. Stedman, Richard Henry and Elizabeth Drew Stoddard, and Bayard Taylor.

The lead poem, or the Pfaffian "text of the moment," did not rely on originality. It instead more broadly highlighted lyrical performances that encouraged response and transmission. Reprints, a regular item in the opening spot, signaled an attentive interest in the day's major writers (for example, Elizabeth Barrett Browning) and popular texts (for example, "The Beautiful Snow"), and two issues (July 28, 1860; September 15, 1860) used more than half of the first page to reprint poems by English writer Dr. James Henry, whom the *Press* had declared perhaps the "greatest" poet of the century.[29] Clapp even recycled poems in this space that he had featured in his earlier *Pioneer* anthology—S. T. Coleridge's "A Christmas Carol" (December 25, 1858) and Robert Herrick's "How to Keep Lent" (March 12, 1859)—as well as work by John Pierpont (November 6, 1858), a local minister from where Clapp had edited the *Pioneer*, who had written what Clapp once called "one of the stars in the *world's* firmament."[30] If Longfellow and G. P. Morris had proved satisfactory as subjects of parody in the early issues of the *Press*, then Clapp further used the performative front-page space to mark the Pfaffian environment as one that moved forward on the familiar and the ready as much as on the original and new.

Clapp's own voice comes through insistently in that lead spot—through his recycling earlier editorial work (the *Pioneer* poems) and through such prose features as his running series in five issues on Paris. But Clapp's poetry offers an especially compelling body of texts to consider, as he apparently had more lead poems than any other author, even accounting for the Whitman parodies that carved out an authorial space by representation rather than authorship.[31] Clapp's dominance in that position challenges Whitman-centered readings of the paper, but even as Clapp apparently engages in like struggles to solidify his authorial image, his poetry explores the relationship between lyric repetition and a collaborative, performative environment. On the one hand, the current record of Clapp's poems in the lead spot establishes the *Press* as a stable haven whereby the editor-author, fresh from a tour of (anonymous) publishing successes on New York's literary scene, sheds anonymity to gain full identity. The inaugural issue opens with the unsigned "The Shadow on the Wall," with Clapp claiming authorship two issues later; and Clapp with one exception subsequently uses the easily identifiable "H.C., Jr." until he signs the final poem—"A Song for the Future"—with a fully articulated "Henry Clapp, Jr."[32] He also during this period reprints earlier anonymous prose pieces from *Harper's*, claiming in the *Press* his authorial identity. One of Clapp's poems, "Nobody's Song," had appeared in other places simply with the signature of "NOBODY"; in the *Press*, Clapp could lay claim to the same poem, overwriting a pseudonym that had erased not only his name, but his significance and very being. This performative space, we might say, allows Clapp to step forward as the King of Bohemia and sit at the head of the Pfaffian table.[33]

However, not only had Clapp already been "somebody" on the temperance and reform circuit; his publishing record in the *Press* also highlights an ambiguity where his identity is concerned. The editor hid facts about his earlier publications when he reprinted his writing in the *Press*. Perhaps most significantly, he offers the pose rather than the act of improvisation, embodying the immediate response and pretense of originality required to participate in a Pfaffian atmosphere. With the series of prose pieces reprinted from *Harper's*, Clapp asserted his authorship in the *Press*, and he also carefully credited the original publication. He apparently followed a different policy where his poetry was concerned, however. "Gold," "Song about Nothing," "Blue and Gold," "All for Lawn," and "Nobody's Song" all appear in the *Press* without proper reprint credit.[34] Moreover, all of these poems, with the exception of "Song about Nothing," are published under "Original Poetry" in the magazine's lead spot, and they follow an earlier piece in the *Press* that criticizes other periodicals for acting similarly. Calling out several periodicals by name, as well as "some two hundred other papers," the *Press* complains that they "have neglected to give us credit for the original poems which they have reprinted from the columns of THE SATURDAY PRESS. You have good taste, gentlemen, but that is no reason why you should not be honest."[35] In Clapp's own case, the theft is hidden when one poem is retitled "Gold" after having been published originally in the *Knickerbocker* (August 1858) and reprinted elsewhere as "The Song of the Worldling." But that gesture, it appears, was rare for Clapp, who lifted wholesale the poems he originally published in the *New York Evening Post* ("Nobody's Song") and *Harper's Weekly* ("All for Lawn," "Song about Nothing," and "Blue and Gold").[36]

Significantly, Clapp's repeated acts of self-appropriation take place in an environment far more conflicted over poetry ownership than the aggrieved editorial note would suggest. Less than one month after its first issue, the *Press* had weighed in on one of the most notable authorship controversies of the 1850s, that surrounding the highly popular "Nothing to Wear," a satirical poem that describes the dissatisfaction "Miss Flora M'Flimsey, of Madison Square," has with her lavish wardrobe, even after "three separate journeys to Paris."[37] Although *Harper's*, the publisher of the poem, sided with authorship claims by William Allen Butler, the *Press* offered sympathetic support to an alternate story circulating, in which a young woman, Miss Peck, said she had lost the poem while riding on public transportation. Miss Peck originally was inspired to write the poem by a tear in her dress, the story went, but the poem disappeared when she carried it "in her pocket."[38] According to the *Press*, "There was nothing improbable in the lady's version of the affair. Before this, manuscripts have been lost and found."[39]

In the case of Clapp's self-reprinted poems, not only did Clapp's "ownership" of his texts set up the *Press* as the locus at which they could be "found" after having been "lost," but a general climate of flexible circulation where poetry was concerned also supported Clapp's theft as a performative act. His poetic record in the *Press* made him seem more immediately prolific than he was, and he becomes part of an improvisatory atmosphere, aligned with the daily production of a periodical that constantly required "quip, and quirk, and queer conceit." Clapp, as he publishes himself in the *Press*, is an author always ready with a poem, an image further solidified by the additional infusion of new material (for example, the parodic "War"). Indeed, the ambiguity where Clapp's signature is concerned so implicates him in the daily production of the periodical that he becomes potentially present every time we see a byline with something less than a certain identity. Others wrote under pseudonyms for the publication, but Clapp always becomes a reasonable candidate for authorship, as read in the image of both his apparently prolific output and his apparent hesitance to claim that byline, from the opening-day publication of "The Shadow on the Wall."

As with his use of reprints in the lead spot, Clapp's self-publication further blurs the line between the originary and the response—that if the "text of the moment" in "Pfaff's" in theory might be separate from what it engendered, such a model in fact often created a feedback loop. Poetry, one *Press* article claims, is derivative; the paper already had accused poet N. G. Shepherd of plagiarizing an Aldrich poem, only to retract the charges a few weeks later because "the similitude between Mr. Shepherd's poem and that of Mr. Aldrich was only in the first verse, and moreover, was one that might easily have been explained without reflecting in any way upon the author."[40] Clapp himself operated to some advantage in a system that encouraged a high level of repetition. In an extreme example, the opening four lines of two of his strikingly similar poems read as follows:[41]

"Song About Nothing"	"Nobody's Song"
I'm thinking just now of nothing.	I'm thinking just now of Nobody,
For there's nothing in all I see;	And all that Nobody's done,
And I am well pleased with nothing,	For I've a passion for Nobody,
And the world is nothing to me.	That Nobody else would own.

In addition to having almost exactly the same first lines, the poems offer like consideration of a single word, writing over traditional topics of love and idealism with placeholders. They also pursue similarly chronological narratives, with "nothing" and "Nobody" getting the credit in explaining the speaker's origins and development. The poems are both "form depleted of content" and "form with the power to cue up content"; to read them is to recollect thousands of conventional "verselets." But each text also contains within it commentary on the nature of the feedback loop. By ironizing the "verselet," Clapp makes it an example of "quip, and quirk, and queer conceit," and he fuses derivation and improvisation.

The formal elements that Clapp and other poets so automatically employ further demonstrate how repetition becomes the means for response. McGill, in her scholarship on reprinting, has associated abstraction, generality, and "openended address" in antebellum writing with its circulation.[42] Similarly, the very production of Clapp's poetry seems heavily dependent on interior repetition through words or refrains or highly distinct sound patterns. The repeated request to "bring me gold" ("Gold") or "spare" "my illusions" ("Mes Illusions"); the progression from "Tick-tick" to "Click-click" to "Quick-quick" as the speaker moves from time marked by a clock to time (mortality) marked by one's heart ("The Old Year"); the employment of rhyme that recalls, to some degree, Poe's "The Raven" ("The Shadow on the Wall")—with these and other formal elements, Clapp sets up his poems as machines, with subjects fed into their gears and the final products appearing in "reams."[43]

As a larger policy, that belief in the role form could play in an improvisatory environment is grounded again in broader cultural expectations toward poetry. In the accounts of competing claims to "Nothing to Wear," both authors had stepped up to perform; Butler added "some twenty-five lines," at the request of *Harper's*, and Peck attempted to prove her authorship by "printing" several lines of verse that she claimed belonged in the original version.[44] The formal properties of "verselets" thus supported a culture of improvisation. Such were the conditions of popular poetry that two people could add lines to the same text, each with some degree of credibility, as well as produce subsequent poetry that might lead reviewers to question an authorial claim. Remove their quarrel, and Mr. Butler and Miss Peck were only one step away from sitting next to each other at the improvisatory "table" at Pfaff's. Even as they argue over ownership, they engage in the virtual performative culture that poetry made possible in the nineteenth century.

A collaborative and performative environment thus supported a system of production on demand. Although Paula Bennett's seminal essay on periodical poetry effectively emphasizes the degree to which commonly derided "space-fillers" were invested with significance and function, poetry, it appears, was valued in part because it *was* space-filler.[45] Thomas Bailey Aldrich writes of his early stint as subeditor of the *Home Journal*, "The cry for 'more copy' rings through my ears in dreams";[46] and given that Clapp was the head of a cash-strapped enterprise in the growing literary culture of New York, the idea that some writing might be "thrown off"—produced on demand and generated in improvisatory moments in response to a key central text—was part of poetry's form-based appeal. Such properties additionally situate the genre in a useful place for considering the associated bohemian work ethos. As Christine Stansell explains, the bohemians had a reputation for being lazy that was not borne out by their actual working lives; she characterizes Pfaff's as "an anteroom to the workshop," and Levin further acknowledges that "perhaps some of [the group's work] realized Balzac's ideal of fusing labor and leisure."[47] The need for content was real, and if the production of poetry embodied the kind of ease valued in the Pfaffians' social circle, then it presented an attractive intersection between creation and labor that eluded critics who complained about the loafing of the group.

After assuming the lead spot so frequently in the *Press*, Clapp ceded the position first to Whitman and then to others, a transfer that further demonstrates the larger generative, collaborative network Clapp had advocated for since his early days with the *Pioneer*. Clapp's final poem for the original run of the *Press*, the first—and only—poem he published in the periodical under his entire name, solidifies the attractions of that network by setting out one of his favorite metaphors. Clapp, imagining an ideal future world, offers "A Song for the Future" where "truth, electric, flies from pole to pole."[48]

The image in Clapp's "Song" echoes his earlier singing birds in "Free Speech," the electric impulse in "Reform Instrumentalities," and the opera singer's song in "Adelina Patti." But after Clapp revived the *Press* following the Civil War, the last poem the journal ever printed was "The Toiler" by George Cooper. If Longfellow had reworked the image of the laborer in the 1840s to articulate the value of "effort for its own sake,"[49] then in Cooper's arguable rewriting of Longfellow's "The Village Blacksmith," labor is reclaimed as an act of necessary drudgery. Cooper's poem, his third published in the *Press*, depicts labor as repetitive and unending. The process also is markedly solitary; the toiler works "In gloomy halls,— / His only friend the hammer that he swings."[50] Such an image thus strips production of the community that Clapp earlier had celebrated; the laborer in Cooper's poem becomes an isolated machine who "neither sighs nor sings." The poem, which ends with the hammer "still," offers a depressing endnote for poetry and for the publication; it also makes a compelling case by counterexample for the vision that had governed Clapp's editorial work. To work by oneself might produce something enduring, but "gold" could result as well, Clapp might have argued, from a community of writers engaged in acts of "quip, and quirk, and queer conceit"—in acts of poetic improvisation.

NOTES

1. Mott, *History*, 520.

2. "Pfaff's," *SP*, Dec. 3, 1859.

3. See Amanda Gailey's essay in this volume.

4. Champion Bissell, "Fitz-James O'Brien and His Time," *Lippincott's Monthly Magazine* (May 1894): 703. American Periodical Series Online.

5. McGill, *American Literature*, esp. 145–51, and Homestead, *American Women Authors*, 150–91.

6. Richards, *Gender and the Poetics of Reception*, esp. 1–27, 28–59, and 107–48; 109.

7. See Richards's "lyric telegraph" in ibid., 109; also, the characterization of "the lyric" as "a tremendously popular technology" in McGill, *American Literature*, 160.

8. Reynolds, *Walt Whitman's America*, 407; Loving, *Walt Whitman*, 237.

9. Winter, *Old Friends*, 97.

10. Ibid., 97, 98.

11. On sociability and poetry, see Russell and Tuite, "Introducing Romantic Sociability."

12. Karbiener, "Whitman at Pfaff's," 2–3, 19, 27, 27–28.

13. Tomsich, *Genteel Endeavor*, 9; Getty Gay, "The Royal Bohemian Supper," *SP*, Dec. 31, 1859.

14. Loving, *Walt Whitman*, 237.

15. Levin, *Bohemia in America*, 26–30. On Pfaff's, and on Clapp's seminal role, in the context of New York's emergence as a publishing center, see Stansell, "Whitman at Pfaff's."

16. Clapp skillfully employed religious rhetoric, although he had harsh words for the institutions of "popular Religion" (Clapp, *Pioneer*, 3). For descriptions of religious publishing efforts as an early form of mass media, see Nord, *Faith in Reading* 5, 7.

17. Clapp, *Pioneer*, 91.

18. *NUPM* 1:454–55.

19. Clapp, *Pioneer*, 118.

20. Miller, *Bohemians and Critics*, 18. For another view of Clapp's career change, see Lause, *Antebellum Crisis*, 3.

21. Amanda Gailey counts forty-six Whitman-related items in the *Press*; see Gailey's essay in this volume.

22. See Joseph Barber's "Peace and War" in the June 11 and 25 issues. Unless otherwise noted, my claims about the *Press* refer to the original run of the paper from October 23, 1858, to December 15, 1860, as there were marked changes in format, contributors, and tone when it was revived after the Civil War.

23. See "Doggerel," *SP*, July 16, 1859, and Rev. J. L. Hatch, "The Dog that Goes in for the Right," *SP*, July 30, 1859.

24. "Editor's Drawer," *Harper's Monthly* (July 1851): 283. Making of America. Mott later repeats the 1912 *House of Harper's* claim that the popular "Editor's Drawer" grew out of "after-dinner anecdotes" shared at "certain foregatherings of Methodist preachers at the home of Fletcher Harper" (*History*, 388).

25. Richards, *Gender and the Poetics of Reception*, 6. Richards highlights poetry's "brevity" as a quality useful for its circulation (6); McGill, *American Literature*, 160.

26. For a description of Clapp's ephemeral output but once-impressive literary

reputation, see "Personalities," *Independent*, April 22, 1875, 6. American Periodical Series Online.

27. Clapp's poetry had been published in religious, agricultural, and children's magazines, as well as in a collection focusing on his writing as editor of the *Pioneer*, an anthology titled *Voices from Prison* (1849), and as a self-published book-length comic work, *Husband vs. Wife* (1858).

28. "Walt Whitman's Poem," *SP*, Dec. 24, 1859.

29. "A Discovery," *SP*, July 21, 1860. I consider poems as lead items when they appear directly after either the masthead or a department (the books list).

30. Clapp, *Pioneer*, 28. Clapp recycled "How to Keep Lent" a second time in the *Press*, as well as three other poems from the *Pioneer* collection.

31. There are barriers to claiming definitively that Clapp was the most frequent lead contributor. Although he published anonymously and pseudonymously, and thus likely has additional writing credits, Charles D. Gardette, also frequently published in the lead position, likewise stands as a candidate for other authorship credits. See Clark, "'Saerasmid.'"

32. For that exception, see NEMO, "All for Lawn," *SP*, Sept. 17, 1859, which is placed directly above another text signed with Clapp's initials and which was reprinted under "Figaro" in 1865.

33. For two dramatically different Thomas Nast cartoons that depict Clapp in this position, see Karbiener, "Whitman at Pfaff's," 18.

34. The poems were published, respectively, on July 9, August 13, September 3, and (the final two together) September 17, 1859.

35. "Literary Notes," *SP*, Jan. 1, 1859.

36. I have established the respective publication dates of the poems as August 13, September 5, September 26, and October 3, 1857.

37. "Nothing to Wear," *Harper's Weekly*, Feb. 7, 1857, 84. The poem, originally published anonymously, appeared with William Allen Butler's name in the November 1857 *Harper's Monthly*. See Mott, *History*, 471–72. Clapp's "All for Lawn" reads as a possible response to the satiric poem; the August 20, 1857, *Evening Post* mentions Clapp's authorship of "A New and Authentic Version of Nothing to Wear."

38. August 8 *Weekly* quoted in Harper, *House of Harper*, 135.

39. "'Two Millions' and 'Aquarelle,'" *SP*, Nov. 6, 1858.

40. "The Individuality of Genius," *SP*, Oct. 29, 1859. For the charges, see "Literary Notes," *SP*, June 25, 1859. For the apology, see "Explanation," *SP*, July 9, 1859. The *Press* published many more Shepherd poems; he became a beloved Pfaffian, according to Winter, *Old Friends*, 65.

41. "Song about Nothing," *SP*, Aug. 13, 1859; "Nobody's Song," *SP*, Sept. 17, 1859.

42. McGill, *American Literature*, 157–60.

43. The poems were published in the *Press* on July 9, August 20, and January 1, 1859, and October 23, 1858. For an argument connecting Robert Browning's "tech-

nical innovations in prosody . . . with new technologies of transportation and communication," see Prins, "Robert Browning," 205.

44. Harper, *House of Harper*, 135; Smith, *Sunshine and Shadow*, 346.

45. Bennett, "Not Just Filler," 216.

46. In Winter, *Old Friends*, 146.

47. Stansell, "Whitman at Pfaff's," 112–13, 117–18; Levin, *Bohemia in America*, 37.

48. "A Song for the Future," *SP*, Nov. 24, 1860.

49. Anderson, "'Be Up and Doing,'" 2.

50. "The Toiler," *SP*, June 2, 1866.

On Puffing
The *Saturday Press* and the
Circulation of Symbolic Capital

LEIF ECKSTROM

From the earliest issues of the *New York Saturday Press* in 1858, Henry Clapp Jr. built its reputation around an ostensibly iconoclastic "No Puffing" policy. At midcentury, puffing, or the promotion of books by editors and critics under the guise of independent criticism and review, was thought to be an intractable problem for American publishing. As Lara Langer Cohen explains, "puffery [had] developed into the literary critical norm" in the United States by the late 1830s, and it had come "to encompass a wide array of ingenious arrangements to promote the fortunes of various literary cliques, including paid reviews, self-reviews, and exchanges of favors."[1] It was against such "cliques," "sects," "parties," and "isms," as well as "publishers," "booksellers," "authors," and "advertisers," that Clapp directed his *Saturday Press* in an attempt to topple "the whole system of Puffing."[2]

The performative aspects of Clapp's position against puffing rang hollow for one reader, however, who, in a notice written for the Boston *Saturday Evening Gazette* about the *Saturday Press*'s debut issues, responded incredulously to the *Press*'s "threats of independence" and "self-conceit," as well as the weekly's implied rejection of commercial interests put forward in its antipuffing campaign, suggesting that from all this bluster "one might presume that the editors [of the *Saturday Press*] . . . come to their place of business in balloons."[3] And yet, Clapp's posture was at least partially the point, because the *Saturday Press* reprinted and extended the *Gazette*'s joke about its material conditions of production, confirming for the *Press*'s readers in "The Palace and Princes of the Press" the "Eastern splendor" and "Oriental magnificence" of the editors' "Fifth Avenue" residences, the balloons "built of the finest Indian silk and inflated with the rarest American gas" for transporting them from home to work, and the wages paid in "diamonds" to the paper's "magnificently" remunerated staff.[4] Evident in this satirical exchange is the understanding that an obvious divide separated the symbolic aspirations of a paper on the make from its actual material conditions; but, as this essay argues, puffing demonstrated the complex nexus between the symbolic and the material, exemplifying for midcentury readers the curious means by which fictions of print capitalism, despite being recognizable as fictions, shaped the literary culture of the day.

While it was easy enough to decry the practice of puffing for the way it undermined criticism's claim to disinterestedness, not to mention literature's implicit claims to be above the crass machinations of the marketplace, it was decidedly more difficult for antebellum print culture to imagine or explain the emergence and circulation of literary distinction without invoking puffing and self-promotion as the primary mechanisms behind a book or paper's perceived merit and financial success. As a mechanism, puffing inspired the idea that symbolic capital, the essence of a puff, could be "inflated with the rarest American gas," circulated, and made to pay "magnificently" once it was converted to hard, economic capital. According to this way of thinking, puffing stood within a mystified nexus where literary value intersected with commercial value, and it suggested a means for managing the vagaries of literary reception and distinction. For all the clamor that Clapp raised around the nefarious practice of puffing, he, too, wanted to see the *Saturday Press*'s symbolic capital converted into dollars if not "diamonds," and the *Press*'s satirical take upon its material conditions of production brought home the idea that literary autonomy and distinction were related to, if not dependent upon, the material transcendence that "The Palace and Princes of the Press" figured as opulent wealth.

If the notice from the Boston *Gazette* thought it ridiculous that a paper like the *Saturday Press* would presume to exist in a world beyond commercial interests, Whitman scholarship has documented a more obvious objection to Clapp's professions against puffing. Clapp mounted, after all, in December 1859, a year-long publicity campaign on behalf of Walt Whitman and his publishers and in the process made the *Press* financially dependent upon Thayer and Eldridge's publishing house.[5] But this contradiction was only one of many circumscribed by the practice of puffing. Indeed, puffing, as practiced and imagined by the *Press*, encapsulated a wider, contradictory set of ideas about how literary value related to economic value and how literature functioned as a commodity. The story of puffing in the *Saturday Press* is not simply, then, a narrative of Whitman's promotion, but rather a set of conflicted exchanges that wrestled with the possibility of autonomy in the literary marketplace and underscored the stakes of symbolic capital production in late-antebellum New York.

PUFFS, BOHEMIAN TWADDLE, AND
A CASE FOR SYMBOLIC CAPITAL

As the *Saturday Press* was preparing to fold (for the first time) in November 1860, it reprinted three proleptic eulogies first published in other papers. Among them, the *New York Sunday Courier* wrote of the *Press*'s staunch refusal to puff and its impending closure:

> This is pure and undefiled Quixotism. . . . To put down the puffing business is about as sensible an undertaking as to attempt to put down crying babies. If the *Saturday Press* had gone into the puffing business, it would not be at the point of giving up the ghost. But its appeal for assistance is pretty good evidence that it has seen the error of its ways, and is now doing a little gentle puffing on its own account.[6]

And from a decidedly more cynical vantage, the *Sunday Atlas* offered the following:

> Before a paper can be worth anything for the insertions of "puffs," it must attain some circulation. . . . All the world does not admire bad imitations of the French journalists and feuilletonists; nor appreciate continual puffs of Walt Whitman's dirty "Leaves of Grass;" nor make a steady pabulum of the lucubrations of the Bohemians of Literature. . . . [W]hen the epitaph of the *Saturday Press* comes to be written, it will have no reference to the "lack of money for advertising," nor yet to the perverted taste of the public, which will pay for advertising in its own way, in papers of circulation and influence. That epitaph will read: "Died of too much Bohemian twaddle."[7]

Beginning with an editorial in its third issue, the *Saturday Press* had staked its reputation upon the idea that it would "never adopt the policy of indiscriminate praise" known as puffing, and it would likewise not be swayed by the warnings from publishing houses that "unless we adopt the puffing system, to which they have all got accustomed (as some people get accustomed to swill milk), we shall not get their advertisements."[8] Moreover, Clapp maintained that refusing the practice of "indiscriminate praise" was the only way for the art and literary weekly's criticism to have any credibility and that the *Press* would therefore pursue independence in its opinions, whatever the cost. As the comments from the *Sunday Courier* and *Sunday Atlas* attest, however, Clapp's editorial and promotional practices did not differ so distinctly from the market-driven publishing practices he criticized.

Five issues later, for instance, in the publishing notice printed in the top left-hand corner of the first page, the *Press* declared itself—in the familiar, hyperbolic tone of a puff—to be an "Independent Journal of the Times," with five principle characteristics and two clear puffs about its audience and contents:

Characteristics of *The New York Saturday Press*.

I. The Saturday Press is, in every respect, AN INDEPENDENT JOURNAL, connected with no party or sect, and tainted with no kind of "ism."

II. The Saturday Press is irrevocably opposed to the whole system of Puffing, and never allows its reading columns to be used for the purpose of serving any private ends.

III. The Saturday Press is not the organ of any Bookseller, Publisher, Theatre Manager, or other Advertiser; nor of any clique of Authors or Artists; nor of any other persons except its avowed Editors.

IV. The Saturday Press is the only journal in the country which gives a COMPLETE LIST OF NEW BOOKS, or anything like a COMPLETE LIST OF BOOKS IN PRESS.

V. The Saturday Press is the only journal in the country which furnishes a COMPLETE SUMMARY OF LITERARY INTELLIGENCE.

VI. The Saturday Press circulates exclusively among thinking and intelligent persons, and is, therefore, the *Best Advertising Medium in the Country* for all persons who wish to reach that portion of the community.

VII. For these and other reasons the Publishers feel justified in saying, that for all intelligent and cultivated gentlemen and ladies, there is no more interesting or valuable journal in the country than THE NEW YORK SATURDAY PRESS.[9]

Functioning as part self-review, part editorial policy, and part advertisement, these characteristics were reprinted in the same prominent location for the next twenty-one consecutive issues.[10]

The contradictory means by which Clapp stridently declared the *Saturday Press* to be "independent" and above the practice of puffing are crucial to understanding the *Press*'s legacy in its day and our own. In much the same way that Christine Stansell has argued, following Jerrold Seigel's work on the bohemians of nineteenth- and twentieth-century France, that "Bohemia . . . was not the thing apart its contemporaries believed it to be, but rather an imaginative enactment . . . of inchoate tensions between bourgeois life and artistic aspiration," I argue that the *Press*'s stance against puffing was not an absolutist or wholly antagonistic literary-critical position against the market.[11] Instead, the *Press* used the problem of puffing to mark its distinction *within* the market, as much as against it. Thus, the *Press*'s characteristic tendency to puff its independence, staged most strikingly in the "Characteristics" quoted above, should not be dismissed as mere humbug or evidence of the paper's baldly transparent hypocrisy. Rather, we should view its antipuffing pose as a performance committed to both imagining a literary-critical paper that could exist beyond the market and, at times, satirizing the sanctimonious disavowals of real market conditions that came along with occupying such a stance.[12]

As the *Sunday Courier* and *Sunday Atlas* suggest, there were plenty of contradictions to be found in the *Press*'s representations of itself and its relation to the practice of puffing. The most obvious was that the *Press* did in fact puff, a point both papers roundly made. The *Sunday Courier* concedes, however, the endemic nature of puffing to the New York literary marketplace and subsequently reads the *Press*'s submission to such a practice as inevitable and excusable in its "gentle[r]" form.[13] The *Sunday Atlas* delves a bit deeper into the *Press*'s contradictory self-image and insists that the *Press* has confused its literary pretensions with actual market value. Accordingly, it writes that the *Press*'s failure has more to do with its content than with its amply promoted virtue of refusing to puff.[14]

As fitting as this criticism might have been, the *Atlas*'s critique was driven by a larger question left unresolved in the antebellum literary marketplace and one made more pressing by the flagrant practice of puffing: how did literary value relate to market value? In the attempt to declare its own value, the *Press* imagined that it could override market value, and the *Atlas* was right to dismiss this as a posture that could only *appear* to make the market disappear. But in making its counter position, the *Atlas* insisted that literary value was synonymous with market value, since the presence of one confirmed the other, and thereby failed to advance any nuanced understanding of the relationship between the two. That said, the *Atlas*'s critique underscored an important distinction between actual circulation and the representations of prospective circulation found in advertisements, notices, solicitations, and puffs for papers and books alike. As the writer for the *Atlas* implies, puffing and advertising could hardly guarantee a rise in actual circulation for the *Press*, though the concerted efforts of a group of like-minded, solicitous editors could present readers and future advertisers with the semblance of a successfully circulating paper or book.

Working within the French context, Pierre Bourdieu has argued that a series of similar disputes over artistic ideals and disavowals of real market conditions within the bohemian revolutions of nineteenth-century Paris proved crucial to the autonominization of its literary field as well as the emergence of a cultural avant-garde. According to Bourdieu, bohemian artists attempted to turn economic value on its head through a symbolic revolution, but in the process, they created an "infernal mechanism" that threatened to undermine the very claims to distinction and autonomy they had sought for themselves within a restricted literary field of their own making. As Bourdieu writes, the moment that artists argue most stridently "that a 'work of art . . . is beyond appraisal, has no commercial value, cannot be paid for,' that it is *without price*, that is to say, foreign to the ordinary logic of the ordinary economy, they discover that it is effectively *without commercial value*, that it has no market."[15] The *Atlas*'s easy dismissal of the *Saturday Press*'s legacy as so much "Bohemian twaddle" suggests an already cynical understanding of the "infernal mechanism" that Bourdieu would later describe in the twentieth century: according to the *Atlas*, then, the *Press*'s commercial failures were entirely predictable, a function of writing to an all-too-narrow audience, and its public demonstrations of the "necessity of . . . [the paper's] . . . virtue" with respect to puffing were transparently feeble attempts to put a sanctimonious sheen on an otherwise unremarkable failure to anticipate market tastes.[16]

But when we put the fact of the *Press*'s financial failings aside for a moment and extend to Clapp and the *Press* Bourdieu's analysis of the symbolic gains achieved by Parisian bohemians through the overturning of market logic, another explanation of the *Press*'s legacy comes into view. Bourdieu's idea that capital takes a number of forms (economic, social, cultural, and symbolic) is helpful because understanding that capital moves through flexible and sometimes competing forms clarifies Clapp's motivation for taking on the puffing system and promoting so heavily the *Press*'s critical independence, whatever the immediate financial costs might have been from potentially rebuffed advertisers. When viewed as an investment in symbolic capital, Clapp's aggressive campaign to define the *Press* in opposition to market protocols takes on a more strategic and less "quixotic" appearance. From this vantage, it becomes clear that Clapp's "Characteristics" of the *Press* do not attempt to rewrite the logic of literary value needing to take on some form of market value so much as they attempt to redefine that market in restricted and prestigious terms, as a weekly that "circulates exclusively among thinking and intelligent persons," for instance.

We can see that Clapp's investment in symbolic capital "paid off" to the extent that William Dean Howells, as a young, aspiring writer from Ohio, perceived the *Saturday Press* to be (in 1860) on par with the *Atlantic*, a magazine with significantly more economic, social, and cultural capital standing behind it. As Howells wrote of the *Press* forty years later in his *Literary Friends and Acquaintance* (1900):

> [T]hat paper really embodied the new literary life of the city. It was clever, and full of the wit that tries its teeth upon everything. It attacked all literary shams but its own, and it made itself felt and feared. . . . It is not too much to say that it was very nearly as well for one to be accepted by the *Press* as to be accepted by the *Atlantic*, and for the time there was no other literary comparison.[17]

As Howells indicates, the *Saturday Press* was an embodiment of the New York publishing scene, and it was in this locale that symbolic capital was more easily appropriated and, at times, fabricated through aggressive acts of self-promotion and puffing. In contradistinction to Boston's print culture, which had developed a reputation for staid, elite publications vetted by long-standing cultural institutions and families, New York publishing was markedly more commercial and volatile.[18] Moreover, its literary culture was more dynamic and open to the interventions of an upstart like Clapp. By describing the *Press*'s bid for legitimacy as a contest of "teeth," a process of making "itself felt and feared," Howells intimates that representations of symbolic capital were contestable and ephemeral performances. But in retrospectively decrying the "literary shams" perpetuated by the *Press*, a reference, perhaps, to Clapp's hypocrisy in puffing the *Press* and Whitman (among other peccadilloes like failing to pay its writers), Howells plays at a similar sort of game of legitimating and, in this case, denying symbolic capital while overlooking the difference that historical perspective makes within such contests. Writing in 1900, Howells knew that the *Press* had failed in the literary coup it announced throughout 1859 and 1860, but it is important to recognize that the *Press*'s original puffs and self-promotions were prospective texts that imagined a future circulation that was still, theoretically, possible. Once that future was known to be foreclosed, as it was when Howells wrote his "personal retrospect" about the *Press*, it became difficult to see its puffs or self-promotions as anything other than "literary shams."[19] Clapp's simultaneous critique and embrace of puffing helps recover a midcentury contest over legitimacy and prestige, the outcome of which was, in this moment at least, far from certain.

The absence of a consolidated cultural elite in New York provided Clapp with two things: it enabled him to access the literary field with relative ease, and perhaps more importantly, it helped him define what was missing within the city's periodical culture, thereby providing him with a niche market for his publication. Although Clapp never defined the *Press* as an elite publication, per se, and mocked the elite posturing of others whenever he could, he nevertheless saw the *Press*'s central task in prestigious terms: to create and curate the literary taste and intelligence that Clapp thought the city (and its readers) needed and deserved.[20] And yet, in attempting such a task, Clapp and the *Press* became entangled in the seeming contradiction of producing an elite taste for (and within) the mass market.

While Clapp and the *Press*'s contributors were very much engaged in the processes of distinction and consecration we have come to associate with elite cultural production, twentieth-century scholars like Bourdieu have had trouble accepting the legitimacy of the journalistic medium to such a task because of its appeals to a mass audience and its ties to the commercial world, which often made for an unstable and porous border between commercial writing and literary writing.[21] According to Bourdieu, nineteenth-century journalism existed in a world that was structurally at odds with "serious" criticism and writing. He describes nineteenth-century Parisian journalists, no matter how bohemian, as an intellectual and literary proletariat caught within an industrialized field of literary production that they could not change from within.[22]

Stansell takes a similar position with the bohemians who gathered at Pfaff's tavern and served as the primary contributors to the *Press*. While she makes the important point that "bohemia was inextricable from the cultural marketplace," she reverses this position when it comes to the literary marketplace and insists upon a hard distinction between commercial, "hack" work and the "serious" work of "artists," a distinction that is decidedly twentieth-century in its perspective and one that misrepresents the actual conditions of literary production and consumption in antebellum New York.[23] Instead, it is important to see that the contemporary producers and consumers of this periodical culture could not and did not distinguish so easily between "popular" and "literary" forms, between "hack" and "serious" work, and that these later distinctions were made possible by symbolic contests waged within the periodicals themselves.[24]

Periodicals were central to literary production and consumption in this moment, and as Stansell writes, they "mixed poetry, short stories and essays with sketches and news" with little differentiation in terms of format. Stansell takes this to mean that the medium "allowed hack writers, unconnected to the powerful institutions of literary taste and approbation, to begin to conceive of themselves as artists," but such a position overstates the exclusiveness, allusiveness, and coherence of "literariness" in antebellum New York, as well as the division of labor that separated the manual "hack" work of journalism from the "serious" creative work of "writing."[25] Her characterizations of literary labor and value nonetheless mark an important "elision" of the numerous and, as Cohen reminds us, often-ignored "processes that bring literature into being"—from "the material processes . . . [of] paper-making, typesetting, printing, [and] sewing" to the "ambiguously literary activities [of] editing," reading, reciting, performing, and even the selling of periodicals and books.[26] Indeed, while scholars have long used the writing of singular authors to define the literary field, Clapp's *Saturday Press* took a different view and underscored the field-shaping power of secondary modes of literary production—editing, compiling, reviewing, advertising, and puffing, among other tasks—that were often strategically ambiguous literary activities and that held sway over the consumption as well as the production of literature. The collaborative and commercial aspects of these activities have often been grounds for the lack of importance granted to them within literary histories of this period, but as Clapp knew well, those characteristics made them all the more powerful in shaping New York's late-antebellum literary field.

PUFFING AMIDST THE PRINT EXPLOSION

By midcentury, New York publishing had well eclipsed that of Boston and Philadelphia, in terms of both the number and variety of publications issued and the circulation those publications received. In fact, by 1860 New York was the nation's largest industrial center and publishing its leading industry.[27] The material conditions of print in New York were heavily oriented toward the mass market, but the city's diverse and expanding population also supported a substantial range of periodicals that helped "create" and stabilize various "subcultures" organized around "social, political, racial, and linguistic difference."[28] And while the often salacious content of New York's daily newspapers prompted an easy critique of the mechanisms and tastes of market-driven publishing, their highly publicized circulation numbers and boasts about their advertising revenues also shifted the ambitions and expectations of smaller, niche publications like the *Saturday Press*. The unprecedented explosion of commercial print in New York encouraged wild fantasies about print and its market potential that became oddly normative in this period and that help to explain the strange mix of fatalism and optimism that suffused both the practice of puffing and its condemnation—even among the most cynical of publishing insiders who wrote for the *Press*.

Clapp's November 3, 1860, editorial, "Card," epitomized this conflicted view on puffing and advertising when he opined: "Our greatest difficulty, all along, has been the lack of means to advertise the paper properly; if we could have done this, it would ere now—judging from what we have accomplished without advertising—have been a triumphant success." Clapp attributed the paper's failing to a lack of capital; he had begun the paper with "less than $1000," and that small sum prevented him from advertising the journal. Clapp's dogged optimism, in the midst of clear financial failure, speaks in part to his ongoing bid to secure a wealthy backer for the *Press.* In August of 1860, Whitman's publisher, Thayer and Eldridge, had arranged to assume ownership of the *Saturday Press* (at Clapp's request and with Clapp remaining as its editor) on September 1, but the firm had rising debts and stagnant sales throughout the summer and fall, forcing Thayer and Eldridge to abandon this deal.[29] Thus, by November Clapp was in search of another "person of means" to save the paper and provide the burst of capital that would, in his mind, secure its financial success.[30] While the fate of the *Press* looked dire indeed, Clapp's statements also point to an unshaken belief in the literary marketplace's responsiveness to a well-timed infusion of capital and advertising. Such a belief is visible in Clapp's optimistic view that should the "character of the *Saturday Press*" become known to a larger readership, it would necessarily turn into "a large and paying business," and in the fatalistic view that "if we would only change the character of the *Saturday Press*, and, in imitation of our con-temporaries, go into the puffing business at so much a line, we might make it pay at once."[31] As Clapp and many of his contemporaries imagined, puff-ing presented another means for turning the economic value of literature on its head. According to this view, puffing ensured that demand, or read-ership, would follow supply, rather than the other way around, and with-out regard to quality. Proleptic in its desire, puffing presented readers with the appearance of a book or paper's successful and prodigious reception before the fact.

Earlier that year in a letter to Whitman, Clapp wrote more explicitly of this understanding of the literary marketplace:

> [*Leaves of Grass*] is bound to sell, if money enough is spent circulating the Reprints and advertising it generally. It is a fundamental principle in political economy that everything succeeds if money enough is spent on it. If I could spend five hundred dollars in one week on the Saturday Press I would make five thousand dollars by the operation. Ditto you with the L. of G. [. . .] [J]ust now I am in a state of despair even in re-spect to getting out another issue of the S.P. and all for want of a paltry two or three hundred dollars which would take the thing to a paying point, and make it worth ten thousand dollars as a transferable piece of property.[32]

The idea that the literary marketplace would respond necessarily and in an instant to the influx of capital and advertising was a central conceit behind both the practice and the condemnation of puffing. This way of thinking about print's market potential grew out of a general recognition of the antebellum print explosion as well as the particular, well-publicized cases of overnight print sensations.[33]

One such well-publicized case was Robert Bonner's *New York Ledger*.[34] By 1855 Bonner had remade the dry-goods mercantile sheet into a literary weekly, the subscriptions of which famously jumped from less than 3,000 upon acquisition to 100,000 by the end of 1855 and 180,000 by the end of 1856.[35] By 1855, Bonner had paired highly visible advertisements of the paper's exclusive content with an equally well-publicized campaign to collect the celebrity and leading authors of the day. Bonner's promotional strategies turned what appeared to be the instantaneous conversion of the symbolic and cultural capital represented by exclusive publications and celebrity authorship into the economic capital of soaring issue and subscription sales, and likewise, he demonstrated that the formula could be made to work in the opposite direction: the extravagant display and application of economic capital appeared to produce and secure symbolic capital as well when he publicized, for instance, the enormous and unprecedented sums of money he paid to Fanny Fern ($100 a column), Henry Ward Beecher ($30,000 advance for his novel *Norwood*), Horace Greeley ($10,000 for his *Recollections* series), Henry Wadsworth Longfellow ($3,000 for the poem "The Hanging of the Crane"), Alfred Lord Tennyson ($5,000 for the poem "England and America in 1872"), and Edward Everett ($10,000 donation to Everett's Mt. Vernon Association in exchange for a series of letters).[36] While Clapp and the *Press* ridiculed the *Ledger*'s poor taste in literature and Bonner's crass commercial tactics, Bonner's example nonetheless encouraged wild fantasies about print's market potential and the equally pervasive idea that market demand responded as much to representations of the supply of literature (in the form of puffs, notices, and advertisements) as to the actual experience of reading that supply. Indeed, Clapp's interest in the symbolic capital to be gained from promoting the *Press*'s antipuffing policy, its discerning criticism and exclusive readership, and its comprehensive reporting on book and periodical publications, as well as his expectation that the *Press*'s distinction would eventually pay out significant sums of money, mirrored Bonner's priorities with the *Ledger* at the same time that Clapp bemoaned Bonner's influence upon the literary field.

Clapp promoted the *Press* as a necessary intervention in a literary market that was saturated with books and periodicals but had no reliable means of discernment. And yet, the very material conditions that helped Clapp claim this distinction for the *Press* were also the conditions in which the puffing system could thrive. Daniel Fineman has argued, more generally, that the high volume of objects produced by industrial capitalism forced individuals into a "specular relation" with most of the objects they consumed; in other words, these objects were "consumed as representations" and "according to their nominal qualities."[37] Thus, at the same time that critics like Clapp were increasingly empowered by readers who could not possibly keep up with the quantity of books and periodicals in circulation and relied upon those critics for accurate representations of their "nominal qualities," editors and publishers who puffed were likewise empowered when the print explosion further complicated the accountability and authenticity of predominantly anonymous reviews and notices. And while the line separating genuine criticism from puffery was not nearly as distinct as Clapp made it out to be in the *Saturday Press*, the scandal that Clapp drew around puffing provided the *Press* with a performative fiction that lent the paper distinction and purpose within a competitive marketplace.

The actual practice of puffing was more complicated and often less mendacious than the *Press* depicted it to be. In addition to the material conditions mentioned above, puffing grew out of a gift economy, whereby editorial favors were exchanged as a means of doing polite business, and the newspaper exchange list system, which encouraged editors to read, share, review, reprint, and promote material printed in other papers since periodicals were exempted from postage charges in the U.S. mail system. As Leon Jackson explains, "Exchange networks . . . had a tendency to generate alliances and networks of likeminded editors."[38] These networks of likeminded editors were ideally suited to the task of puffing and often grew into mutual admiration societies. One of Clapp's earliest editorials marked the slight trepidation he felt in refusing to reciprocate the praise other journals had given the *Saturday Press* at its debut:

[W]e trust we shall not be accused either of ingratitude or of jealousy, when we say, as we do most distinctly, that praise from papers which are equally ready to laud the first vulgar and flashy journal that comes along, is not an honor which we at all covet. Furthermore, nothing is more humiliating than to receive favors which one cannot reciprocate;

and we may as well announce, once for all, that we shall never adopt the policy of indiscriminate praise.[39]

The *Press*'s earliest declarations of independence were meant to excuse the paper from the textual and social relationships that otherwise might have led to "a potentially endless cycle of mutual indebtedness" and interfered with the autonomy of its criticism.[40] Thus, while puffing was yet a social practice with objectives and rewards that extended beyond the initial exchange of money in the literary marketplace, the *Saturday Press* chose to emphasize the technological and market-driven aspects of the practice in order to aggressively set the terms of its relations with other editors and papers. In other words, and as Whitman's treatment in the *Press* makes clear, the paper's "No Puffing" policy was actually an expedient way to control what and how it puffed rather than an abstemious rejection of the practice.

PUFFING IN THE *PRESS*: APPLETON'S *CYCLOPAEDIA*, BOOK-MAKING SYSTEMS, AND WHITMAN

Beginning with its third issue, the *Saturday Press* built its case against puffing by consistently excoriating the *New American Cyclopaedia: A Popular Dictionary of General Knowledge* (1857–1866), a multivolume encyclopedia edited by George Ripley and Charles A. Dana and recently published by D. Appleton and Company in New York.[41] According to the *Press*, this encyclopedia was widely judged "on both sides of the Atlantic, to be a miserable failure," and yet, because of the veneration accorded to the Appleton publishing house and its editors, the puffs for the volumes (and the advertisements of their increasing sales) threatened to drown out the necessary criticism of them.[42]

As a general practice, puffing collapsed the difference between advertising and criticism, but the *Cyclopaedia*'s continued success despite having its faults "laboriously set before the public" appeared to make that criticism irrelevant.[43] The *New American Cyclopaedia* was a special case in the *Press*'s view because the incredible sales it achieved through the puffing system—as well as the material conditions of writing the text itself—ran roughshod over the critical labor and scholarship that the *Press* valued so highly. Thus, in the pages of the *Press* the *Cyclopaedia* came to represent an abomination within the secondary order of literary production.

The *Press* traced the encyclopedia's numerous errors and self-contradictions to the below-market wages that the Appleton publishing house paid its writers. In "Literary Pay," the *Press* announced that *Harper's Magazine* paid ten to twenty "dollars a page" for "light contributions," while "for the carefully digested and laboriously condensed articles which a national Cyclopaedia demands from its contributors," the publishers of the *Cyclopaedia* paid "*two dollars* a page!"[44] "Two dollars a page," the writer continued, "are offered for scholarship, power of combination, condensation of information from a hundred sources, and the mechanical labor of putting the materials into literary form!" For this writer, "mechanical labor" is in no way antithetical to "literary form." Instead, the writer implies that "hack" work is a function primarily of "hack" pay, and that "literariness" is a quality that any print genre, medium, or worker might aspire to and achieve. And while the charge of puffing was most often invoked on behalf of deserving artists (in the abstract) who failed to secure a wide readership, not for lack of merit but for lack of social connections with the editors who mattered, the *Press*'s extended coverage of the *Cyclopaedia* controversy took a different tack and underscored its greater interest in the way puffing compromised periodical culture and criticism as a collective enterprise. The *Press* felt there was more at stake in its intervention against puffing than rescuing individual artists from obscurity or deflating the reputations of undeserving writers and their works that had been puffed up by friends and publishing houses; instead, the *Press* attempted to refine the literary field by first refining the periodical culture that gave literary culture its shape and made literature recognizable as such.[45]

In a hoax piece titled "The Japanese Book System," which doubled as a satire of encyclopedia-making, the *Saturday Press* imagined a crisis not just of systematic and mechanized book production, but of consumption as well. The piece reported that in Japan "there is but one publishing house," and that this lone house had developed a system of book-making—distinct from book-writing—that recombined the text and type of a primary text in order to produce a series of secondary texts that doubled as primary, authoritative, and autonomous texts themselves.[46] The reporter likened the process to a chemical recombination of atoms, offering the example that setting one text, hypothetically described as "*The History of Modern Philosophy*" and primarily concerned with the subjects "*History, Modern, and Philosophy*," would, in turn, produce "four books" from "these three elements." The books would differ "entirely in character as the components differ in arrangement," as we can see from the four titles produced in this example:

1. The *History of Modern Philosophy*
2. The *Philosophy of Modern History*
3. The *Modern History of Philosophy*
4. The *Modern Philosophy of History*

The writer continued to explain:

> When the work contains many elements, the number of combinations, and hence the number of works, is enormous. It is true that many of them seem nonsensical; but so firm is the faith of the people in the unerring certainty of the principle, that they reject none. The incomprehensible they regard as prophetic, and hence sacred, and not to be understood until the events unfold. . . . So if any work should contradict their preconceived opinions, they never contend, but submit as to an oracle.

While this hoax betrays an obvious anxiety about a mechanized system of production that replaces the genius of an author with the genius of a system, it also imagines a book-making system that has excised the shaping force of writers, critics, and compilers upon the consumption practices of readers. Such a literary field would have no use for the selection and consecration of texts provided by an institution like the *Saturday Press* because "the people" "submit" directly to these texts as if they were "an oracle." In a similar way, publishing house puffs attempted to collapse the difference between literary value and commercial value, and in this dystopian vision that was "The Japanese Book System," the *Saturday Press* imagined a world in which whatever the system or the publishing house could produce, no matter how nonsensical, would be read, valued, and consecrated as literature. For the *Press*, the scandal of "The Japanese Book System" was forged not only in the loss of authentic moments of inspired and autonomous literary production, the loss of an author and an aura, but also in the loss of the secondary agents and institutions that would otherwise give shape to that literary field.

By article's end "The Japanese Book System" reveals itself to be a satire aimed at the dubious production and circulation practices of the *New American Cyclopaedia*. In attempting to be both hoax and satire, "The Japanese Book System" was able to extend the *Press*'s critique of the *Cy-*

clopaedia scandal and puffing as a general practice, while also pointing to the hyperbolic aspects of that critique. The satirical reading of "The Japanese Book System" called into question the ideological underpinnings of the puff that were, however inadvertently, preserved in the *Press*'s criticism of the practice: namely, that readers were compliant masses open to the direction of critics and publishing houses, and likewise, that print markets were easily manipulated, responding, in an instant, to the flow of money and advertising. As the writer of this piece explicitly notes, "The Japanese Book System" and puffing, more generally, imagined (and relied upon the idea of) an incredibly "docil[e]" reading public that hardly aligned with the *Press*'s characterization of its public in other contexts as an intelligent and discerning collection of readers.[47] But if the *Press*'s faith in its readers' intelligence (not to mention the experience of its contributors as skeptical readers themselves) threw doubt upon the presumed gullibility and easy compliance of readers put forward in puffs, Clapp and the *Press* nonetheless found it harder to dismiss the intoxicating possibility that puffing would produce an inevitable and enviable success in the market.

This conflicted desire to both critique and enjoy the supposed benefits of puffing found its greatest extension in the *Press*'s treatment of Whitman throughout 1860. By Amanda Gailey's count, the *Press* printed "no fewer than seventy-two Whitman-related items" (notices, reviews, advertisements, parodies, and reprints from other papers) throughout that year, and while Gailey and Ted Genoways have advanced our understanding about what this promotion meant for Whitman's reception, I want to offer a reading of what that promotion meant for Clapp and the *Press*.[48]

If Clapp staked the *Press*'s reputation upon its antipuffing policy, how are we to understand the apparent contradiction between this policy and the *Press*'s flagrant puffing of Whitman? One explanation would be that the *Press* reserved the right to puff whom it pleased. Clapp prized authentic opinions in the *Press*'s editorials and once joked that its editorial "we" would signify not "men in general, including the speaker," as Webster defined it, but rather "the speaker alone excluding men in general."[49] Clapp later defended what he thought to be Juliette Beach's "unfavorable view" of *Leaves of Grass* along these lines, writing, "It always gives us pleasure to print every variety of opinion upon such subjects, especially when . . . the careful reader can have no doubt as to the writer's meaning."[50] These comments open up the possibility of a "gentle[r]," more sincere form of puffing that supported a variety of opinions and the individuals who wrote them in contradistinction to the repetitive message of a publisher's puff distributed through multiple papers.[51]

For Whitman scholars, the fact that the *Saturday Press*'s numerous puffs for Whitman coexisted alongside negative reviews of *Leaves of Grass* has exemplified the principle that all press was good press for the likes of Whitman and Clapp. A longer view of the *Press*'s antipuffing campaign suggests, however, that a more complex understanding of the contradiction was available to readers of the *Press*. Much like "The Japanese Book System," which presented readers with two contradictory modes of reading at once (a report that asked to be read as hoax *and* satire), the *Press*'s puffing of Whitman performed a similar contradiction. On one hand, Clapp's puffing of Whitman reflected the very kind of cronyism and "clique"-ishness that his "Characteristics of *The New York Saturday Press*" explicitly rejected.[52] Similarly, Clapp's financial dealings with Thayer and Eldridge's publishing house mirrored the relations between other publishing houses and periodicals and likewise blurred the line between criticism and advertising.[53] But on the other hand, the *Press*'s outspoken rejection of the practice made its puffing of Whitman performative and self-reflexive in ways that common puffs were not.

Take, for instance, the failed reading of Whitman performed by Umos within the paper's Washington correspondence section, which carried forward the manufactured controversy that followed the 1859 Christmas Eve publication of Whitman's "A Child's Reminiscence."[54] Here, Umos echoed the conclusions of the Cincinnati reviewer in declaring that he had not "poetry enough to understand Walt's Yawp," but he also connected the automatic, inauthentic writing imagined in "The Japanese Book System" to Whitman's poem when he suggested "that Whitman [had] found a lot of dictionary-*pi* going off at auction, bought it for a song, employed a Chinese typesetter from the Bible House to set it up in lines of unequal length, and then sold it to you [Clapp] as an original Poem."[55] Umos's editorial about another failed reading of Whitman further satirized the reader—in this case, himself—who "didn't get" Whitman, but his performance also questioned the notion of a docile, compliant reading public, which, as I have noted, was a crucial part of midcentury thinking about puffing. Like the Cincinnati reviewer before him, Umos resisted the presumed force of the *Saturday Press*'s endorsement of Whitman and thereby represented, in part, the general unruliness of the antebellum reading public that would have been dubious of a concerted puffing campaign.

However strategic Clapp's intentions might have been with the *Saturday Press*'s promotion of Whitman, the print campaign that actually transpired was hardly as calculating or devious in its effects as the *Press*'s criticism of puffing might have led its readers to expect.[56] Far from determining a uniform reception for the third edition of *Leaves of Grass*, the *Press*'s puffing of Whitman produced and reproduced a range of responses to the poet that proliferated outwards in multiple directions and troubled the notion that puffing yielded reliable, predictable results. Rather, in puffing Whitman, the *Saturday Press* played at and played with representations of Whitman's reception. At the same time that the positive reviews of Whitman were in line with those of traditional puffs, there was also an emergent sense that periodical readers were savvy to editorial hype and had the ability to spot and resist the feedback loops created by puffs. Umos's critique (and its placement in the *Saturday Press*) reveals the *Press* trying to encourage and represent that kind of savvy reader while also hoping to score a windfall in popular readership.

These distinctions from the common practices of puffing did not save the *Press* from charges of hypocrisy, but they did provide the paper with a means of drawing more attention to the context of its circulation and further extending its claims to distinction within a competitive periodical marketplace. Its Whitman puffs remained idiosyncratic as well, both for the simple fact that no other paper could have been accused of *wanting* to puff Whitman and for the more interesting forms this puffing assumed within the pages of the *Press*. In this way, Clapp's puffing of Whitman did not explicitly compromise the *Press*'s independence, but rather asserted its editorial prerogative to champion what and whom it pleased.

The *Press*'s treatment of puffing—and the attendant vagaries of literary reception and profit—has consequences for the current critical narrative surrounding the production of the 1856 and 1860 editions of *Leaves of Grass*. If, as this narrative suggests, these editions demonstrate Whitman's evolving response to the inadequate reception of his poetry, we must recognize, first, that Whitman's sense of failure was predicated upon the hyperbolic market potential ascribed to books in puffs, and second, that Whitman himself not only embraced the culture of puffing and reprinting, but also integrated these practices into his own poetic project.[57] As Meredith McGill has argued (with respect to the 1856 edition), Whitman's poetic and promotional strategies increasingly reinforced one another: he developed "techniques for extending his poetic voice, using poetic and publishing strategies that draw our attention elsewhere for an account of origins, cultivate a range of possible responses, and allow a voice we will come to recognize as Whitman's to emerge in their very midst."[58] And yet, speaking with Horace Traubel in 1889, Whitman idealized reception as a direct exchange between the poet and "the people," while disparaging the indirect means that, by default, introduced him to the reading public: "[the people] have no way of getting acquainted with me: I get to them through the falsifying interpretations of the newspapers: through slander, even: which is not getting to them at all."[59] Built on the distortions of "literary shams," "falsifying interpretations," and the manipulation of symbolic capital, the publishing context that the later Whitman aims to disavow is the very context in which puffing—and *Leaves of Grass*—had originally taken root.

NOTES

I am grateful for the contributions made by the earliest readers of this essay: Greg Beckett, Virginia Jackson, Edward Whitley, Joanna Levin, Eleanore Eckstrom, and the Medford School Writing Group.

1. Cohen, *Fabrication*, 33.

2. "Characteristics of *The New York Saturday Press*," *SP*, Dec. 11, 1858.

3. "The Palace and Princes of the Press," *SP*, Nov. 27, 1858, which reproduces the portion of the Boston *Saturday Evening Gazette*'s notice quoted above.

4. Ibid. In Poe's writings the balloon became an apt figure for a print culture bloated by puffs, countering the idealized, Habermasian image of print as a public sphere constructed through rational debate. See Cohen, *Fabrication*, 56–64.

5. For more on this publicity campaign, see Amanda Gailey's essay in this volume.

6. "A Failure to Be Regretted," *SP*, Nov. 17, 1860.

7. "Alas! Poor 'Saturday Press,'" *SP*, Nov. 17, 1860.

8. "To Whom It May Concern," *SP*, Nov. 6, 1858.

9. "Characteristics of *The New York Saturday Press*."

10. The final reprint of this notice appeared in *SP*, May 7, 1859.

11. Stansell, "Whitman at Pfaff's," 110. See also Seigel, *Bohemian Paris*, 5–13; and Levin, *Bohemia in America*, introduction.

12. See, e.g., "The Palace and Princes of the Press."

13. "A Failure to Be Regretted."

14. "Alas! Poor 'Saturday Press.'"

15. Bourdieu, *Rules*, 81 (Bourdieu's emphasis).

16. Ibid.

17. Howells, *Literary Friends*, 70.

18. Levin, *Bohemia*, 66. Stansell makes a similar point when she writes that in Clapp's New York (as opposed to in Boston) the "rules of writerly entrepreneurship" were "predicated on manipulating money and publicity rather than social connections and patronage" ("Whitman at Pfaff's," 122).

19. Howells, *Literary Friends*, 16.

20. Clapp's ambitions for the *Press* as a journal of record, as well as his disdain for the flood of "flash," "trash," and inconsequential literature that circulated in staggering proportions thanks to the popularity of other literary weeklies like Robert Bonner's *New York Ledger*, are evident in his editorial comments. See *SP*, Jan. 8, 1859.

21. For more on the porousness of this border and newspaper culture in nineteenth-century France, see Terdiman, *Discourse/Counter-Discourse*, chap. 2.

22. Bourdieu, *Rules*, 53.

23. Stansell, "Whitman at Pfaff's," 114–15. See also, Jackson, *Business of Letters*, chap. 1.

24. Stansell, "Whitman at Pfaff's," 114–15.

25. Ibid. See Levin, *Bohemia in America*, 67–68, for a related critique of the significance Stansell accords to the "gatherings at Pfaff's."

26. Cohen, *Fabrication*, 12.

27. Dowling, *Capital Letters*, 18.

28. Henkin, *City Reading*, 128.

29. Genoways, *Walt Whitman and the Civil War*, 74. On December 5, Thayer and Eldridge informed Whitman that the firm was bankrupt.

30. "Card," *SP*, Nov. 3, 1860.

31. Ibid.

32. "Letter to Walt Whitman," May 14, 1860, *WWC* 2:375.

33. See Greenspan, *Walt Whitman*, 24.

34. See Mott, *History*, 356.

35. Smith, Introduction, xvii.

36. Figures found in Dowling, *Business*, chap. 3.

37. Fineman, "Parodic and Production," 76.

38. Jackson, *Business of Letters*, 123.

39. "To Whom It May Concern," *SP*, Nov. 6, 1858.

40. Jackson, *Business of Letters*, 125.

41. Perry Miller reports that the *Cyclopaedia* "sold into the millions, earning Ripley over $100,000." See Miller, *Raven*, 341; and "To Whom It May Concern."

42. "Literary Pay," *SP*, Nov. 13, 1858.

43. Ibid.

44. Ibid (emphasis in original).

45. For more on the exemplary relations shared between Ticknor and Fields's literary publishing house and the periodical press, see Charvat, *Profession*, 168–89; and Brodhead, *School of Hawthorne*, 48–58.

46. "The Japanese Book System," *SP*, Feb. 12, 1859.

47. Ibid.

48. See Amanda Gailey's essay in this volume; and Genoways, *Walt Whitman*, 44.

49. "Editorial," *SP*, Oct. 23, 1858.

50. "Notes of the Week," *SP*, June 2, 1860; see also, Genoways, *Walt Whitman*, 48–50.

51. "A Failure to Be Regretted."

52. "Characteristics of *The New York Saturday Press.*"

53. The strategic blurring of this line is evident in the notices that Whitman wrote and submitted to Brooklyn and New York newspapers regarding the Christmas Eve publication of "A Child's Reminiscence" in the *Saturday Press*. See Amanda Gailey's essay in this volume; and Genoways, *Walt Whitman*, 19–20.

54. See Jackson, *Before Modernism*.

55. Umos, "Waifs from Washington VI: The Setting of a Jewel," *SP*, Jan. 14, 1860.

56. See Genoways, *Walt Whitman*, 42–78.

57. For an exemplary version of this general argument, see Reynolds, *Walt Whitman's America*, 339–82.

58. McGill, "Walt Whitman and the Poetics of Reprinting," 56.

59. *WWC* 3:467.

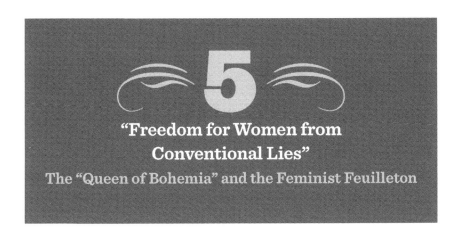

"Freedom for Women from Conventional Lies"

The "Queen of Bohemia" and the Feminist Feuilleton

JOANNA LEVIN

In his "Street Yarn" of 1856, Walt Whitman observes: "A lady—slender and elegant—in black from head to foot. That is Miss Ada Clare, called by many a perfect beauty; questionless of decided talent; one about whom many interesting stories might be told."[1] If "interesting" operated as code for "scandalous" in 1856, by the time Whitman reminisced with Horace Traubel about a gathering at Ada Clare's Forty-second Street brownstone, Clare's name, once invoked, immediately prompts Whitman to reflect on her (and other female bohemians') dubious creditworthiness and the question of how her support of *Leaves of Grass* redounded on him: "I think it [the gathering] was at Ada Clare's: and by the way, it is very curious that the girls have been my sturdiest defenders, upholders. Some would say they were girls little to my credit. I disagree with them there, and I suppose that's not the only place where we disagree either!"[2] After raising doubts about the respectability of "the girls," Whitman breezily defends his defenders and aligns himself against the unspecified naysayers who looked askance at the female bohemians—and, by extension, at the volume of poetry that they collectively championed.

For her part, Ada Clare's one recorded reference to Whitman occurs when she was in fact defending him in the *Saturday Press* against those who doubted his poetic bona fides: "Whitman's 'A Child's Reminiscence' could only have been written by a poet, and versifying would not help it. I love the poem."[3] Appearing in the larger context of the bohemian publicity blitz on behalf of the 1860 edition of *Leaves*, this declaration also emerged from the more immediate context of Clare's weekly column, "Thoughts and Things." This particular column begins with satiric commentary about the "agitating" subject of "women's dress" and segues into a short, pithy comparison of Whitman's poem and William Winter's "Orgia: The Song of a Ruined Man." Of the latter poem, Clare declares, "I cannot admire it," explaining that it is reducible to a rote formula: "With the text he begins with, a practiced versifier might go on rhyming until the seas were dry." Predictable patterns of invention and verse provide the binary opposite of "A Child's Reminiscence," the more organic and romantic emanation of the true "poet." One poem translates the voice of the sea, and the other threatens to dry it up.

The opposition between the natural and the unnatural organizes both sections of this column, but it is the all too weighty artificial "thing"— women's dress—that generates the most "thoughts." Emerging as the objective correlative of patriarchal control, female fashion, according to Clare, presents abundant material for an ongoing battle between the sexes, culminating most recently in the furor over the "Bloomer": "One thing above others pleases me: it is to see men annoyed by the prevailing fashion . . . Because, when women proposed to wear a truly sensible and beautiful dress, men opposed it, not only by argument, but by brute force." And yet, though she charts the sexual fault lines in the fight over "the Bloomer," Clare ultimately takes the role of mediator rather than combatant. She emphasizes the aesthetic appeal the costume would have when modeled by "a beautiful young woman," adding that comfort and sexual attractiveness would mutually reinforce each other, and by extension, the interests of men and women in female dress might harmonize instead of conflict: "Add to this picture the health which so comfortable a dress, conducing to open-air exercise, would bring . . . and men can hardly help melting before this vision of loveliness."[4] Further elaborating on the utopian potential of "the Bloomer," Clare extends the hope that by relieving women "from the continued burden and fretfulness of unnatural attire," the costume could potentially "bring with it a freedom for women from conventional lies."[5]

This column thus allows us to see how Clare's support of Whitman fit into *her* larger bohemian agenda. Following her argument on behalf of less restrictive dress, her praise of Whitman's ability to eschew traditional "versifying" unites free verse and "the Bloomer" in a combined space of bohemian freedom. On the pages of the *Saturday Press*, at Pfaff's, and in her informal salon on Forty-second Street, Clare fashions *la vie bohème* as a liberatory zone for women, all the while musing on how it could be used more broadly to reconstruct relationships between the sexes.[6] As the widely recognized "Queen of Bohemia" during the late 1850s and 1860s, Clare pioneered new intersections between women's rights and bohemianism, synergistically redefining both movements in relation to the other.

SEPARATE SPHERES, HIDDEN DEPTHS, AND THE LITERARY WOMAN

The future "Queen of Bohemia" was born Ada Agnes Jane McElhenney in 1834 to an aristocratic South Carolinian family.[7] Ada fled her apparent destiny, however, refusing to play the part of the Southern Belle and eventual plantation mistress. She ran off to New York and financed her trip by stealing the money her grandfather had collected for a John C. Calhoun monument. She did leave a note, however, vowing to pay interest on this sum. Nonetheless, by appropriating funds intended to honor Calhoun, a distant relative and one of the leading representative men of Southern patriarchy, Ada weighted her departure with considerable symbolic baggage. She later explained her action in a letter to a Charleston friend: "I have unfortunately one of those active, restless minds which must have some steady and exciting occupation. . . . I . . . will try to find an active sphere for myself."[8] She legally changed her name to Ada Clare in 1857, with a nod to the Charles Dickens character from *Bleak House*, another blonde, blue-eyed beauty who struggled over a family inheritance.[9] By the time Whitman observed Clare in his "Street Yarn" of 1856, she was "possessed of some wealth," and her search for an "active sphere" had led her to the theatrical stage and to the publication of essays and poems in such periodicals as the *New York Atlas*. Some of the "interesting stories" referenced by Whitman in his "Yarn" were eventually told in print by Clare herself. In a series of articles published in the *Atlas* between November 1856 and January 1857, she revealed her consuming passion for the famed international heartbreaker and concert pianist Louis Moreau Gottschalk. She first veiled her own identity, but she boldly revealed her authorship in the title of the last of these articles, "Ada Clare on Suicide." Clare had already rejected one preexisting cultural script, refusing to play the part of the Southern Belle; in this article, she reveals that she will reject another: she will not be the suicidal Victorian heroine who takes her own life after being seduced and abandoned. "I say to myself, my poor Ada, this is a short play and you may as well see the end of it," she declares. Clare arrives at this conclusion after one last reference to the identity of her seducer, however, wondering, "Are doubt, despair, and Gottschalk, things of which the soul in death takes no cognizance . . . or do they loom up in the untraveled country as eternal torture?"[10]

Between the time she penned these words and the beginning of her reign as queen of New York's bohemia, Ada Clare spent a couple of years in Paris. When the *Saturday Press* described the "Royal Bohemian Supper" given by the newly appointed "Queen of Bohemia" in her "palace" brownstone on Forty-second Street on Christmas night in 1859, we know that among "Her Majesty's subjects" was an "infant Prince of Bohemia."[11] The details surrounding the birth of Clare's son Aubrey remain shrouded in a degree of mystery, but it was widely assumed that Gottschalk was the father and that Aubrey was born out of wedlock.[12] This then was the celebrated and notorious Ada Clare whom the New York correspondent of the *Philadelphia Dispatch* observed one night in a private box at the Winter Garden in 1860:

> About a year ago Bohemia had a grand banquet at the house of a certain lady who is an amateur actress and a brilliant writer for the SATURDAY PRESS—which journal par example is the organ of Bohemia. The lady is dashing in her appearance, gay, light-hearted, a genuine blonde, and reported to have "moneys." . . . At the banquet in question this lady was chosen "Queen of Bohemia," and it was this fair monarch whom I beheld in the theatre . . . Near her sat . . . the editor of the SATURDAY PRESS, to whose columns the "Queen" contributes such bewitchingly audacious, such sparkling wicked, such subtly dubious communications, a la Madame Dudevant [George Sand].[13]

This dispatch reveals that Clare's exalted status as "Queen of Bohemia"— the title the *Saturday Press* had first introduced in print the previous year—had begun to gain traction beyond the pages of the house "organ of Bohemia." Yet, while Clare no doubt appreciated the *Philadelphia Dispatch*'s nod to her brilliance as a writer and probably embraced the characterization of her columns as "bewitchingly audacious," the notion that her columns were "wicked," even if modified and tempered by the adjective "sparkling," would likely have given her pause. Much like Whitman, Clare braved and even courted scandal, but only in the name of what she saw as a higher moral ground, one that she explicitly linked to the combined social energies of feminism and *la vie bohème*.

The first American bohemians, like their French counterparts, dedicated themselves to a life centered around artistic production and defined themselves and their community in relation to their (sometime) antithesis, "the bourgeois"—especially as embodied in "the respectable sort," or "Mrs. Grundy," the moralizing matron from the eighteenth-century play *Speed the Plow*.[14] Ada Clare followed suit, both challenging and adapting contemporary bourgeois discourses of "True Womanhood" while fashioning herself "Queen of Bohemia."[15] With respect to bohemian Paris, Jerrold Seigel has argued that bohemia "grew up where the boundaries of bourgeois life were murky and uncertain,"[16] and for Clare, bohemia helped to map an unstable terrain between men and women, the public and the private, the conventional and the authentic, the absurd and the commonplace, the passionate and the sentimental, the virtuous and the chaste, the subversive and the genteel, and the European and the American. Alternately upholding and collapsing these divisions in the name of what was itself an unstable compound—a feminist bohemia—Clare combines "Thoughts and Things," the title of her weekly columns, in a lively mixture of reflection and description.

The very title of her weekly column suggests a tribute to one of her important feminist precursors, Margaret Fuller, whose own dispatches to the *New York Daily Tribune* were called "Things and Thoughts in Europe."[17] For her part, Clare wrote from "bohemia," that mobile cultural territory that she and her contemporaries defined as existing within and without the United States. Clare's most general description of the content of her columns appears when she defends her (and by extension, the *Saturday Press*'s) refusal to engage in the practice of "puffing": "I will . . . take the liberty of saying here, that this series of articles commenced with a view of stating my honest convictions about the passing events of the day, and that in the same course I will strive to continue."[18] Just as the Pfaffians imported "bohemia" from France, so many *Saturday Press* columns emulated the structure of the nineteenth-century French feuilleton. Like feuilletons, Clare's weekly columns move fluidly, sometimes abruptly, through a variety of topics: they engage in literary, artistic, and dramatic criticism; chronicle the latest fashions; and comment on cultural, social, and ethical issues. Their style is often witty, parodic, and explicitly subjective.[19] Traversing the wide territory of *la vie bohème* and its moral and artistic coordinates, her otherwise apolitical columns frequently center on questions of gender and women's rights. If Fuller's dispatches dealt with a broader range of social and political issues, Clare nonetheless shared her predecessor's commitment to reimagining gender roles and to developing a national/international culture that would improve the position of women.

Many of her columns are self-reflexive, and Clare herself tells us how to read "Thoughts and Things." She bares one of her central rhetorical devices when she announces: "Humor is the true 'reduction to the absurd,' of the false social problem. When the foolish human throat wears itself out with shrieking its pitiful platitudes about talent, and love, and women, and religion, humor takes pride in displaying the ludicrous side of the argument." Implicitly connected to the playful spirit of *la vie bohème* and its ability to uncover the absurdity of the commonplace, she further legitimates her choice of humor over linear argumentation with a simple rhetorical question: "When men argue about the incapacity of women, with the works of George Sand and Elizabeth Browning and Charlotte Bronte . . . under their eyes, of what avail will it be to argue with them?"[20] Similarly, she applauds a female speaker at a "Woman's Rights Convention" for injecting humor into the otherwise dry proceedings: "If indeed there is anything capable of being treated in a broad comic vein, it is the position in which woman stands towards man, his assumption of her inferiority, etc. The subject is as closely connected with humor as it is with pathos."[21] Tapping this "broad comic vein" in yet another column, Clare simply turns the tables on her male readers, reversing expectations in an extended satire of the doctrine of separate spheres. "I confess that though I often admire the writings of men, it always pains me to see a man exposing himself to general remark and to the gaze of women, by coming publicly forward," Clare writes. "The sacred precinct of home is the true sphere of men. Modesty, obedience, sobriety, are the true male virtues." However playful, this parody also allows Clare to insinuate, quite pointedly, that the ideology of separate spheres is motivated more by male fear of having to compete with women in public pursuits than by an honest attempt to slot the sexes into their proper roles: "It must not be supposed we do not love men; in their proper sphere we are willing to love, cherish, and protect them. But we do not want them as rivals—we wish to be able to unbend to them. Their strength must lie in their weakness. . . . Besides the question is not what the man is, but what we women wish him to be."[22]

As Clare was well aware, her humor might also have the effect of softening her arguments, making them more palatable to a potentially hostile audience. As she notes in another column, no doubt with a certain amount of irony, "I am apt to take extreme views on all subjects, so I think humor is the smiling, rounded, flesh-filled form."[23] Thus likened to a conventionally attractive womanly visage and shape, humor implicitly feminized Clare's columns, even as those columns challenged prescriptive gender roles. Yet, rather than compromising her message, this fleshy personification of humor is very much in line with her larger feminist-bohemian agenda, one that sought to build a vibrant heterosocial space that accommodated the erotic while advancing the position of women in the public sphere. Alive to the difficulties of this agenda, Clare rises to the rhetorical challenge, addressing herself to both male and female readers through a cunning blend of humor, charm, and provocation.

Indeed, her playful rhetoric contrasts with more direct critiques of the separate spheres published elsewhere in the *Saturday Press*. One editorial, perhaps written by Henry Clapp Jr., states bluntly, "Our notion is that woman's peculiar sphere is whatever field of action she finds herself best adapted to," adding that the *Press* supports women's "complete emancipation from the silly laws of society, which prescribe to them, now, as their first duty, to learn the art of administering to the pleasures of a sex which does all in its power to degrade them."[24] Clare's own tactic was to highlight the absurdity of these "silly laws" and to reduce the potential for defensive reactions through humor. The artist A. L. Rawson suggests that Clare's manner in the semipublic sphere of the bohemian salon she held at her Forty-second Street brownstone was much like that of her authorial persona, and it counteracted Clapp's sharper tendencies: "She was a royal and dear little woman, whose saving grace and sweetness outshone and overpowered for good the king's evil influences of pipe, beer and cynic joke."[25]

From her image of the rosy young "Bloomerite" to her evocation of humor as a voluptuous form, Clare sought to celebrate female sensuality and eroticism. She did not subscribe to ideas of female "passionlessness," the complex Victorian sexual ideology that had both feminist and antifeminist adherents. As Nancy Cott has argued, many women found this ideology serviceable "in gaining social and familial power"; however, Cott also observes, "feminists were the first to question and oppose the ideology once it was entrenched. When prudery became confused with passionlessness, it undermined women physically and psychologically by restricting their knowledge of their own sexual functioning."[26] Clare was among the first early feminists to speak out against this ideology, and she was likely influenced in part by the bohemians' interest in Fourierism. For Charles Fourier and his bohemian adherents, "passionate attraction" is "the impulse, given to us by nature prior to any reflection," a potent force that could resist social prejudice and propel change.[27]

Clare dedicated herself to the recognition and legitimation of such impulses. In one column, for example, she belies the very notion of female passionlessness, slyly noting the avid, though covert, attention lavished by various respectable women on William Page's painting of a naked Venus, then on display at the Dusseldorf Gallery. She asks, "If the Herald's suggestion, that the Venus on exhibition outstepped the lines of modesty, caused such an influx of ladies to the Gallery, what multitudes would have flown there, in case there had been a hint that an immodest Apollo was to be seen?"[28] In many other columns, Clare affirms the importance of the passions, broadly defined, including but not limited to those related to romantic sexual love. Indeed, for Clare, the female performer, often celebrated in her columns, became the ultimate representative of an unfettered, passionate female nature: "It is only on the stage that the woman is taken out of the world's straight-jacket, and left with free limbs and free soul. The actress, the singer, may put away convention, cant, and hypocritical moralities . . . Her beauty, her talent, her instinct, her oratorical or vocal powers, her grace, her passions, are all to be used to the utmost and godlike extent. She is to go forth and be great without illustrating any moral tract."[29] It was the stage that released the performer, suspending the mandates of "the world," counteracting the artifice of traditional femininity, and creating the space for freedom. According to Rawson, Clare "often said in after years when on the stage that the mimic life of the theatre was more real than any other," its theatricality, paradoxically enough, revealing a path to the authenticity she sought.[30] Consummate art remained the surest point of access to an essential soul that might free the individual from the trappings of restrictive convention—something like the "soul of revolt, source of all rebellions, or pure law of the revolutionary" that Michel Foucault described (and rejected as a theoretical possibility), but which Clare upheld, again and again, as "the free, fearless, untampered with convictions of the soul [that] are in themselves the purest and largest logic."[31] For the romantic Clare, it was not so much that the stage foregrounded the basic truth that women are always already playing a socially constructed role; or if it did, it at least freed women from constrained or banal role-playing and allowed them to assume the full dignity of tragic heroism. Clare herself pursued a career as an actress, and she used her columns to praise many of her female contemporaries in the dramatic arts. She had exacting demands: "Let the artist beware . . . that she lead us into no puny, conventional circle of art . . . She must lead us to the brink of those fiery deeps which underlie the cold crust of human existence."[32]

Providing a passport to these previously inaccessible realms, "the illustrious prima-donna Adelaide Cortesi" was one who, for Clare, numbered among the "splendid types of genius which sweep stormily through you, revealing to you the depths of your own nature, even as the whirlwinds drive asunder waters of the sea, till you can almost see the dim sands beneath them." The best actresses and singers could reveal elemental truths of human nature to such a revelatory degree that they generated "a certain sentiment of intoxication."[33] Unlike most sentimental discourse, the uncanny "sentiment of intoxication" that Clare identifies does not dissolve the self in sympathetic identification with the other; rather, the performer provides the romantic mirror that allows the individual to come into greater focus.[34]

In thus privileging the hidden "depths of your own nature," Clare participates in the emerging "semiotics of 'depth'" that, according to Joel Pfister, "gave weight to the premise that there exists a deeper, truer, precultural self that is more essential than the social self."[35] Pfister also adds that the recovery (or production) of such a self galvanized the early-twentieth-century bohemia of Greenwich Village at a time when the release of "suppressed desires" seemed to presage a broader social transformation, and Marx and Freud, in the hands of the Greenwich Villagers, emerged as plausible coconspirators in a bohemian revolutionary moment.[36] The first American bohemians anticipated this desire to access and release a liberatory stratum of psychic depth. Indeed, what Clare saw in Cortesi and other female performers, the bohemians also revered in Whitman. As Rawson later recalled, "it was the general conviction of the coterie that Whitman had torn off the conventional geegaws from human nature and glorified man," adding that Henry Clapp, the "King of Bohemia," was wont to urge, "'Come, Whitman, you savage, open a page of nature for us.'"[37] For Clare, this larger bohemian effort to circumvent cultural encoding in the name of hidden depths and natural impulse promised a specifically feminist wind-fall—the "freedom for women from conventional lies" that propelled her bohemianism.[38]

Though Clare highlighted the value of the female performer in locating transformative depths, she maintains that most women writers were not given, or did not take, the same amount of license: "in literature, in science, in the other arts, the opposite principle prevails [from that of the stage]: the woman who attempts to work, must wrench out all that is truly passionate from her nature, before she can be considered the respectable and useful worker." Instead of reinscribing the "moral dogma, the conventional dogma, the social dogma," Clare calls on women writers to "draw from the deep current of love, of passion, of grief, that boils down under their own silent hearts."[39] As part of her feminist-bohemian agenda, Clare had long dedicated herself to "admiring the capacities of my sex" in her literary and dramatic criticism, yet she was ready to criticize when women writers failed to advance the position of women or to deliver the literary qualities she admired. Augusta Evans's *Beulah*, for example, allegedly a "waxen" imitation of *Jane Eyre*, spurred Clare's harshest criticism. "'Jane Eyre' was a breathing, blood-warmed being. . . . In her wrists, you felt the beatings of purple pulses; and troops of passionate longings," Clare notes, before adding these devastating comments (which seem to have led *Beulah*'s publisher to pull its advertisements from the *Saturday Press*): "But 'Beulah' is a wearisome, artificial piece of pasteboard, in whose troubles you cannot sympathize, whose pride is obstinacy,—whose grief, sentimentalism of the blabbiest sort."[40]

Jane Eyre, unsurprisingly, stands as an exemplary text for Clare, a standard of excellence against which other works by women writers must be measured. As Nancy Armstrong has argued, the fiction of the Brontë sisters was a leading force in the production of passionate depth from within "a recognizably modern form of consciousness." If Jane Austen's novels represented a harmonious blend of social convention and individual desire, the Brontës, on the contrary, promoted a new "relation of surface to depth" since "their heroines typically desire the one man whom society forbids them to marry, giving rise to the notion that social conventions are, in an essential way, opposed to individual desire."[41] *Jane Eyre* thus provides a likely template for feminist-bohemian desire, but *Beulah* leaves Clare cold, its variety of sentimentalism at odds with the bracing and catalytic passion that she sought.

For Clare, women writers who met patriarchal expectations were simply sellouts, though she makes a halfhearted attempt to sympathize with women who chose more traditional paths in life and literature: "Few women are strong enough to choose between truth and the world's good opinion. For in the latter path though it lead them away from immortal truth, it leads them to some monotonous, leaden respectability and much lazy peace."[42] Only honesty, in Clare's view, could promote more fulfilling relationships between the sexes, ultimately enabling better friendships and love affairs and promoting cooperation in the public sphere. Earning Clare's praise, one woman writer who did not "wrench out all that is truly passionate from her nature" was Harriet Prescott. Upon reading the first installment of "The Amber Gods" in the *Atlantic Monthly*, Clare enthuses: "I am so dazzled by a reading of the first number, that I hardly dare express my opinion of it . . . Is there no redundance in all this blaze of glowing rhetoric, in this passionate outpouring of wildering words?"[43] In a later column, Clare confesses: "I am awaiting the developments of her story, the 'Amber Gods,' with some agitation, chiefly because I am cherishing a tender, let us hope not fatal passion for its hero." However tongue-in-cheek, this confession then yields a reflection that speaks directly to one of the central conflicts explored in Clare's early autobiographical writings and later novel: the question of how to reconcile self and other, female autonomy and romantic passion. "Let Miss Prescott beware how she introduces as heroes into her romances, those ravishing darlings of reality, whom men must always sneer at, and women ever adore, since in loving these only, can she learn the vast and self sustaining resources of her own deep heart," Clare writes, insisting on the paradox that romantic ravishment can lead to greater self-realization and independence.[44]

Still, though Clare demands passion and honesty from women writers, she recognizes the difficulty of winning support from the male literary authorities who demanded "conventional lies" instead of passionate depths and literary realism: "But O! my brothers, if you were not here to persuade her to betray herself, to sell herself for your patronage, if she were let loose from lies, and could speak that she knows and feels and suffers,—sneers, contempt, misconception, would die on your lips, and we two sexes would be better friends; we could love each other better."[45] And yet, preferring their own fictions of femininity, even when faced with contradictory evidence, these male literary gatekeepers, according to Clare, "hold truth [to be] of no consequence" when assessing the work of female contemporaries: "Does he not insist that the woman's efforts are weak, when the one he is criticizing rises up into the heavens for very strength? Does he not stop to state that the queen of the poultry-yard, the divine muffin-maker, is his divinity?"[46] In her capacity as the "Queen of Bohemia" rather than the "queen of the poultry-yard," however, Clare urges men, once again, to overcome their prejudices, to support female artistic productions, and not to view female writers as potential "rivals" who must be confined to a private sphere. Appealing to their "manly honor" and expressing the very love she hopes they will reciprocate, Clare insists: "The man should exalt and assist the woman, even as she should exalt and assist him. The two sexes need have no jealousies, no injustice, no hatred between them in the abstract. Nature divided them into two sexes, that they might the better love each other."[47] Variations of this refrain, this hope that the sexes "might the better love each other" reverberate throughout Clare's columns. Sexual divisions need not necessitate a separation of spheres of influence or gendered endeavors, and honesty (when widely disseminated in print) could promote more satisfying intimate relationships; once free from the "conventional lies" that had been foisted upon them—and that they may well have internalized—women would receive public recognition for who they really were, and such recognition would in turn provide the basis for the reconstruction of as private an emotion as love. Like the model recently theorized by Elizabeth Dillon, Clare's conception of "the public sphere blurs the distinction between public and private in part because it points toward the mutual constitution of public sphere recognition and private subjectivity"; Clare's sense of the inextricability of the public and private— and the role of print and such social spaces as "bohemia" in meditating between the two—is at the core of her feminist bohemianism.[48]

Ruled by its queen, bohemia became a space of possible reconciliation. Clare insists, for instance, that the monstrous "Blue-Stocking" of yore no longer terrorizes the literary field; instead, under the (somewhat ironic?) guise of mourning the demise of this gender-bending, part Amazonian, part Gorgonian beast whose pen had "dried up the source of milk in her breasts," Clare announces the arrival of the benign (though "amusing"!) literary woman, who is also the exemplar of true womanhood:

> Now, alas! How painful the contrast. The literary woman is hardly to be distinguished from the rest of her sex, except in the small matter of being a trifle more amusing. . . . The whiteness of her breast shines like

stars, and the most limpid blue of heaven courses itself in veins thereon, giving sweet entertainment to the holy angel of love.

She is full of warm aspirations, deep longings, kindly sentiments, entertaining thoughts, and above all others proveth the glory of the master-passion. The male feareth her no longer; he knoweth how prone she is to love him.[49]

Of course, like the Blue-Stocking, who, according to Clare, had "mocketh at [men] in her wrath . . . snorting tempest-making words," Clare herself does her fair share of parodying men in her columns, but she claims that her motivation is love rather than anger, and she refuses to see any fatal contradiction between grace, beauty, and romantic devotion—the "master-passion"—and female advancement in the public sphere.

And yet, in another column, Clare suggests that the reputation of literary women remains very much in doubt precisely *because* of their susceptibility to the "master-passion." She takes issue with Rose Terry's quaint "Matilda Muffin," a sketch that, Clare notes, wastes time debunking the Blue-Stocking instead of taking on a more current target:

A thing has passed away here, long before it ceases to be visible in Connecticut [Terry's home]. . . . In metropolitan cities the literary woman is no longer accused of sternness toward the other sex: frailty is what they accuse her of now. The male, who is always the protector of virtue, follows vindictive in her footsteps, to dry the tears no longer of the betrayed mutton-chop, but of injured propriety: her crime he says is no longer a domestic, but a moral one.[50]

A later column makes it apparent that Clare was speaking of herself and other female bohemians when complaining that the "literary woman" was now accused of moral "frailty."

SCANDAL, VIRTUE, AND THE BOHEMIENNE

Much as Clare sought to open the public sphere for women, she insisted that she wanted to protect her own personal privacy from the proto-tabloid intrusions that were part of the emerging culture of metropolitan celebrity. "The taste for exploiting the private lives of those who have rendered themselves in any way famous, is becoming more and more confirmed in America," Clare complains, specifying, "For several years my own private life and character have been made the subject for all manner of malicious and false statements. . . . What the individual does or says in a public capacity, is all that belongs to the public."[51] Of course, Clare had helped to promote her own celebrity by writing openly about her infatuation with Gottschalk a few years earlier, but she never addressed the paternity of her son in print; before the birth of Aubrey, in 1856, Whitman had noted that "many interesting stories" might be told about Clare, yet he declined to print those stories. The illustrator and journalist Thomas Butler Gunn, for his part, did not publicly print any scandalous stories about Clare, but he did note them, several times, in his diaries. Regarding her "illegitimate child," for example, Gunn wrote in 1860: "Affecting the Bohemienne and Georges [*sic*] Sand business she acknowledges maternity, and is the centre of a circle of the Clapp style of men. Possessing some intellect and ability as her writings attest, she is I suppose bedeviled to all intents and purposes—self outlawed from decent womanhood."[52] Gunn further claimed, "the Briggs'es of the press and others praise her on the principle that its always safe to praise a woman," but Clare herself did not believe that most editors were so circumspect, insisting: "Most journals prefer in publishing a scandalous lie . . . that relate[s] to a woman rather than to a man. They would rather, for instance, calumniate Ada Clare than John C. Heenan; is it that the female fingers are considered inconvenient or inadequate to the tweaking of the editorial nose?"[53] Singling out the pugilist John C. Heenan as representative of the men who had avoided the censure that she herself incurred, Clare also insinuates that Heenan's alleged wife, Adah Isaacs Menken, had fared comparatively poorly in the press. Erupting in January 1860 when the *Spirit of the Times* publicly disputed Menken's claim that she had married the sportsman, the Menken-Heenan scandal played out in the press over several months, during which time Menken joined the bohemian circle, became close friends with Clare, and issued her "self-defense" at a public poetry reading on August 20, 1860: "I read and write . . . for those who honor a woman for her purity of motives, her aspirations, and her sufferings, wherever she may be found."[54] With "purity of motives" trumping standard notions of sexual chastity, Menken sought to redefine true womanhood in a manner similar to Clare, also refusing to see herself as "self outlawed from decent womanhood."

Much like her fellow female bohemian, Clare did not entirely reject the sentimentalized rhetoric of female goodness but rather sought to protect it from the likes of the narrow-minded, all-purpose bohemian adversary

"Mrs. Grundy." Indeed, extracting what she calls the "divine law of love" from the debased "laws of society," Clare's feminist feuilleton becomes what we might term a sentimental jeremiad, one that eschews "sentimentalism of the blabbiest sort" in favor of firmer moral foundations and prepares the way for another hybrid compound—what a later commentator would term "feminine bohemianism":[55]

> Virtue . . . only exists where there is freedom of action. So necessary is this element of freedom, that the constrained woman can never be said to be virtuous, however pure she may be. The laws of society, the social and religious code, may construct a quality called morality, but they have no acquaintance with virtue. . . . Virtue is that quality that keeps a woman pure and incorrupt through whatever scenes in life she may pass, whatever knowledge she may acquire, whatever she may do. . . . As it is, the great body of men persist in believing against all record and the witness of their own eyes that the woman who can accept one man can accept all men. . . . One strong love, and a physical looseness of character, are the two things farthest apart in this globe.[56]

Differentially defining her terms, Clare seeks to oppose "one strong love" and "physical looseness of character," true "virtue" and the reified "morality" of social and religious doctrine. She posits "freedom of action" as the precondition for "virtue" (though it is unclear whether the free woman can make any choice other than to honor "one strong love" if she is to remain virtuous); "one strong love" emerges as the source of the sentimental "virtue" she defends; and Clare derides any attempt to equate such pure feeling with "promiscuity."[57] Sexual chastity or marital monogamy might follow the letter of the sentimental law but still fail to honor the true spirit of virtuous love. Moving from the sentimental to the satirical, Clare then provides a laundry list of ever more absurd and incongruous signifiers of female "physical looseness of character": "An acquaintance with general literature, a frankness of speech and manner with men, a disposition to dress becomingly, a sensitiveness to dramatic pathos, a good appetite, a cheerful expression of countenance, . . . a longing for sugar-plums, a love for piano-music, an occasional acquaintance with Lubin's powder rouge, an aversion to lying, an ability to think for one's self . . . are all set down as sure symptoms of an invalid moral system."[58] Her columns reveal that she herself exhibited many of these "symptoms" (as any regular reader of "Thoughts and Things" would know), but she rejects the notion that an "invalid moral system" is their cause—or the explanatory core of her identity.

Thus, even though some tried to depict Clare as a "sparkling wicked" specimen of the demimonde, she represents herself as the *true* true woman—or, in her formulation, the French "Bohemienne." She defines this figure as one who is adept at distinguishing the authentic and natural from the conventional and artificial. In a column that takes issue with the "received" views of bohemianism that would link it to debauchery and rabid irreverence (that the bohemian "must take pleasure in keeping his boots and his cheese in the same drawer"), she describes "the highest type of a Bohemienne":

> When I was in Paris I saw a woman who appeared to me to be the incarnation and the highest type of a Bohemienne. . . . And thou, loveliest image of womanly grace, if thou art not the type of the Bohemian, thou shalt be to me the type of all that is noble among women; for thou hast taught me, that in the midst of every narrow thought, and unvirtuous morality, and uncharitable harshness of code, one woman can spread forth the white wings of an angel, and rising above them all, draw up to her own ardent height those who assemble around her; for thou hast taught me how near beauty, and truth, and purity, and passion, are to God![59]

As Edward Whitley has noted, in this column Clare boldly employs the iconography of the domestic angel of the house, "reinvented here as the essence of bohemianism."[60] Given Clare's earlier mockery of the rhetoric of separate spheres, this reinvention might seem perverse, at odds with the tenor of her social critiques. And yet, for Clare, "bohemia" was precisely that liminal social space between the public and the private that could purify and extend some of the essential values associated with the domestic sphere—not the "modesty, obedience, and sobriety" she lampooned, but instead the love, generosity, and spiritual elevation she championed (and it is important to note that in the passage cited above, Clare added "passion" to the end of her more familiar list of ideal womanly attributes.)

If the traditional true woman uplifted the domestic sphere and exerted an undefined "influence" over the public at large by refining the males in her midst, "the Bohemienne," as embodied by Clare herself, presided over a transnational countercultural realm that extended from Paris to New

York, and from the semiprivate sphere of her Forty-second Street literary salon to such semipublic spaces and forums as Pfaff's (though not everyone was welcomed at the bohemians' exclusive "Long Table"[61]) and the *Saturday Press*. Just as Clare celebrated the Parisian "Bohemienne," her own loyal subjects extolled their queen's ennobling virtues. Clare's "Bohemienne" was an "angel of love and mercy . . . to those who came within her immediate sphere," and Clare herself garnered such tributes as this poem:

> All her sympathy share,
> If to her they repair,
> Though wretched and lone,
> With friends and hope flown;
> A gem, sparkling and rare,
>
> .   .   .   .
> Is the lovely and loving
>   Sweet Ada Clare.[62]

Rawson echoes the discourse of true womanhood that Clare herself adapted to her bohemian context, writing of Clare, "when the Pfaffians gathered at her Sunday night receptions it was to do her homage as a woman, and, therefore, their moral uplifter." In praise of Clare's generosity of spirit, Rawson also provides an anecdote about the time Whitman had "met an outcast young woman far down Broadway and walked with her all the way up to Forty-second Street to commend her to Ada Clare's good graces, on the idea that she was the friend and patron of all sorts of unfortunates."[63] For the likes of Thomas Butler Gunn, however, Clare was herself one of the "unfortunates"—he referred to her and her female friends, collectively, as "literary-unfortunate females and Bohemiennes."[64] To support this judgment, Gunn elaborates on a rumor that some of the male bohemians seem to have perpetuated about Clare and her friend Getty Gay (the scribe of the "Royal Bohemian Supper," whose young death from consumption adhered all too closely to the cultural script written by Henri Murger in his *Scènes de la vie de bohème*).[65] After Getty Gay died in 1860, he observed:

> She was one of the Allie Vernon stamp, a married woman, her maiden name Gertrude Louise Vultee, her married one, Wilmhurst. Her husband edits a feeble weekly, entitled the "Traveller," in this city; both he and she lived with "Ada Clare" otherwise Miss Micklehenning—the

fast literary woman. Shepherd [likely the Pfaffian Nathaniel Graham Shepherd] tells me that the Bohemians had a whispered rumor that the affection between these women was of a Parisian, Sapphic charater [*sic*]—it may be so, or only a monstrous canard originating in the depraved minds of such men as Clapp or O'Brien. Judging from "Ada"'s writings, one might credit it. This wretched "Getty" "quitted this world of care and pain, and found rest and peace with her Creator" . . . on the 21st, being about twenty years old and dying of consump-tion. What a life, and what a termination to it! Bohemianism! were there no Bohemmians in Sodom and Gomorrah, I wonder?[66]

Whatever the bohemians may have "whispered" to Gunn (and whether or not they, or Clare herself, viewed the possibility of a Sapphic relationship between the two women as something entirely more positive than a "monstrous canard"), his description of Clare as the "fast literary woman" explicitly contradicts her self-representation in the *Saturday Press*. As for Whitman, even though he later remembered Clare as among his "sturdiest defenders," he nonetheless equivocated in his assessment of the goodness of her life when first learning of her death from rabies at age thirty-eight in 1874; he wrote to Ellen O'Connor: "Poor, poor Ada Clare. I have been inexpressibly shocked and saddened by the horrible & sudden close of her gay, easy, sunny free, loose, but *not ungood* life."[67] Following the adjective "loose" (as we have seen, Clare herself addressed rumors about her "physical looseness of character") that final double-negative would appear, specifically, to characterize her sexual morality, and it fails to resolve into the strong affirmation of her "virtue" that Clare had insisted upon in the *Saturday Press*. Whitman supported the "entire redemption of woman out of these incredible holds and webs of silliness, millinery, and every kind of dyspeptic depletion," but his not unkind judgment of Clare still bears a residual trace of the double standard.[68]

Even within "bohemia," the sexual conflicts and gender asymmetries that Clare mocked, parodied, and pleaded against in her columns resurfaced, if in a more muted form. As Daniel Cottom argues:

Clare's writing accomplishes something that Whitman's could not begin to do: it works to explain the power of Mrs. Grundy as the embodiment of all opposition to America's bohemians. . . . The reality was that women had more to lose in bohemia than did men. This was especially true for middle-class women, for whom bohemia's rejection of convention generally entailed a decisive loss of their social position, not a vacation from it or a lever for raising it, as was often the case with men.

Cottom further underscores the "imaginary singularity" of Clare's status as "Queen of Bohemia" (as opposed to the "metaphysical universality in Whitman's assertion of bohemian identity"), a "mock title" that smacks of bravado but obscures, or perhaps highlights, a lack of real world consequence: "All know that she has no kingdom and only such power as [the bohemians] may decide to pretend she has at any given time."[69] Yet Clare knew that such acts of make-believe could transform the real, however slowly or partially, and her reign helped suture a bohemian community and alternative living structures, which lasted, in part, until her death.[70] She set the stage for later bohemian adventures and for the emergence of fabulous bohemian queens.

Her feminist feuilleton of the mid-nineteenth century was a discourse of mediation. "Thoughts" would reconfigure "things"—the apparently intransigent structures of the real—and reveal new ways of seeing and being. Men and women might come together, sheltered under the sympathetic wings of the "Queen of Bohemia," and learn to "love each other better." Carefully constructed paradoxes might replace contradiction and conflict. Rhetorically fusing true womanhood and bohemian nonconformity, Clare synthesized both discourses, deploying each to compensate for the potential limitations of the other. Sentiment was freed from the social hierarchies that would distort it, and bohemianism eschewed rebellious nihilism in favor of recontextualizing and democratizing still vital social values and aims. In assessing the "unfinished business of sentimentality," Lauren Berlant asks, "Is moving past a form's historical dominance the same thing as witnessing its breakdown? If not by substitution, how do new metacultural figures of the emergent subject of history—the hybrid, the queer, the feminist, the migrant—transact with previously ascendant patterns of normative identification?"[71] Clare shows us how one new metacultural figure, the female bohemian, transacts with older patterns of identification, providing a fraught but progressive encounter between feminism and sentimental convention, bohemianism and the genteel tradition. In her hands, disparate literary genres and cultural discourses collide and jostle toward freedom.

NOTES

1. Whitman, *New York Dissected*, 131.

2. *WWC* 3:117.

3. "Thoughts and Things," *SP*, Jan. 14, 1860.

4. On the Bloomer debate, see Smith, "Antebellum Politics," 79–81.

5. "Thoughts and Things," *SP* Jan. 14, 1860.

6. As Sherry Ceniza has demonstrated, other women associated with the *Saturday Press* and its bohemians also embraced *Leaves*, and for similar reasons. Ceniza, "Being a Woman," 118–19.

7. The artist A. L. Rawson, Clare's friend, later recalled that her "family name was McIlhenny, of South Carolina, where her grandfather was one of the richest cotton planters in the Sea Islands" ("Bygone," 100). See also Goldblatt, "Queen of Bohemia," 10–11.

8. As Gloria Goldblatt recounts in her unpublished biography of Ada Clare, Ada's family held several conferences in Edward McCrady's law office regarding Ada's conduct (quoted in Goldblatt, "Ada Clare," 44, from Papers of Edward McCrady Sr., Manuscript Collection of the South Carolina Historical Society, Charleston). Ada wrote to her friend Julian Mitchell of her search for an "active sphere." See Ada Agnes McElhenney to Julian Mitchell, March 12, 1855 (quoted in Goldblatt, "Ada Clare," 73, from Julian Mitchell Papers, South Carolina Historical Society Manuscript Collection, Charleston).

9. Starr, *Bamboula!*, 250. Goldblatt, "Ada Clare," carefully reconstructs Clare's correspondence with the lawyers who handled her inheritance (Papers of Edward McCrady Sr.).

10. "Ada Clare on Suicide," *New York Atlas*, Jan. 4, 1857, 1.

11. Getty Gay, "The Royal Bohemian Supper," *SP*, Dec. 31, 1859.

12. Clare's close friend Marie Howland later wrote to Edmund Clarence Stedman that she and Clare had "frequent talks about Gottschalk" and that Ada "said nothing to deny that Gottschalk was the father of Aubrey" (quoted in Goldblatt, "Ada Clare," 108; Marie Howland to Edmund Clarence Stedman, June 21, 1894, Columbia University Special Manuscript Collections, Edmund C. Stedman Collection).

13. "The Queen of Bohemia," from New York Correspondent of the *Philadelphia Dispatch*, reprinted in *SP*, Nov. 10, 1860.

14. Levin, *Bohemia in America*, 44.

15. On this discourse, Barbara Welter's "The Cult of True Womanhood, 1820–1860" remains indispensible. Welter, *Dimity Convictions*, 21–41.

16. Seigel, *Bohemian Paris*, 10–11.

17. For a collection of Fuller's "Things and Thoughts in Europe," see Fuller, *"These Sad but Glorious Days."*

18. "Thoughts and Things VII," *SP*, Dec. 10, 1859.

19. Clare did not use the term "feuilleton" to describe her articles in the *Press*—though she titled her later columns for the *New York Leader* "Literary Feuilletons." Other *Press* columns used this term.

20. "Thoughts and Things," *sp*, Jan. 7, 1860.

21. "Thoughts and Things," *sp*, May 19, 1860.

22. "Thoughts and Things No. V," *sp*, Nov. 26, 1859.

23. "Thoughts and Things," *sp*, Nov. 17, 1860.

24. "Woman in the Kitchen," *sp*, July 21, 1860, 2.

25. Rawson, "Bygone," 100.

26. Cott, "Passionlessness," 175.

27. Fourier quoted in Zwarg, *Feminist Conversations*, 146. On the roots of American bohemianism in the Fourierist-inflected activities of the Club at 555 Broadway, see Lause, *Antebellum Crisis*, 21–43.

28. "Thoughts and Things No. II," *sp*, Oct. 29, 1859.

29. "Thoughts and Things," *sp*, June 2, 1860.

30. Rawson, "Bygone," 102.

31. Foucault, *History of Sexuality*, 95–96; and Clare, "Thoughts and Things," *sp*, June 2, 1860.

32. "Matilda Heron in Geraldine," *sp*, Aug. 27, 1859.

33. "Thoughts and Things," *sp*, June 2, 1860.

34. On "the experience of sympathetic identification as the narrative and affective core of a sentimental structure of feeling," see Hendler, *Public Sentiments*.

35. Pfister, "Glamorizing," 174.

36. The phrase "suppressed desires" was the title of a play written by the bohemians Susan Glaspell and George Cram Cook in 1915. See Pfister, "Glamorizing," 177.

37. Rawson, "Bygone," 105.

38. "Thoughts and Things," *sp*, Jan. 14, 1860.

39. "Thoughts and Things," *sp*, June 2, 1860.

40. "Thoughts and Things No. IV," *sp*, Nov. 12, 1859. On advertisements being pulled, see "Thoughts and Things," *sp*, Dec. 10, 1859.

41. Armstrong, *Desire and Domestic Fiction*, 191–93.

42. "Thoughts and Things," *sp*, June 2, 1860.

43. "Thoughts and Things," *sp*, Jan. 7, 1860.

44. "Thoughts and Things," *sp*, Jan. 21, 1860.

45. "Thoughts and Things," *sp*, June 2, 1860.

46. "Thoughts and Things," *sp*, Jan. 21, 1860. Clare also subjects male authors to critique when they fail to validate the "truly passionate" woman. One column, for example, takes aim at Hawthorne for his privileging of angelic Hilda over "womanly" Miriam in *The Marble Faun* ("Thoughts and Things, *sp*, Mar. 10, 1860).

47. "Thoughts and Things," *sp*, Jan. 21, 1860.

48. Dillon, *Gender of Freedom*, 6–7.

49. "Thoughts and Things No. VII," *SP*, Dec. 10, 1859.

50. "Thoughts and Things," *SP*, Jan. 28, 1860.

51. "Thoughts and Things," *SP*, Apr. 21, 1860.

52. Thomas Butler Gunn Diaries, vol. 11 (1859): 161, Missouri History Museum, St. Louis.

53. "Thoughts and Things," *SP*, Apr. 21, 1860.

54. Quoted in Sentilles, *Performing Menken*, 78.

55. The phrase was used in Emilie Ruck De Schell, "Is Feminine Bohemianism a Failure?," *Arena* 20, no. 104 (1898).

56. "Thoughts and Things," *SP*, Mar. 17, 1860.

57. For an instance of this tendency, one had only to look at contemporary parodies of Menken's poem "Come to Me" (see Sentilles, *Performing Menken*, 57). Interestingly, in a later feuilleton for the *Leader*, Clare writes that women rarely get over their first loves, noting that subsequent loves are but replacements for the original lost love object: "Jones, Brown, Grey, Smith, Simpkins, Thomkins, and Whiffles . . ." Technically speaking, this laundry list of lovers still supports her dedication to the "one strong love" she had earlier celebrated in the *Press*, though with a transgressive twist. See Clare, "Some False Proverbs," *New York Leader*, Mar. 7, 1863, 1.

58. "Thoughts and Things," *SP*, Mar. 17, 1860.

59. "Thoughts and Things," *SP*, Feb. 11, 1860.

60. Edward Whitley, "The Queen of Bohemia and *The Saturday Press*," paper presented at the Society for the Study of American Women Writers Conference, Philadelphia, October 24, 2009.

61. Rawson, "Bygone," 98.

62. Sue Littie Lator, *Flag of Our Union*, Feb. 6, 1858, 48.

63. Rawson, "Bygone," 105.

64. Thomas Butler Gunn Diaries, vol. 14 (1860): 16.

65. Gunn writes that "Getty Gay has still more of the core of the bitch in her, as Smollett's Trunnion would say. By [George] Arnold's account she adds direct prostitution to her 'literary' pursuits." (See Thomas Butler Gunn Diaries, vol. 11 [1859]:152.) Arnold was a regular Pfaffian, and Winter insisted that he was "the most entirely beloved member of that group," noting, "There was a sentiment of fraternity among those Bohemian writers." On the basis of Arnold's alleged comments, his "sentiment of fraternity" may well have been aptly named, describing homosocial fraternizing rather than the heterosocial bonds that Clare cultivated (Winter, *Old Friends*, 94).

66. Thomas Butler Gunn Diaries, vol. 14 (1860): 12–13.

67. Whitman quoted in Loving, *Walt Whitman*, 351 (emphasis in original).

68. Whitman, "Democratic Vistas (1871)," 463.

69. Cottom, *International Bohemia*, 172, 184.

70. In her brownstone, Clare created a more informal version of the "unitary household" that fellow bohemians had begun as a Fourierist-inspired experiment (Goldblatt, "Ada Clare," 403). Later, when Clare pursued her career as an actress, her son Aubrey often lived with other members of her extended bohemian family (Goldblatt draws on Marie Howland's unpublished memoirs, Fairhope Public Library, Fairhope, Alabama; ibid., 342). Clare continued to blend the professional and personal when she married the actor-manager Frank Noyes in 1868 (ibid., 427).

71. Berlant, *Female Complaint*, 235. Cottom convincingly argues that with its "self-divided . . . narration," Clare's later novel *Only a Woman's Heart* (1866) seeks a "language adequate to the experience of conflict" (*International Bohemia*, 172, 184). I would add that she remains ever committed to *mediating* these conflicts and contradictions.

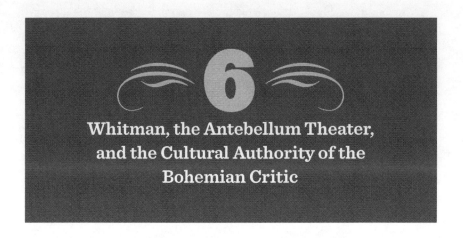

Whitman, the Antebellum Theater, and the Cultural Authority of the Bohemian Critic

EDWARD WHITLEY

The bohemians of antebellum New York were theater people. Some of the most prominent—not to mention infamous—of Manhattan's playwrights, actors, and stage managers gathered at Charles Pfaff's beer cellar to drink and talk with the writers and artists who made the Broadway nightspot the center of America's bohemian counterculture.[1] Pfaff's was situated at the heart of the theater district, making it an ideal location not only for the after-parties of actors such as Lola Montez, John Brougham, and the notorious Adah Isaacs Menken (who famously appeared "nude" on stage in a flesh-colored body stocking; see Figure 9) but also for the conversations of the drama critics from the *New York Saturday Press*, who routinely stopped by the bar to discuss the city's theatrical offerings.[2] These critics cultivated a public image as avant-garde commentators whose tastes and sensibilities exceeded those of both the general public and the powers-that-be in the theater industry. The elitist posture that they adopted in the weekly "Dramatic Feuilleton" column by dismissing popular opinion out of hand and relying instead on the judgments of a select few appears to be an exception to what Joanna Levin has called the "democratic egalitarianism" of the *Saturday Press*, which "often editorialized against the development of a restricted high culture."[3] Despite this elitist posturing, the *Saturday Press* theater column often betrayed the anxieties these critics experienced as they sought to establish themselves as tastemakers of American culture against the democratic judgment of theatergoers who voted for their favorite actors and plays with their feet (and their dollars). At a number of key moments in the antebellum run of the "Dramatic Feuilleton"—moments surrounding issues of creativity, celebrity, aesthetics, and critical judgment—they attempted to allay these fears by anchoring their claims to cultural authority to Walt Whitman's emerging status as an American icon.

Given that the critics for the "Dramatic Feuilleton" preferred to distance themselves from their readers rather than join with them in a common cause, it is curious that they turned to the poet of democracy to ground their authority as tastemakers. Nevertheless, on a number of occasions they invoked Whitman's poetry (and persona) to reinforce the notion that a closed circle of bohemian elites was uniquely qualified to pass judgment on the American theater, despite the fact that Whitman himself was at the time cultivating his reputation as the poet of common people. Whitman has always meant different things to different people. This effort to enlist him in the cause of bohemian theater criticism is one of the earliest examples of how his status as a cultural icon was made to serve an agenda that he may or may not have fully supported. As such, the ways that the bohemians used Whitman to articulate a set of concerns and anxieties about their cultural authority require that we backdate to the late 1850s Kenneth M. Price's observation that Whitman's iconic status has made him "so central to practices and formulations of American culture, past and present, that we may use his life, work, ideas, and influence to examine major patterns in our culture."[4] Long before Whitman's status as a cultural icon was securely in place, a group of bohemian critics used him in their efforts to direct the course of the American theater.

BOHEMIAN TASTEMAKERS AND THE "DRAMATIC FEUILLETON"

When Henry Clapp Jr., the founding editor of the *Saturday Press*, returned to the United States after a decade-long sojourn in Europe, he brought back with him the critical temperament of French periodicals such as *Le Figaro*, whose motto *"Sans la liberté de blâmer, il n'est point d'éloge flatteur"* ("Without the freedom to criticize, there can be no true praise") could serve equally well to describe the *Press*'s attitude toward the actors and playwrights of New York.[5] Clapp adopted the penname of "Figaro" to signal his allegiance to this French critical tradition and recruited a trio of likeminded theater critics to write a weekly "Dramatic Feuilleton" column that pulled no punches in its reviews of the current theater.[6] The first of these critics, Fitz-James O'Brien, had only a brief, six-month tenure with the *Press*, but his style and demeanor left a lasting impression on subsequent contributors to the column. O'Brien, like many of the bohemians who gathered at Pfaff's, was an admirer of Edgar Allan Poe; indeed, the Irish-American writer came to be known as the "Celtic Poe" for his experiments with gothic and speculative fiction as well as for his harsh critical tone. Somewhere between the Parisian critical temper of *Le Figaro* and the unapologetic attack mode Poe made famous, the "Dramatic Feuilleton" critics found their voice, a voice that their contemporaries said was "much too independent" to appear anywhere other than the bohemian *Saturday Press*.[7]

Following O'Brien, Edward G. P. "Ned" Wilkins and William Winter wrote the remainder of the "Dramatic Feuilleton" articles in the years leading up to the Civil War. The cheeky French pseudonyms under which they wrote—Personne (No One) and Quelqu'un (Someone), respectively—complemented the Parisian style of the free-form feuilleton genre and defined the whole endeavor as an effort to bring continental style to New York and turn Pfaff's into America's answer to the Latin Quarter.[8] Ned Wilkins took great pleasure in alienating his American readers with both the European style and irreverent tone of his feuilletons. In February 1860 he reprinted the letter of one especially irate reader who complained: "I have never been so much disgusted with anything in the whole course of my life as your last what-do-you-call-it Feuilleton (just as if you couldn't get an English heading or signature!). Why don't you take and read the beautiful critiques in the Boston and Philadelphia papers, and write like them?"[9] William Winter similarly relished the alienating nature of the feuilleton genre, as well as its connection to French culture. Adopting the disoriented posture of his imagined (and uncultured) readers, he wrote: "Why, man, I don't even know what a Feuilleton is. What is it? A treatise, an essay, a disquisition, a criticism, a sermon, a lampoon, or what?"[10] In a later column he answered: "All I know of it is that it is something more or less droll about theatres and things, written in a saucy, nondescript, 'you're another' sort o' style, and leaving actors, actresses, managers, play-wrights, play-goers, and ye general reader, in a state of utter despair. . . . It is the same thing in France,—where, I am told, the Feuilleton originated."[11] The self-conscious and deliberately alienating elitism of the "Dramatic Feuilleton" was one of its hallmarks: it allowed O'Brien, Wilkins, and Winter to elevate their status while thinly veiling fears about their own cultural relevance.

In the "Dramatic Feuilleton" column that appeared in the inaugural issue of the *Saturday Press*, Fitz-James O'Brien attacked the melodramatic conventions of the theater in a way that did little to cover up his own frustrations at receiving neither popular nor critical acclaim. O'Brien was a playwright as well as a critic, and he offered his own struggle to find a playhouse willing to take a chance on his work as proof that New York's theater managers were a craven and venal lot who did little more than rehash the same tired dramatic conventions for an unthinking public. "I declare," he wrote, "that some day or other—when I have found a manager of weak mind who will produce it—I will write a comedy of modern life which shall be constructed on the following principles." He then proceeded to give a laundry list of the stock characters and plot points that his own, presumably groundbreaking, production would turn on their heads:

> I will have my nobleman a virtuous honest person, who has never been a seducer or a fop, and who is not the victim of any impending disclosure relative to his past time. My lawyer shall be a decent man, whose enjoyment in life does not altogether consist of absorbing the nobleman's property and enveloping him in a network of mortgages and promissory notes. . . . One of [the nobleman's] daughters shall marry the rich man who her family wishes her to marry, and, what is more, marry him willingly. The other shall refuse to elope with the ruthless villain who plans her destruction. . . . I will have no lost wills turning up in the last act. The people who are rich in the first act shall keep their wealth, and remain wealthy at the fall of the curtain.

Impatient with what he saw as the formulaic nature of popular melodrama, O'Brien longed for a theater that would not only be more entertaining, but more in line with his own artistic sensibility. He continued:

> I am driven to this desperate resolve—he who becomes a dramatic author in New York must, indeed, be desperate—by having witnessed, for these last few years, a succession of comedies and dramas all founded upon the same model. Everything going wrong in the first act, everything going right in the last. . . . It is continual partridge on the stage. By way of a change, give me even a piece of ostrich.[12]

The critical persona that O'Brien created in this first "Dramatic Feuille-ton" column is that of a connoisseur of the dramatic arts whose expertise is wasted on both an uncultured public and the theater managers who cater to their whims. He knows the theater inside and out, but this knowledge, rather than helping him see one of his own plays through to production, serves instead to underscore his status as an outsider to a culture that ulti-mately does not deserve him. The metaphor of drama-as-food that he ends with—theater managers across the city are content to feed their audiences an inoffensive diet of partridge rather than surprise them with the radical new taste of ostrich—is particularly apt given that O'Brien and the other drama critics for the *Saturday Press* thought of themselves as tastemakers who would, in Russell Lynes's classic formulation, "discipline everyone to a higher appreciation of the arts."[13] As Richard Butsch has shown, by the 1840s "theatrical knowledge . . . began to be important in the dominant culture" among "audiences who distinguished appreciation of art (taste) from enjoyment of entertainment."[14] While sharp distinctions between highbrow and lowbrow art would not fully take shape until after the Civil War, the antebellum period witnessed an increasing demand for taste-makers to preside over Americans' habits of cultural consumption.[15] The theater critics for the *Saturday Press* were happy to oblige.

In a "Dramatic Feuilleton" column from 1860, Ned Wilkins also used a similar metaphor comparing the theater to food when he lamented that a stage manager as well regarded as Laura Keene "has to cater for Peoria. No Clarendon or Fifth Avenue dinners for her audiences. Sweeney's and the Fulton Market, and plenty of it, is the word for them."[16] Laura Keene had more than earned Wilkins's respect ("I believe she has the true artis-tic pride in her vocation," he wrote[17]), but he also knew that the theatri-cal equivalent of the "humble dishes" at Sweeney's Restaurant and the Fulton Market were more appealing than the upscale fare at restaurants on Fifth Avenue and the Clarendon Hotel to the uncultured palates of theatergoers visiting from Peoria.[18] Prescient of the Vaudeville refrain from a generation later, "Will it play in Peoria?," the drama critics for the *Saturday Press* were already using the Illinois town and its "pastoral" resi-dents as shorthand for the tastes and prejudices of Middle America.[19] So when Wilkins complained about "a dull week in the theatres," he could blame this tedium on the fact that "the playhouse is given over to the children and the Peorians."[20] Similarly, when Keene found success with *Jeanie Deans*, a sentimental adaptation of Walter Scott's *The Heart of Mid-*

lothian, Wilkins predicted that this success would continue thanks to an influx of visitors from the Midwest and rural South: "I see that there is already a good deal of Peoria and Attakapas in town, so *Jeannie* [*sic*] is good for another month."[21] If bohemian New York was the center of the cultural universe, middlebrow Peoria and Louisiana's backwater Attakapas County were its "barbarous" counterparts.[22]

William Winter was also dismissive of middlebrow theatergoers. He wrote many of his "Dramatic Feuilleton" columns as open letters to "the General Public" and referred to this imagined reader with faux obsequiousness as "My Dear General." Winter's general public was forever ignoring his advice to patronize the subtle and nuanced performances of the actors whom he admired, preferring, instead, those who were "noisy, and funny, and full of action."[23] He implored them to take in the performances at a poorly attended production of Molière's *The Hypochondriac* (*The Imaginary Invalid*) on the recommendation that "nothing could be more natural and simple, and yet nothing more artistic." As he signed off on the column, he begged, resignedly,

> The Hypochondriac is splendidly performed, and I am glad to see that it is to be kept on another week.
> Go and see it, General.
> Yours, moderately (because you won't do what I tell you),
> Quelqu'un[24]

Winter's frustration with the public for not "do[ing] what I tell you" betrayed an anxiety about the cultural authority of the bohemian critic that permeated the "Dramatic Feuilleton" columns. Winter and the other *Saturday Press* critics were horrified at the prospect that the preferences of the general public—and not their own expert opinions—would determine the fate of the theater. "What I most dislike in you," Winter wrote to the general public, "is your ridiculous way of claiming to make and unmake people, especially theatrical and operatic people."[25] Upset that uncultured theatergoers could, and routinely did, "make and unmake" the careers of actors and singers by choosing to patronize (or not patronize) their performances, Winter inadvertently revealed the fear that he and his fellow critics were less relevant as cultural tastemakers than they believed themselves to be.

One of the ways that both Winter and Wilkins responded to this fear was by describing for readers of the *Saturday Press* the theater discussions that took place among the bohemians at Pfaff's. Because Peoria and Attakapas were not invited to participate in such conversations—indeed, the bohemians made it clear that they went to Pfaff's precisely to escape the tedious presence of the general public—readers were led to believe that the real power to "make and unmake" theatrical careers lay beneath the pavement at 647 Broadway. For example, Winter wrote in one column about his reaction to what he considered the histrionic performances of popular actors Charlotte Cushman and Edwin Forrest: "Nine persons in ten who see Cushman's Meg Merriles, go home and have the nightmare after it. A good dose of Forrest produces the same effect. I generally neutralize it, in my own case, by going straight from the theatre to Pfaff's, and listening to a discussion about something; very likely about dramatic art."[26] In comments such as these, Winter was able not only to register his contempt for what he called the "muscular business" of acting (which, he believed, achieved its effect by "bullying" audiences into an emotional response), but also to present Pfaff's as a space where enlightened conversations on the theater could take place among critics who refused to be "bullied" by the theatrical establishment of New York.[27]

In a similar anecdote, Winter wrote about seeking refuge at Pfaff's to counteract the negative effects of seeing Dion Boucicault's *Dot*, a popular play whose plot he deemed so incomprehensibly bad that it left him mentally disheveled:

> The next day I didn't know the multiplication table from the breakfast table, and a jolly Briton who went with me the last time was reduced to such a condition that he couldn't distinguish between the British Lion and the American Eagle (dear bird!). . . . And half a dozen lagers taken at Pfaff's immediately after, didn't help him in the least. Nor me either. We loafed there, and talked over the piece and its nonsensicalities, for over an hour.[28]

An hour-long discussion (and a half-dozen beers) may not have been enough to purge the taste of bad theater from Winter's mouth, but it did reinforce the image of the bohemian beer cellar as a locus of cultural authority. A number of details in this account point specifically to those aspects of bohemian identity that Winter and his fellow "Dramatic Feuilleton" critics emphasized as central to their authority as tastemakers. Pfaff's is depicted here, as it is elsewhere, as a European space combining the German festive culture of drinking and loafing with the intellectual atmosphere of a Parisian café—complemented, no less, by having a "jolly Briton" as a drinking companion. Contemporary accounts report that Pfaff's beers, wines, and coffees represented the best imports that Europe had to offer; patrons were similarly promised that they would "find at Pfaff's the best German, French, Italian, English, and American papers."[29] Pfaff's may have been a short walk from the "children and Peorians" who overran New York's theaters, but passing through its doors transported its patrons to the salons of Paris and the festive atmosphere of Germany.

RECRUITING WHITMAN TO THE BOHEMIAN CAUSE

The loafers who gathered at Pfaff's to talk about the theater also counted among their number the poet who wrote, "I loafe and invite my soul, / I lean and loafe at my ease observing a spear of summer grass," and who was identified in 1855 as "a perfect loafer."[30] While Whitman was by no means the central figure at Pfaff's, he was a respected participant in the bohemians' discussions on dramatic art. In one of several references to Whitman in the "Dramatic Feuilleton," Ned Wilkins cited Whitman's disdain for *Jeanie Deans* to reinforce his own opinion that Scott's story worked better on the page than it did on the stage. Wilkins wrote in the January 14, 1860, column, "Walt Whitman, and various other competent critics, declare that the beauty, the force, and the power of [Scott's] delightful romance cannot be expressed dramatically; and they may be, possibly are, quite right." When Wilkins name-checks Whitman alongside "various other competent critics," it sounds, at first blush, like the references he routinely made to the opinions of critics writing about the theater for other periodicals. It is unlikely, however, that Wilkins was referring to a published theater review by Whitman about Boucicault's adaptation of Scott's novel. The few comments that Whitman made about Walter Scott in the *Brooklyn Daily Times*—the newspaper he regularly wrote for during this period—have nothing to say about stage adaptations of the Waverly novels, and the theater criticism that he wrote earlier in the 1840s is similarly silent on the issue.[31] It is more likely, then, that Wilkins was referring to a private conversation with Whitman at Pfaff's.

Had Wilkins been responding to some published commentary by Whitman, this reference to "Walt Whitman, and various other competent critics" would have been merely another example of nineteenth-century journalists using mass-circulated newspapers to engage with each other in a print-mediated public sphere. But rather than use the *Saturday Press* to address Whitman in the public sphere of print journalism—a sphere to which anyone with access to a newsstand could, theoretically, participate—Wilkins was instead using the paper to report on a conversation that took place in the invitation-only space of the bohemian beer cellar. Printing a conversation from Pfaff's in the *Press* did not serve to open up a discussion with the general public; instead, it was a way for Wilkins to locate his cultural authority within a closed circle of bohemian elites and the wisdom that Whitman imparted to a select few. It bears asking, however, why Whitman should merit top billing among this cohort of "various other competent critics." He had little-to-no reputation as a theater critic, and the relatively modest success of the third edition of *Leaves of Grass* was still several months away.[32] What credibility was Wilkins hoping to gain by citing the opinion of a minor poet about matters in the New York theater?

The other references that Wilkins made to Whitman in the course of his tenure as theater critic for the *Saturday Press* point toward a potential answer to this question. In the February 18, 1860, column, Wilkins's review of the New York opera scene included an offhand comment identifying Whitman as an innovator of unparalleled power: "The only thing worth mentioning in the Operatic way,—because the only thing that could claim the merit of novelty (a great merit in these latter days, when everybody is continually doing the same thing over and over again, except Walt Whitman, who does nothing as nobody ever did it before),—is the presentation of *Der Freischutz*, Opera by Carl Von Weber." This image of Whitman as the lone bulwark against a universal decline in artistic creativity recalls Fitz-James O'Brien's initial critique of the antebellum theater as "continual partridge on the stage" and his desperate request, "By way of a change, give me even a piece of ostrich." For Wilkins, Whitman is O'Brien's ostrich. Like Emily Dickinson's "only Kangaroo among the Beauty," Whitman is something strange and wonderful amid the tame ordinariness of everyday life.[33] And while Whitman would remember Ned Wilkins as a devoted supporter—"Ned was courageous: in an out and out way very friendly to Leaves of Grass," he told Horace Traubel—it is not entirely clear why Wilkins would cite Whitman's poetry as an example of creative innovation in the context of the New York opera.[34] Granted, it was only a few months earlier that Whitman had published "A Child's Reminiscence" (later titled "Out of the Cradle Endlessly Rocking") in the *Saturday Press*, which he would describe in an anonymous self-review as being structured according to "the method of the Italian Opera."[35] Despite the attention that "A Child's Reminiscence" generated in the *Press*, writing a poem made up of arias and recitatives hardly seems enough to qualify someone as an innovator in the performing arts. Taken alongside Wilkins's other reference to Whitman as a "competent critic" of the theater, however, it becomes apparent that Wilkins was not merely responding to a reputation that Whitman had acquired; he was helping to create it. Wilkins was building an image of Whitman as both a critical authority and a creative force, as someone as competent at evaluating art as he was at creating it.

The "Dramatic Feuilleton" of January 7, 1860, reveals that Wilkins was not only concerned with depicting Whitman as an artist and a critic, but also a celebrity. After announcing his plan to produce a new play of his own, Wilkins mentioned Whitman alongside the most popular performers of the current season: "My new five-act tragedy, *Anna Maria*, is nearly ready for the stage, and it is probable that a young lady of brilliant personal attractions, rare accomplishments, and aristocratic conjunctions will make her first appearance upon any stage, etc., etc. Where, I ask, where will the *Octoroon, Jeanie Deans, Geraldine, Lesbia*, Mr. Bateman, Walt Whitman, Miss Agnes Robertson, and the Shu-shu-ga, be, after that?" It is one thing for Wilkins to say, with mock bravado, that his new play will overshadow blockbusters like *The Octoroon* and *Jeanie Deans*, and that his leading lady will steal the applause of actors such as H. L. Bateman and Matilda Heron (whom Wilkins playfully called "the Shu-shu-ga" after the multiple references in Henry Wadsworth Longfellow's *Hiawatha* to "the heron, the Shuh-shuh-gah").[36] It is quite another, however, for him to say that his play will outshine Whitman in the popular imagination when Whitman had yet to earn a reputation that would put him in the same constellation as these A-list stars. Wilkins was no doubt joining with other *Saturday Press* contributors in rallying around Whitman as the bohemians' cause célèbre: "A Child's Reminiscence" had been published only two weeks earlier, and as Amanda Gailey has shown, *Press* editor Henry Clapp labored to get the poem reprinted in newspapers throughout the country and used the *Press* to publicize this and other of Whitman's works.[37] Within the context of the "Dramatic Feuilleton," though, this campaign to elevate Whitman to the status of bohemian celebrity took on an added layer of significance.

As David Haven Blake has argued, nineteenth-century "celebrities served as a kind of representational technology, their identities pieced together in a collaborative performance between their individual selves and the supporting community." Nineteenth-century Americans, he continues, chose "among a group of actors, musicians, writers, and promoters a few select individuals whom they would vest with sociopolitical meaning."[38] When Clapp, Wilkins, and other *Saturday Press* contributors threw their support behind Whitman, they did so not only because they believed in him and his poetry, but because he was someone whom they could "vest with sociopolitical meaning" through a "collaborative performance" that involved elevating him to iconic status and then drawing on the power afforded by that status to confirm their own cultural authority. For theater critics whose claims to prominence were perpetually undercut by a disobedient populace, Whitman served as something of a stabilizing force—particularly when references to him as an artist, a critic, and a celebrity presented him as someone who had mastered every aspect of the arts from production and analysis to popular appeal.

Only one of the antebellum theater critics for the *Saturday Press* would live long enough to see Whitman achieve anything resembling the kind of prominence attributed to him in the "Dramatic Feuilleton." Ned Wilkins died from pneumonia in 1861, and Fitz-James O'Brien died in 1862 from wounds sustained while fighting for the Union Army. William Winter, however, had a long and productive life as a poet and critic. He started his forty-year career covering the theater for the *New York Tribune* in 1865 and was, according to Bruce A. McConachie, "the foremost drama critic of his day by 1870."[39] Winter turned his back on bohemia and embraced what came to be known as the "genteel tradition" in American culture, but he retained from his experience at the *Saturday Press* an elitist disposition and a disdain for the aesthetics of antebellum melodrama. During his run on the "Dramatic Feuilleton," Winter made only one reference to Whitman. And while this continued Wilkins's tendency to use Whitman as a touchstone for the theater, Winter instead chose to align Whitman with the tired conventions of melodrama rather than present him as an artistic visionary. Winter had unkind things to say about Whitman, referring to him later in life as a "commonplace, uncouth, and sometimes obnoxiously coarse writer, trying to be original by using a formless style." Whitman, for his part, called Winter a "miserable cuss," "a dried up cadaverous schoolmaster," and "an arrant damned fool."[40] It comes as no surprise, then, that Winter's sole reference to Whitman in the "Dramatic Feuilleton" had the

35. "All About a Mocking-Bird," *SP*, Jan. 7, 1860, 3. See also Skaggs, *Overtones of Opera*, 13–33.

36. Longfellow, *Longfellow*, 139, 150, 170, 171, 188, 262, 266, 271.

37. See Amanda Gailey's essay in this volume.

38. Blake, *Walt Whitman*, 58, 27. My thanks to David Blake for his feedback on this and other sections of this essay.

39. McConachie, *Melodramatic Formations*, 235. See also Ackerman, *Portable Theater*, 16.

40. Winter, *Old Friends*, 140; *WWC* 1:61, 2:93, 3:431.

41. "Dramatic Feuilleton," *SP*, Oct. 23, 1858.

42. *LG*, 30.

43. "Thoughts and Things," *SP*, Jan. 14, 1860, 2.

44. *PW* 2:693–94; Ackerman, *Portable Theater*, 42. See also Reynolds, *Walt Whitman's America*, 154–93.

45. *WWC* 4:189–90.

46. *WWC* 7:177.

47. Whitman, *Gathering of the Forces*, 2:319.

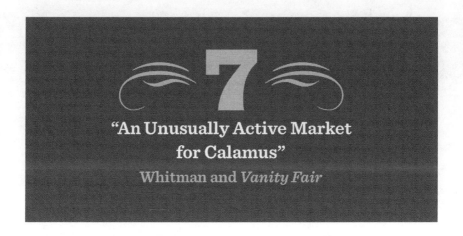

"An Unusually Active Market for Calamus"

Whitman and *Vanity Fair*

ROBERT J. SCHOLNICK

On March 9, 1861, the New York humor magazine *Vanity Fair* unhesitatingly addressed what it called "The Great Literary Question of the Day": "What will Walt. Whitman's *Leaves of Grass* be when they are dried, and posterity has raked 'em—Hey?" While *Vanity Fair* got a laugh by poking fun at Whitman—his *Leaves* are but fodder for bovines—it also complemented him by recognizing that succeeding generations would continue to chew on *Leaves of Grass*. Lest the editors be held liable, *Vanity Fair* warned that reading Whitman's poetry carried risk. Six months earlier, on September 15, 1860, under the title "Curious if True," the weekly reported: "'A young lady who graduated recently at an institute in Virginia, has been committed to the Insane Asylum at Raleigh. Her friends attribute her mental aberration to the reading of Milton's *Paradise Lost.*—Exchange.' Good gracious—what would have become of her had she read—say for instance Walt Whitman, or one of Isaac Adah Menken's [Adah Isaacs Menken's] high pressurisms?" Given the friendship between Whitman and the actress and poet Menken, fellow habitués of Pfaff's, the bohemian cafe at 647 Broadway much favored by *Vanity Fair* editors and writers, the comparison is apt.[1]

Frank Luther Mott writes that *Vanity Fair* was "born in Pfaff's cellar, bohemian gathering place of the wits of the fifties."[2] A regular at Pfaff's from 1859 through late 1862, Whitman most likely was present when ideas for a humorous weekly were being considered. Just who conceived the idea remains unknown, but the responsibility for creating and sustaining the magazine was assumed by three brothers of the Stephens family: William Allan became editor-in-chief, Henry Louis served as principal cartoonist, and Louis Henry was its "Publisher for the Proprietors." During its short existence—from December 31, 1859, to July 1863—*Vanity Fair* published at least twenty-two references to Whitman. The fact that *Vanity Fair*, which Mott describes as "this best of the early comic papers," gave positive and revealing attention to Whitman suggests that it saw its function as a worldly New York humor magazine dedicated to poking fun at the pomposity, hypocrisy, and cant of politicians, preachers, and literary highbrows who controlled public discourse.[3] Both Whitman and his fellow Pfaffians were determined to resist a culture that sought to limit sexual expression to the marriage bed—and then only for procreation. In Whitman the weekly had a powerful symbol of liberation, someone quite willing to lead his readers "In Paths Untrodden," as he wrote in the first poem in the "Calamus" sequence, added to *Leaves of Grass* in 1860.[4] Not surprisingly, certain of the references to Whitman in *Vanity Fair* call attention to his willingness to experiment with alternatives to heterosexual marriage.

No one could charge the *Vanity Fair* writers with not knowing Whitman's work or the influences that had shaped him as the "originator of the grass school of poetry," as one contributor wrote in May 1862.[5] On December 15, 1860, in "The Aesthetics of the Boot," a writer identified as Aldi Borondi Fosca Phorniosticus testified that he too had "travelled through the Wilt Waterman, the Weller and Fowls, and the R.A.F. Waldersonian Schools" of poetry, phrenology, and philosophy. Phorniosticus assumed that the reader knew of the phrenological publishing firm Fowler and Wells, the "silent" publishers of the 1855 and 1856 editions of *Leaves of Grass*, and of Whitman's friendship with Ralph Waldo Emerson. Phorniosticus too had "sat on the lap of Paumanok, and heard the little Child say softly—amid the hoarse, heaving breaths of the Old Mother, as W. W. put it:

O what am I?
O I don't know anything about it.
O that I did,
Or you,
Or any other man.

The parody echoes "Out of the Cradle Endlessly Rocking," published as "A Child's Reminiscence" on December 24, 1859, in another New York periodical aligned with the bohemians, Henry Clapp's *Saturday Press*. Searching for "the outward manifestations of the divine ME," the writer confesses his frustration. Not Whitman's poetry, not the phrenologists at Weller and Fowls—who had, he reports, actually examined his head—and not even the great philosopher of the R.A.F. Waldersonian Schools had satisfactorily answered the question of questions: what is the meaning of life? He had no choice but to develop his own philosophy, not, as had Thomas Carlyle, by devising a philosophy of clothes, but by formulating "The Aesthetics of Boots." Here too Whitman's example offered the essential lesson: "I had noticed that mysterious Something about Boots myself. I remember thinking at first that it was like what the *Saturday Press* said about Mr. Whitman's poems, 'The meaning is subtle and well enveloped, eluding definition,'—I think that was it."[6] Not counting the five-line echo of "Out of the Cradle" quoted above, *Vanity Fair* published at least five parodies of Whitman. These parodies—along with *Vanity Fair*'s running series of comments, puns, comic asides, and other references—paint a revealing picture of Whitman as a poet whose "barbaric yawp" already was being heard, at least by the readers of a weekly that quickly "created a considerable stir" by offering "live, topical, substantial fare."[7] The contributors behind *Vanity Fair* expressed their affection for Whitman even while poking fun at him, both in the pages of the comic weekly and around the tables at Pfaff's.

At Pfaff's it was "give and take . . . by the brightest minds in New York. The retold story and the repeated bon mot were rigorously barred, but the new good thing was sure of applause," Ferris Greenslet has written in his biography of Thomas Bailey Aldrich, who contributed to both the *Saturday Press* and *Vanity Fair*.[8] Regulars and occasional visitors at Pfaff's also included Clapp, George Arnold, Fitz-James O'Brien (who tragically died of battle wounds on April 6, 1862), Charles D. Gardette, N. G. Shepherd, Henry Neil, Charles Farrar Browne (Artemus Ward), Frank Wood, Ada Clare, Charles Dawson Shanly, Fitz Hugh Ludlow, William Winter, Richard Henry Stoddard, and Edmund Clarence Stedman, who called *Vanity Fair* the nation's "first measurably successful comic and literary weekly."[9] "There was not much of a literary market at that time," Stedman recalled. "Newspaper salaries were very low. There were few magazines, and scarcely any but *Harper's* and the *Atlantic* paid much of anything. New York itself was not literary and looked with distrust, if not contempt, upon working writers."[10] Still, the New York bohemians "were all very merry at Pfaff's," Aldrich wrote in "At the Cafe," published in *Vanity Fair*'s first issue, December 31, 1859. They created a supportive community, even as they satirized one another and the respectable press. "These people were mostly from the country," Stedman recalled in 1890, following Clapp's death. "They had scarcely any acquaintance in the city outside of their profession. You can easily see that they were thrown back upon themselves and made the most of that artistic, happy-go-lucky *bonhomie* and comradeship."[11] Don C. Seitz points out that Artemus Ward came to Pfaff's "as one to the manner born. The evenings were gay with converse and many libations of Pfaff's brew. . . . The members were men of genius, kinsmen in the world of light, who came here to meet their brothers."[12] The Pfaffians sought to infuse that light, humorous, but pointedly satiric style into *Vanity Fair*. What better way to get back at the pretentious periodicals and newspapers that didn't pay them or hire them or notice them other than with satire? What better way to promote each other's work, Clapp saw, than with a barrage of press notices—even negative ones—that could make a public personage of a writer like Whitman? As Christine Stansell writes, "Clapp's prescience lay in his comprehension of how publicity and celebrity could, within a changing literary market, obviate the need for critical and moral approval."[13]

The cause of sexual liberation united the bohemians. Clapp had been arrested for leading a free-love rally; Ada Clare gave birth out of wedlock; and Menken, who had appeared onstage in a translucent body suit (see Figure 9), flouted conventional morality. It was at Pfaff's that Whitman socialized with members of the "Fred Gray Association," an informal group of young male friends with whom he tested the boundaries of homosocial intimacy.[14] Whitman left an unfinished poem, "The Two Vaults," describing the irreverent, largely masculine atmosphere of "beautiful young men" at Pfaff's.[15] Similarly, the "Calamus" section of the 1860 *Leaves of Grass* called attention to a new style of urban life, one in which men gathered in drinking establishments such as Pfaff's. In "City of Orgies" Whitman praises Manhattan as the place where "the frequent and swift flash of eyes" offer "me the response to my own—these repay me, / Lovers, continual lovers, only repay me."[16]

Vanity Fair satirized the sanctimoniousness of the religious press and the hypocrisy of the self-appointed guardians of public morality, such as Henry Ward Beecher, who was a favorite target. In "The Town" from its first issue, the magazine asserted, "If it be true that . . . God made the country and man the town, then the town needs some one to take care of it." Who better to take care of New York than a smart humor magazine? "The town, too, is the centre of *Vanity Fair*, the point where all its good and all its wickedness is sublimated, where everybody . . . is travelling in the broad road that leads first to the Battery and afterward to no matter where." Here is a new cast of characters—New Yorkers to the core—that included a former showgirl, "Carrie-Jane, or Jennie, as they modernise it," and that wealthy young man about town, "J. Coupon-Dore, Esq . . . neither of whom you, sir, or madam, would be surprised at meeting any place outside the Tombs."[17] Whitman, it would show, was a product of this environment.

Little is known about Whitman's relationship with *Vanity Fair*'s first editor, Frank Wood, or about Wood himself. His successor, Charles Godfrey Leland, had a strong interest in Whitman's work, as Whitman did in Leland's. Leland translated Heinrich Heine's *Pictures of Travel* (1855), which Whitman cherished, telling Horace Traubel that the translation was "a joy and a delight."[18] In 1849 Whitman clipped four articles by Leland on literature and art from *Sartain's Union Magazine*.[19] Leland's younger brother Henry was also a friend of the poet, sending him two articles on his work that he had published in Philadelphia papers. On June 12, 1860, Whitman wrote to Clapp requesting that these pieces be published in the *Saturday Press*.[20] Stricken by heat prostration during his war service, Henry Leland died in 1868. Some twelve years later, Charles Leland recounted that Whitman had told him that during a period of despondency, "in the darkest years of his life"—evidently after the failure of the 1856 edition—he had received from Henry Leland "a cheering letter, full of admiration, which had a great effect on him, and inspired him to renewed effort." Charles Leland recalled that Whitman "sent my brother a copy of the first edition of his *Leaves of Grass*, with his autograph, which I still possess. I knew nothing of this till Whitman told me of it. The poet declared to me very explicitly that he had been much influenced by my brother's letter, which was like a single star in a dark night of despair, and I have no doubt that the world owes more to it than will ever be made known."[21]

Did Whitman publish in *Vanity Fair*? An anonymous entry on the poet in the *National Cyclopedia of American Biography*, published at the end of the nineteenth century, asserts that Whitman "wrote for *Vanity Fair* and other comic or satirical papers in New York, and was a recognized member of a group of young 'Bohemians,' as they were called, made up of musical, dramatic and literary critics attached to the daily and weekly press. At this time he led the life of a free-lance."[22] Since the volume includes John Burroughs's name as a contributor, he may well be the author—in which case the source could be Whitman himself. Charles Glicksberg concluded that "Whitman was probably a contributor, though none of his material has as yet been identified."[23] Whitman would not have been comfortable producing the sort of comic pieces that were the periodical's mainstay. But since *Vanity Fair* satirized figures such as the corrupt mayor of New York, Fernando Wood, and included articles on cultural life, book reviews, sketches of the city, and other material, it is quite possible that Whitman published there.

On February 10, 1860, Whitman accepted a proposal from the Boston publisher Thayer and Eldridge to bring out a new edition of his work. During March, April, and May of that year he was in Boston supervising the edition, which appeared in May.[24] Nevertheless, he remained in touch with Clapp and possibly other New York friends while he was in Boston. Clapp wrote him on March 27, "I need not say, we are all anxious to see you back at Pfaff's, and are eagerly looking for your proposed letter to the crowd."[25] During the first half of that year, *Vanity Fair* published five references to Whitman. Two of these, a parody on "counter-jumpers" and a reference to the calamus root, bear importantly on the new volume.

Published on March 10, 1860, the first reference to Whitman is part of an article on "Ages of American Authors," which satirizes an emerging style of treating authors—especially New Englanders—as hallowed figures. *Vanity Fair* playfully criticizes these puff pieces as violations of journalistic ethics. But if such pieces were to appear at all, then *Vanity Fair* would correct the record and ensure that all the important writers— especially New Yorkers such as Whitman and Fanny Fern—were included. Singled out for criticism is "the Boston *Transcript*, that great authority in literary matters," which has been "favoring the world with the ages of several American literary notabilities. . . . The *Transcript* having made a few blunders and several omissions, we have fortified ourselves with diverse facts on this highly interesting subject, which we proceed to lay before our expectant readers." The expectant readers learn that "the author of *Leaves of Grass* is 81 (his youthful appearance may be attributed to vegetable diet)." Fanny Fern is nineteen, and Stoddard and Aldrich "will be 21 on the 4th of July next." Clapp is 101. The paragraph concludes with a statement vouching for the factual truth of the information, but "if we have mis-stated the exact age of any literary lady or gentleman we shall be most happy to correct the mistake on the receipt of refuting vouchers."

A week later, on March 17, *Vanity Fair* published a revealing twenty-five-line parody, "Counter-Jumps. A Poemettina.—After Walt Whitman," in which Whitman is identified as a "counter-jumper," a term apparently coined by the magazine to refer to the well-dressed male clerks who worked in the fashionable stores catering to women. The term "counter-jumper" became one way of speaking about the emergence of an urban gay culture, as the historian Bert Hansen has demonstrated.[26] The *Vanity Fair* parody includes a large drawing of Whitman as a bearded poet standing above and behind a seated younger man (see Figure 1). The poet holds an enormous hat in his left hand as if ready to envelop the seated figure. Would the denizens at Pfaff's have recognized this as a depiction of his relationship with a particular individual, perhaps Fred Vaughan? According to Charley Shively, Vaughan "lived with Whitman while the poet finished his 'Calamus' poems which their love helped to shape. . . . In 1860 Whitman sent Vaughan galleys from Boston when the 1860 edition went to press."[27] Is the pictured plant meant to be the calamus root itself? If the drawing is meant to carry sexual overtones, then the poem itself reinforces those suggestions:

> I am the Counter-jumper, weak and effeminate.
> I love to loaf and lie about dry-goods.
> I loaf and invite the Buyer.
> I am the essence of retail. The sum and result of small profits and
>   quick returns.
>   .   .   .   .
> I am the crate, and the hamper, and the yard-wand, and the box of
>   silks fresh from France,
> And when I came into the world I paid duty,
> And I never did my duty,
> And never intend to do it,
> For I am the creature of weak depravities;
> I am the Counter-jumper;
> I sound my feeble yelp over the woofs of the World.

The poet who presents himself as "Walt Whitman, an American, one of the roughs, a kosmos," here confesses to be just another "weak and effeminate" counter-jumper.[28] This clerk-writer refuses to do his "duty," because he is "the creature of weak depravities." The timing of the parody is intriguing; two months later, with the publication of the "Calamus" section of *Leaves of Grass*, the poet himself would publicly celebrate the world of intense male attachments.

The parody did not necessarily undermine this celebration. Though the figure of the "counter-jumper" might adumbrate some of the cultural stereotypes that accompanied the emergence of the "homosexual" as a social type in the last third of the century, what Bert Hansen describes as the "new public discourse, primarily medical, about the homosexual as a type of person" had not yet developed.[29] Significantly, then, *Vanity Fair* could still publish the parody without affecting Whitman's reputation. During 1860 *Vanity Fair* included some fifteen articles on "counter-jumpers." The parody also explores the way that literature had become part of the new commercial culture—or, as the parody puts it, "the essence of retail." By 1860, as Justin Kaplan has written, Whitman's "dealings with editors reflected a new self-regard and assertiveness" on the economic value of his work.[30]

The *Vanity Fair* issue for April 14, 1860, contained two references to Whitman. The first occurs in the course of a satire on Senator Louis T. Wigfall of Texas, an aggressive Secessionist. *Harper's Weekly* had described him as a masterful "orator—probably the most charming in the Senate."[31] *Vanity Fair* satirizes Wigfall by contrasting him, ironically, with Whitman. Wigfall is called "one of the embodiments of the Republican idea, one of the mighty bulwarks of the constitution, one of the living illustrations of the beauty and majesty and ease of self-government," despite his well-known contempt for the Union. *Vanity Fair* concludes the satire with the note, "Go to, Walt Whitman, thy slabs of wisdom are all in a crumble compared with the granitic chunks that fall from Wigfall!" That same issue contained another brief Whitman reference in the form of a bon mot, one of many such witticisms that appeared in the magazine: "A True 'Barbaric Yawp.' / The milkman's morning cry." This casual allusion suggests just how well-known Whitman's work was among readers of *Vanity Fair*, who knew the sound of his "barbaric yawp over the roofs of the world."[32]

On May 19, as if in preparation for the new edition of *Leaves of Grass*, *Vanity Fair* published "Our Agricultural Column: Crop Prospects for 1860," meant to welcome Whitman back from Boston. A parody of the familiar newspaper and magazine articles on the prospects for various agricultural crops, the piece comments on the prospects that year for pork, peanuts, old rye, bowie knives, and the calamus root, for which an outstanding crop was expected. Evidently the bohemians at Pfaff's knew that in the new edition Whitman would introduce the calamus as the primary symbol of male friendship. Here is *Vanity Fair*'s entry on the "Calamus" crop:

> There will be a heavy crop of this health-giving root. We observed its graceful blossoms in many a meadow. Some of the farmers complain of the effects of heavy rains, and others anticipate a falling-off on account of the severe drought; but the general feeling is one of pride and hope. In consequence of the failure of the tobacco crop an unusually active market for Calamus is expected this season. The rates will rule higher. We believe roots will be held at more than one cent each. But we shall be well prepared to bear this slight advance, the effects of the Crisis of '57 having entirely passed away.

It is impossible to read this reference as anything other than a statement of "pride and hope" from the bohemian community on the prospects for Whitman's new edition. His friends at Pfaff's well understood that he, like the market for calamus, had been depressed following the failure of the 1856 edition. They shared his newfound optimism and confidence in his literary prospects in 1860; this notice is a way of wishing him the best at a pivotal moment in his career.

On July 7, 1860, *Vanity Fair* published a full-scale parody of Whitman as a patriotic poet in a piece that deploys Whitmanian catalogues to reveal a nation of sharpers, prostitutes, drunkards, and corrupt politicians. Titled "The Torch Bearer. A Paean for the Fourth of July. (After Walt. Whitman)," the parody appeared in the *Saturday Press* that same day, suggesting the close connection between the two periodicals:

> 1. I celebrate the Fourth of July!
> And what I celebrate you shall celebrate,
> And all together we'll go in strong for a celebration.
>
> . . . .
>
> 3. When, terrible in the midnight, begins the wild roar of cannon;
> When the ear-cracking cracker awakes me with its continual cracks;
> When punch and confusion are in the house and the "morning call" is
>   brought to me in a tumbler;
> When the stars and stripes hang round in a very miscellaneous
>   manner;

When Broadway is entirely given up to patriotic youth—then Young
    America bristles;
When the police are in a state of mind and the Aldermen in a state of
    body;
When in point of fact there is the devil to pay generally;—
Then is the Fourth of July, and I, rising, behold it.
I descend to the pavement, I swerve with the crowd, I roar exultant,
    I am an American citizen, I feel that every man I meet owes me
    twenty-five cents.
Selah!

.   .   .

5. The shapes arise.

.   .   .   .

Shapes of the bulky Germans, slow of appreciation, drinking their
    Lager Bier;
Pipe shapes; shapes of the smoke-cloud, Irish persons enveloped;
Shapes of the Irish persons brawling, the whiskey mastering their
    brains;
Shapes of the "stars" and "shadows," alert for the wranglers and those
    who fight;
Shapes of the sharpers, courtesans, whiskered persons, collecting
    revenue;
Shapes of counter-jumpers, redolent shades, mint juleps attending;
Shapes of women, fair and otherwise, hungry for ice-cream and for
    lemonade;
Shapes of the ice-cream and the lemonade—disappearing shapes, the
    contact of sweet lips assisting;
Shapes of adventurous persons in balloons, my own shape soaring in
    the balloon of my fancy;—
And then, beautiful to see, the stars and stripes proudly fluttering
    over all.

The poem recalls Whitman's tribute for the visit of the Japanese em-
bassy to Manhattan in "The Errand-Bearers" (later retitled "A Broadway
Pageant" for inclusion in *Leaves of Grass*), which he had recently published
in the *New York Times*.[33] Unlike "The Errand-Bearers," however, "The
Torch-Bearer" focuses on those citizens of New York who most resemble
the habitués of Pfaff's: "bulky Germans . . . drinking their Lager Bier";

"Irish persons brawling" (no doubt a reference to Fitz-James O'Brien, known for his pugilism[34]); "counter-jumpers"; and drunken, entitled revelers who believe that the world owes them (at least) "twenty-five cents."

On August 4 and September 22, 1860, *Vanity Fair* returned to Whitman in the course of a two-part satire called "Private Libraries of New York," provoked by James Wynne's 1860 book of the same name. Exposed are the pretensions of wealthy bibliophiles who spend lavishly on foreign books that they never read. Mocking Wynne's reverential tone, *Vanity Fair* celebrates a number of recent publications, including those by Whitman: "To begin with the collection of Mr. Furnace. Among its curiosities are *The Sinless Child*, original edition, published by Keese; *The Rape of the Lock*, written by Pope . . . the prose works of Walter Whitman, the great American Kosmos, (no connection of Humboldt's); the complete works of Paul de Kock edited by Tome, and the new edition of *Casanova*, a decoction lately recommended by the *World*."[35] Incongruously sandwiched between Alexander von Humboldt's scientific *Kosmos* (published in English as *Cosmos* in 1860), Charles Paul de Kock's ribald fiction, Elizabeth Oakes Smith's sentimental poem "The Sinless Child" (1843), and the memoirs of Giacomo Casanova, Whitman's presence in "Private Libraries of New York" suggests that the wealthy book collectors were not, after all, readers: "the bibliopole seldom gets beyond the cover of his books. To do more than this is to become a reader, which your true bibliopole never is."[36] The readers of *Vanity Fair*, however, would be more attuned to the incongruities in this collection of books than the book owners themselves.

The next reference to Whitman appeared a week later, on August 11, as part of a series titled "Telegraphic Tour" that poked fun at travel writing. It would take readers across "the whole Manifest Destination of the Universal American Continent." Readers learn that an outrageous old widow "has been for seven years like my prose, and Walt Whitman's poetry, Beecher's theology and Andy Davis' Harmonicon, outside of all criticism—'might as well criticise porcupine'—so people let her slide in peace and exclaim in cheerful awe 'did you ever!!'" These references connect Whitman with Beecher and Andrew Davis, a spiritualist, who, David S. Reynolds has written, helped bring to "the fore new kinds of mysticism and spiritual eroticism that Whitman would experiment with in *Leaves of Grass*." Further, Davis's popularization of "mesmeric healing, trance writing, and mental space-time travel through what Davis called 'traveling clairvoyance' . . . were manifested in Whitman's poetry."[37] Similarly, in forming his style, Whitman "paid considerable attention to the oratory of influential ministers like Henry Ward Beecher."[38]

Published on September 29, 1860, "Song of the Barbecue" satirized both Whitman and Henry Wadsworth Longfellow (indeed, the poem's subtitle is "Not by Walt Whitman, nor Professor Longfellow"). The author may have been aware of Whitman's apparent reference to Longfellow in "Poem of the Heart of the Son of Manhattan Island": "And who has projected beautiful words through the longest time? By God! I will outvie him! I will say such words, they shall stretch through longer time!"[39] "The Song of the Barbecue" conflates Chapter XI, "Hiawatha's Wedding Feast," and Whitman's "A Broadway Pageant," published in the *New York Times* on June 27, 1860, as "The Errand-Bearers." Longfellow listed the "Haunch of deer and hump of bison," along with other foods served on the occasion. "The Song of the Barbecue" speaks of the "haunches" of the "bloody ox" served at a political gathering for Stephen A. Douglas. Whitman's poem commemorated the visit of Japanese ambassadors to the United States—and the huge parade in their honor up Broadway on June 16, 1860—with paeans to the triumph of "Libertad" through the joining of American liberty with "venerable Asia, the all-mother." Douglas gave his major speech at Jones Wood outside the city on September 12. *Vanity Fair* satirizes the confusion surrounding Douglas's speech and attendant barbecue, which, according to the *New York Times*, attracted "an unprecedented multitude," drawn "largely . . . by the savor of roast beef, mutton and pork."[40] These stanzas, taken from the middle of the poem, humorously illustrate this confusion through the overblown language of both Whitman and Longfellow:

> Soon the ox came, Libertad!
> I sing of the fatted ox,
> I sing of the ancient ox,
> I sing of the smelling ox,
> I sing of the bloody ox.
>
> Ax inserted in his haunches,
> Libertad! how it squelched.
> Crowds crowd close around the tables,
> Bread-trays wander to the crowd,
> Small boys carry aforesaid Bread-trays.

Jerk it off from sirloin, rump,
Ribs or shoulder, haunch or quarter,
Throw it to the starving crowd,
Bloody, half-cooked, though it may be
Each Bite is a Bite for Douglas!

Libertad! Redad! Whitead! Bluead!
I sing of Douglas, little giant—
Travelling Duggy from the prairies
Ever shouting, ever bawling
"Tell me, pray thee, where's my mother!"

In this case, it is not so much the policies of the "Little Giant" that are being gored or the styles of Whitman or Longfellow, but the chaos attendant on turning a political event into an "immense barbecue."

On November 10, 1860, *Vanity Fair* ran a comic paragraph in which it suggested sending boatloads of notable Americans—including P. T. Barnum, Abraham Lincoln, and James Gordon Bennett—off to a stream in England thought to have rejuvenating properties (as well as high concentrations of arsenic). A report in *Little's Living Age* had attributed the "old age which a large portion of the population attain" to their habit of drinking "the arsenic in the water."[41] *Vanity Fair* had no trouble identifying Americans who would benefit from traveling to the village of Whitbeck where the waters are to be found. And who would be the poet to proclaim the health benefits of drinking the water? None other than Walt Whitman, although even he "could hardly catalogue the probable delights of it. Elfland, Elysium, Lalla Rookh, ducks and green peas, Madeline the *battle*, Shrewsbury oysters, you, whoever you are, ourselves—all upon the half-shell, would be nothing to it." Yes, "Whitman, indeed, should be the bard of Whitbeck, the newly published fountain of perpetual delight. Let us hope that he will indulge us with a hymn to the aresnicated Undin of the rejuvenating river." There is no evidence that he took the advice.

On November 17, 1860, the periodical began an essay, "J.B.," by informing its "Friend reader—your Uncle has a lot of trouble in these receding, seceding, bleeding . . . times." *Vanity Fair* complained, "We are going to lose James." Could the periodical survive without Buchanan, its model do-nothing president? "We are out of Ossian, and Adah Issacs [*sic*] Menken &c. has wailing enough to do for herself in poetry, while Walt Whitman is engaged, or else the world should see a lyric of despair which would drive to raving lunacy the infant in the cradle, and the crow on the housetop." On December 1, 1860, the magazine mentioned Whitman in reference to a disputed statue of George Washington, which, it had been decided, would be removed from City Hall Park to Tompkins Square. So bad was the sculpture, the magazine opined, that many citizens owed their nervous complaints to having to pass it daily. Once the sculpture would finally be removed, "we may 'celebrate ourselves,' as Whitman says; only let us not be too riotous on the occasion, but act as becomes a moral and religious people." Other discussions of Whitman in the first half of 1861 were brief. On April 13, under the title "The Cab-Age," the magazine commented on a bill being considered in Albany, New York, to regulate cab fares in the city. Should passengers be charged by the mile or by a set price for trips within certain zones? As an expert on meters, a poet must be consulted: "Will Walt Whitman, who is said to understand long measures, favor the public with his valuable opinion?"

Civil War hostilities broke out on April 12, 1861, with the firing on Fort Sumter. On June 29, in "A Short 'Loaf,'" *Vanity Fair* reported that "Captain Baker, the pirate commander of the privateer 'Savannah,' seems to have had quite a select library on board his craft. But he didn't have Walt Whitman's 'Leaves of Grass,' although from the nature (and result) of his cruise, it would appear he intended to 'loaf' (on the high seas) 'and invite his soul' (to a speedy flight-wards). It has, however, turned out a very unprofitable Loaf to this Baker we opine. Hardly 'half a loaf,' in fact." The reference is to the capture on June 5, 1861, of the *Savannah*, commanded by T. Harrison Baker, by the USS *Minnesota*. There are no references to Whitman during the second half of 1861, but there are four in the first half of 1862. On February 15, in "Wanted—A Poet," *Vanity Fair*, satirizing the bits of poetry that the *New York Herald* used to spice up its obituaries, provided some samples of its own. After a few lines in the pre-Raphaelite mode, it remarked that "the reader cannot fail to recognize the peculiar versification and melody of that great innovator of modern poetry, Walt Whitman. Are we wrong in laying this tender topaz, this pathetic pearl at the door of the distinguished?"

A gem of human form is gone to the realms of grace,
A princely pearl to enrich the kingdom of God's selected race.

Oh, Araminta dear, she is no longer here to solace the lonely hours of
   father and mother, dear devoted ones of thy world's latest ends.
She, blessed of the three, no longer waits the caressing of parents'
   anxious care. She, she is there with God's selected gems.

On April 12, 1862, the magazine published a full-scale parody under the
title "Bath Oriental" that is much more successful than the obituary verse
in capturing the poet's style:

1. Oh a mixed community of persons! O Manahattanese!
Sauntering on Broadway, or loafing out beyond the ferries, here are
   unwholesome faces.
The lamentable face of the money-broker—the man whose victuals
   don't seem to agree with each other, neither with him, except he
   speculates well.
The face of the down-town merchant, who has passed several
   suffering nights disturbed by the agonizing cries of the
   shapeless child.

   .   .   .   .

3. Take off your duds, and I will mine, and we will go in for a righteous
   wash.
We will take sixty baths, including the process of shampooing, at one
   dollar.
Or one hundred baths, dispensing with the services of the tellaks, at
   fifty cents.
I swear I will not shirk any part of the process.
The peculiar substance which closes up the pores of the skin cannot
   be removed by simple immersion in soap and water, but here there
   is no stoppage, and never can be stoppage.
Large and melodious thoughts descend upon me with the slender,
   spasmic jets of the tepid, blue-white water.
I see the butter-colored chips flying off in great flakes and slivers.
By Jingo! they are like little rolls of human vermicelli.
Dulcemente! Dulcemente!

   .   .   .   .

I would see this Moslem institution established . . . in every city of
   These States . . .

   .   .   .   .   .   .

Celebrate with me, O enfans prepared for the Turkish Bath!

Was Whitman the author? The parody demonstrates a remarkable knowledge of the poet's style. There are precise references to what would become Section 44 of "Song of Myself" and "Salut Au Monde!" Furthermore, the parody looks back to Whitman's editorial days in calling upon the New York authorities to establish public bathing houses. In "Cheap Baths—Health and Beauty" for the *New York Sun* on March 30, 1843, he celebrated the "wholesomeness of frequent ablutions of the body." Charging that the American bathing habits—or lack thereof—were a national disgrace, he urged the "municipal fathers" to establish "*free baths.*"[42] Now, however, the poet looks upon the establishment of Turkish baths as a sound private investment.

The last reference to Whitman in *Vanity Fair* occurred the next month, May 17, 1862. With commencement time approaching, the graduates-to-be were in need of subjects for their final orations. *Vanity Fair* offered its assistance by listing twelve subjects under the heading "To Young Gentlemen who are preparing for Commencement Day." Here is Number III: "For a Philosophical Oration. The Stuck-Eichen-Dummer-Junger-Kleinbocker of Immanuel Kant in its Influence on Walt Whitman."

Rising costs during the war took a heavy toll on *Vanity Fair*, as it did on all periodicals. On December 27, 1862, William A. Stephens announced that the magazine would become a monthly. But after only two months it ceased publication, except for a run of ten weekly issues beginning in May. For two and a half years Walt Whitman figured prominently on the pages of *Vanity Fair*. During 1861, when, apparently, Whitman had otherwise disappeared from the press, *Vanity Fair* helped keep his name alive. The magazine's writers demonstrate a remarkable knowledge of Whitman's work—as we might expect from his close friends and supporters from Pfaff's. Furthermore, in *Vanity Fair* these writers found a vehicle to express their own free and open sensibility: they could joke about sexuality and make fun of the pious religious press. To understand Whitman's presence in the magazine is to see that by 1860 he had found a congenial, supportive community of professional writers who understood the magnitude of his achievement and did their best to promote him. They wanted to make sure that *Leaves of Grass* would be read long after he and they were dead and buried—even at the risk of sending overly sensitive younger readers to the insane asylum.

NOTES

This essay originally appeared, in longer form and with illustrations, as "'An Unusually Active Market for Calamus': Whitman, *Vanity Fair*, and the Fate of Humor in a Time of War, 1860–1863," *Walt Whitman Quarterly Review* 19 (winter/spring 2002), 148–81. See also its companion piece, also by Robert J. Scholnick, "The Fate of Humor in a Time of Civil and Cold War: *Vanity Fair* and Race," *Studies in American Humor* 3, no. 10 (2003): 21–42.

1. Allen, *Solitary Singer*, 262.

2. Mott, *History*, 520.

3. Ibid. The Baltimore merchant Frank J. Thompson, a friend of Henry Louis Stephens, was the essential financial angel.

4. *LG60*, 341.

5. *VF*, May 10, 1862.

6. "The Aesthetics of Boots, Part II," *VF*, Jan. 12, 1861. The reference apparently is to "All About a Mocking-Bird," *SP*, Jan. 7, 1860. The author speaks of Whitman's music carrying with it "all the subtle analogies of our own associations."

7. Glicksberg, "Charles Godfrey Leland," 311.

8. Greenslet, *Life of Thomas Bailey Aldrich*, 45.

9. Stedman and Gould, *Life and Letters*, 1:208. *Harper's Weekly* on April 26, 1862, published an extensive obituary notice with an analysis of O'Brien's contributions to American letters and courageous service as a Union soldier.

10. Stedman and Gould, *Life and Letters*, 1:209.

11. Ibid.

12. Seitz, *Artemus Ward*, 99.

13. Stansell, "Whitman at Pfaff's," 121.

14. Ibid., 107–26.

15. *NUPM* 1:454–55.

16. *LG60*, 363.

17. *VF*, Dec. 31, 1859.

18. *WWC* 2:53.

19. Stovall, *Foreground*, 146.

20. *Corr.* 1:55. Letter dated June 12, 1860. The items included a parody, "Enfans de Soixante-Seize," and a review.

21. Leland's memoirs quoted in Stovall, 224–25.

22. *National Cyclopedia of American Biography* (New York, 1898) quoted in Glicksberg, "Charles Godfrey Leland," 315.

23. Glicksberg, "Charles Godfrey Leland," 315.

24. For a full description of these events, see Allen, *Solitary Singer*, 236–44.

25. *WWC* 1:236–37.

26. Hansen, "American Physicians' Discovery," 16, and note 14, 28.

27. Shively, "Vaughan, Frederick B."

28. *LG55*, 29.

29. Hansen, "American Physicians' Discovery," 17.

30. Kaplan, *Walt Whitman*, 246.

31. *Harper's Weekly*, Mar. 16, 1860.

32. *LG*, 78.

33. See Whitley, *American Bards*, 170–85.

34. Parry, *Garrets and Pretenders*, 50–51.

35. *VF*, Aug. 4, 1860.

36. *VF*, Sept. 22, 1860.

37. Reynolds, "Whitman and Popular Culture," 535.

38. Worley, "Principal Influences," 312.

39. *LG56*, 256.

40. "Douglass and Fusion," *New York Times*, Sept. 13, 1860.

41. *Little's Living Age*, Oct. 5, 1860.

42. Whitman, *Journalism*, 1:172–73.

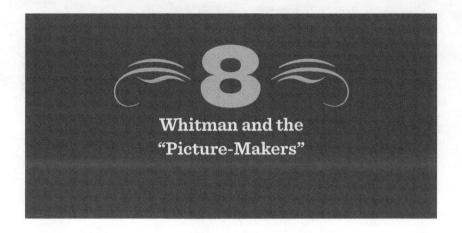

Whitman and the "Picture-Makers"

RUTH L. BOHAN

In the February 11, 1860, issue of the *Saturday Press,* writer and actor Ada Clare assured readers in her column "Thoughts and Things" that "the Bohemian was by nature, if not by habit, a Cosmopolite, with a general sympathy for the fine arts." Both sympathizers and practitioners of the fine arts were well-represented among the regulars at Pfaff's beer cellar, where a congenial atmosphere encouraged interpersonal and cross-disciplinary sharing. Walt Whitman was a great admirer of the arts and forged personal friendships with several of these artists, particularly those who drew for *Vanity Fair.* This essay seeks to recover these artists' presence among their bohemian colleagues while assessing their contributions to the mid-century discourse on bohemianism. Like those around them, the artists were particularly concerned with matters of identity and proved especially adept at deploying their skills in caricature and other forms of visual representation in the construction and reinforcement of bohemian identity. Several such images, including caricatures of the poet, animate the pages of Whitman's notebook, raising important questions about the extent to which Whitman modeled and encouraged pictorial formulations of the bohemian type.

Before his associations with the artists at Pfaff's, Whitman cultivated friendships with a range of artists, including members of the Brooklyn Art Union, an artist-run cooperative intent on stimulating interest in the fine arts through public display and discussion. At the organization's first distribution of prizes, Whitman praised this country's considerable potential in the arts while urging artists to form "a close phalanx, ardent, radical and progressive" to assure its growth and continuity.[1] Whitman also participated in the lively gatherings of artists, writers, and arts patrons who frequented the Brooklyn studio of sculptor Henry Kirke Brown in the early 1850s. Among the participants were Launt Thompson, an Irish émigré who would later become a regular at Pfaff's, and painter William Page, a future participant in Ada Clare's Forty-second Street coterie. In recalling his experiences years later, Whitman remarked, "They were big, strong days—our young days—days of preparation: the gathering of the forces."[2]

If Whitman's associations with the Brooklyn Art Union and Brown's studio constituted "the gathering of the forces," his association with the artists and writers at Pfaff's gave renewed impetus to his concerns with matters of identity and its pictorial manifestations. In the democratic marketplace of New York's expanding literary community, Pfaff's provided Whitman and his fellow bohemians with what Christine Stansell has termed "a theater of democratic, esthetic camaraderie."[3] The rapid rise in book and magazine illustration, facilitated in large part by the substitution of wood engraving for older forms of intaglio engraving, opened up increasing opportunities for artists and writers to explore their talents in a mutually supportive environment that was at the same time reaching new and broader audiences. The phenomenal success of *Harper's New Monthly Magazine*, which began publication in 1850, can be credited in no small measure to its expanded use of illustrations made possible by the new wood engraving process.[4] Whitman was quick to praise *Harper's* for "the beauty of its illustrations," which he termed "an example of what American enterprise and talent can do."[5] He expressed special delight in its comic and seriocomic illustrations, judging them "rich, rare and racy."[6]

Several of the artists who gathered at Pfaff's were among the leading comic illustrators of the period. Thomas Nast, who would become the best known of the group, was scarcely twenty years old and at the beginning of his artistic career when he joined Solomon Eytinge Jr., Frank Henry Temple Bellew, Edward F. (Ned) Mullen, and others around the table at Pfaff's. In the years after the Civil War, Nast would achieve national prominence for his scathing cartoons attacking government corruption and greed, while Eytinge was recognized for his illustrations of the work of Charles Dickens. Bellew, also known as "the triangle" for the distinctive way he signed his cartoons, was familiar to Whitman even before their paths crossed under the vault at Pfaff's. Whitman had entered Bellew's name and address in a notebook, probably in early 1857.[7] A talented and highly respected comic illustrator who contributed drawings to virtually all of the leading illustrated magazines of the period, Bellew would later include Whitman among the twenty-eight figures whose comic portraits he drew for the *Fifth Avenue Journal*.[8]

Whitman's closest friend among the artists at Pfaff's was Ned Mullen, a figure about whom little is known. Even the spelling of his name was in dispute among Pfaffians, who often spelled it "Mullin." Elihu Vedder, a painter who joined Pfaff's in the early summer of 1861,[9] remembered him with great fondness and appreciation. Vedder considered him a "good artist" and praised his drawings for their "delightful freedom and a style of his own," terming them "veritable little gems [that] offered the greatest contrast to the drawings of all about him." Still, Mullen's life was marred by drinking problems that resulted in frequent absences. His landlady termed him "a holy terror," and Vedder recalled that "he was ever on the verge of a fight." Once, after a severe bout of drinking, Vedder and a friend intervened to have the talented but troubled artist admitted to a hospital, even supplying him with fresh undergarments.[10] In 1881, on a return visit to New York, Whitman recalled how he and the former proprietor Charles Pfaff remembered Mullen and the others at Pfaff's in a style all would have appreciated, "namely, [with] big, brimming, fill'd-up champagne-glasses, drain'd in abstracted silence, very leisurely, to the last drop."[11]

Whitman also took an interest in Vedder, who shared with Clapp the distinction of having experienced bohemianism directly in Europe. "If the Bohemia I belonged to in Paris had been divided into classes," Vedder recalled, "I think I could have been returned as a Member for Upper Bohemia. Not that I was proud or rich,—on the contrary, I was poor: but I had a washerwoman and I paid her bills."[12] In New York, Vedder found lodging at 48 Beekman Street in the heart of the city's publishing district. Whitman visited him there, and it is there that Vedder got to know several of the regulars at Pfaff's, whom he affectionately called "the Boys."[13] Whitman no doubt enjoyed conversing with the young artist about his experiences in Paris and perhaps also about his imaginative art of sphinxes and sea serpents.[14] Vedder, however, seems to have been less enamored of the poet. In his autobiography he remembered Whitman as someone who "used to sit with his beard and open collar and hairy breast and beam upon the Boys, [but] his beams remained on the outside of you."[15]

By his own account, Whitman frequented Pfaff's "nearly every night" for about three years, proclaiming the "good talk" among the twenty-five or thirty nightly participants equal to that found "anywhere in the world."[16] This author of a temperance novel thrived in the alcohol-fueled atmosphere of the cellar that he celebrated in an incomplete and unpublished poem drafted in one of his notebooks. The poem praised the "beautiful young men!" who frequented the cellar, joyfully describing it as a place "where the drinkers and laughers meet to eat and drink and carouse." In contrast to the "thick crowds" traversing the sidewalks overhead, where "all is but a pageant," in the "vault at Pfaffs" the focus was on conversation and camaraderie. Whitman was particularly encouraged by the ease with which those present would "Toss the theme from one to another!"[17] Whether writers, critics, actors, or artists, those present found intellectual sustenance and an enriched sense of community in the lively give-and-take that was the hallmark of New York's bohemian gatherings.

Vanity Fair, like the *Saturday Press*, drew heavily on the regulars at Pfaff's for their witty, fast-paced critiques of bourgeois life. Ada Clare, Fitz-James O'Brien, Thomas Bailey Aldrich, George Arnold, Frank Wood, Artemus Ward, and Charles Dawson Shanly all wrote for the comic weekly, while Mullen, Bellew, and Vedder (to a lesser extent) produced many of its illustrations. An additional contributor was the highly respected illustrator and native Pennsylvanian John McLenan, who settled in New York around 1850. Although not known to have frequented Pfaff's, McLenan earned the respect of those present with his well-crafted illustrations for a variety of publications, including several authored by Pfaffian writers. *Vanity Fair*'s publisher, Louis Henry Stephens (not to be confused with his brother, Henry Louis Stephens, the journal's art director), recalled the camaraderie and collaborative effort that characterized the group's early days, mirroring the group spirit at Pfaff's. "It was a custom," he wrote, "in the old editorial rooms at No. 113 Nassau Street, New York, for the writers and artists who were then associated with it to assemble every Friday afternoon, and, over a glass of wine and a cigar, submit and discuss suggestions for subjects for the next issue."[18] Vedder, whose rigorous training in art made it difficult for him to accept what he termed the "touch-and-go style then in vogue," spoke favorably about the democratic procedures that enabled artists to have as much input as writers in determining the content of each issue.[19]

Whitman attracted considerable attention on the pages of *Vanity Fair*, both for the unconventionalities of his verse and for his growing bohemian stature. Robert Scholnick has identified some twenty-three parodies, cartoons, and satirical references to the poet across a two-year period.[20] The attention followed the announcement that the Boston firm of Thayer and Eldridge would publish a new edition of his verse. Not only did this venture have the potential to propel one of New York's rising bohemians into a position of greater national prominence, but from there he could more publicly challenge the cultural hegemony of the Boston elite. Just days after Whitman left for Boston to oversee the new publication, two Pfaffians devoted nearly half a page to satirizing the poet in word and image. The parody is unsigned but has been safely attributed to Fitz-James O'Brien;[21] the accompanying caricature is almost assuredly Mullen's work (Figure 1). Titled "Counter-Jumps. A Poemettina. —After Walt Whitman," the twenty-five-line parody continued a theme O'Brien had first introduced in the magazine two months earlier. In an unmistakable riff on the style and first-person narration of "Song of Myself," the parody boldly exclaimed:

> I am the Counter-jumper, weak and effeminate.
> I love to loaf and lie about dry-goods.
>
> . . . .
>
> I am the Counter-jumper;
> I sound my feeble yelp over the woofs of the World.[22]

A "counter-jumper," literally "one who jumps over a counter," was a term commonly used to refer to a male clerk in a dry-goods store, an occupation many regarded as unmanly. As such, it was one of the new urban stereotypes for men who were attracted to other men.[23]

In Mullen's caricature Whitman stands tall and dignified, not "weak and effeminate," in a coat with distinctively large buttons, such as Whitman wore at the time, a white-collared shirt, and a loosely tied cravat. With one hand in his pocket, he holds in the other an outsized tall hat that is poised to drop over a small, seated male figure in plaid pants. The composition is framed by a long, leafy stalk bearing a strong resemblance to the calamus plant. Whitman would introduce the "Calamus" poems, with their theme of male-male friendship and sexuality, in the soon-to-be-published 1860 *Leaves of Grass*. The visual reference to it here, two months before the book appeared, strongly suggests that Whitman and his Pfaffian colleagues had discussed his use of the term and its sexual

COUNTER-JUMPS.

A POEMETTINA.—AFTER WALT WHITMAN.

AM the Counter-jumper, weak and effeminate.

I love to loaf and lie about dry-goods.

I loaf and invite the Buyer.

I am the essence of retail. The sum and result of small profits and quick returns.

1. Edward F. Mullen, caricature of Walt Whitman,
Vanity Fair, March 17, 1860, 183. Courtesy of the Rare Book and
Manuscript Library, University of Illinois at Urbana-Champaign.

implications before his departure for Boston. Most significant is the way the plant intertwines, even seems to grow out of, the enlarged "I" of the parody's first word, connecting the theme directly to the poet and thus moving beyond the stereotyping image of the counter-jumper that both Mullen and Bellew addressed head-on in cartoons elsewhere in the magazine.[24] Although it has been suggested that the small figure about to disappear under Whitman's hat was a counter-jumper, perhaps a member of the Fred Gray Association, which included several male clerks,[25] it is far more likely that the figure represents O'Brien, the author of the parody and the originator of the journal's counter-jumper theme. With a broken nose, a receding chin, and a distinctive mustache, O'Brien was a frequent target for caricatures by his Pfaffian friends. He also favored plaid pants such as those worn by the small, seated figure.[26] In the act of silencing O'Brien, Whitman asserts his independence from the negative implications of the counter-jumper theme, aligning himself instead with the "aromatic" blades of the calamus plant, whose leafy spears form a gentle arc above his head.[27]

Whitman's upright posture and distinctive attire, together with the way he towers over the diminutive figure of O'Brien, focus additional attention on the poet's rising bohemian stature and celebrity appeal. Whereas Whitman had chosen to represent himself as a working-class poet in the 1855 *Leaves of Grass*, now, on the eve of a new edition of his verse, he assumed a more urbane and complex mode of self-representation, one more representative of the ambiguities and dualities that distinguished bohemians from their contemporaries. "Bohemianism," as Joanna Levin has written, "self-consciously defined itself against the opposition of a bourgeois press dedicated to cataloguing urban types and assessing their relation to desirable social norms."[28] Just before leaving for Boston, Whitman commissioned his friend the painter Charles Hine to paint his portrait, an image that would become the basis for the frontispiece of the 1860 *Leaves*. Whitman mentions Hine in two of his notebooks, including one containing his unfinished poetic tribute to Pfaff's.[29] Mullen's caricature shares with the Hine portrait a focus on the poet's shift toward a more prosperous and distinctly urban identity. At the same time Mullen suggests that the poet's working-class sensibilities have not been entirely subsumed by these personal refinements, for peaking beneath the lower border of the poet's neatly buttoned coat is an unruly shirttail. By projecting the qualities of two such distinct urban types simultaneously—the aristocratic dandy and the working-class loafer—Mullen's Whitman effectively embodies the bohemian ideal of "socioeconomic indecipherability,"[30] which aligns neatly with the poet's own goal of being "Both in and out of the game and watching and wondering at it."[31]

A similar focus on Whitman's bohemian indecipherability characterizes McLenan's caricature of the poet from about the same period (Figure 2). Although not published during Whitman's lifetime, the caricature and its accompanying text would have fit comfortably within the pages of *Vanity Fair*. Even more than Mullen's, McLenan's drawing exudes the cocky self-confidence Whitman projected during his stay in Boston when he gloated to his friend Abby Price, "I create an immense sensation in Washington street. Every body here is so like everybody else—and I am Walt Whitman!"[32] McLenan's caricature represents Whitman wearing a coat, open-necked shirt, and loosely knotted cravat similar to those in both the Hine and Mullen images, but his hair and beard are much less tamed, and the hat he holds in the Mullen image is now perched jauntily atop his head in an echo of the 1855 *Leaves* frontispiece. The result is a creative fusion of the bohemian dandy and the working-class rough. An arc of text below the poet's head humorously reinforces the working-class elements of the image. Loud and boisterous, with several crossed-out and misspelled words, it reads like the comic script for one of P. T. Barnum's buskers. Addressed to the "Ladies and Gentlemen" of the public, it describes the poet as "gifted by nature" but "with a head—that is swollen with literary talent— . . . [and] alowed [*sic*] to go to grass—." Both text and image seem closely allied with an anonymous review reprinted in *Leaves of Grass Imprints*, the pamphlet Thayer and Eldridge had printed and distributed with the 1860 *Leaves of Grass* to publicize the poet and his work. The review, probably written by Whitman and first published in the *Brooklyn Daily Times*, describes the poet as "a rude child of the people! . . . a growth and idiom of America," while acknowledging his "strong clothes," "mottled" beard, and "hair like hay after it has been mowed in the field and lies tossed and streaked."[33]

Drawings in a notebook Whitman used during his time at Pfaff's reinforce the bohemian focus of the caricatures. The drawings range from caricatures and costume studics to the representation of an Irish harp, a nod, no doubt, to the large number of Irish who frequented Pfaff's. Twenty-four in all, the drawings are scattered throughout the notebook identified as "81 Clerman."[34] By their very existence they imply Whitman's

RUTH L. BOHAN {139

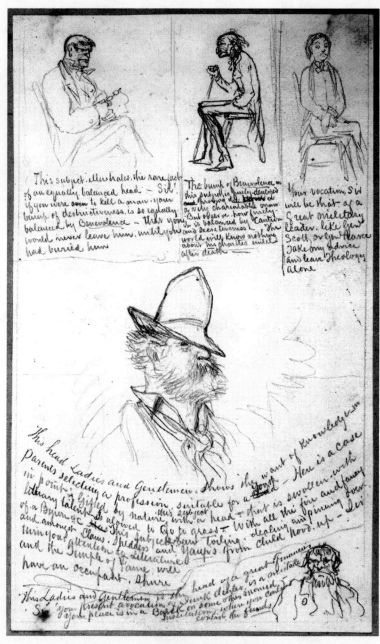

2. John McLenan, caricature of Walt Whitman, ca. 1860.
Pencil. Print Collection, Miriam and Ira D. Wallach Division of Art,
Prints, and Photographs, The New York Public Library;
Astor, Lenox, and Tilden Foundations.

knowledge of and perhaps collusion in their construction, but probably not in their execution. The drawings were presumably made in the course of the nightly discussions at Pfaff's by one or more of Whitman's artist friends. The informal and unfinished nature of the drawings suggest that they were tossed off in very preliminary fashion as a way of working out ideas to be perfected later, much the way Whitman used the notebook to record passing thoughts and ideas for future poems. None of the drawings is signed, but it seems likely that several were done by Mullen. A central theme that emerges from the drawings concerns matters of identity, especially bohemian identity, with its myriad manifestations and attributes. When viewed in the aggregate they suggest that the question of bohemian identity and its pictorial manifestations were a recurring focus of the nightly discussions at Pfaff's.

One of the drawings, the head of a gentleman in a top hat, presents the standard of bourgeois dress and respectability that Whitman and his bohemian colleagues adamantly resisted. The man's chiseled features and upright posture, the antithesis of bohemian indecipherability, complement the straight-sided verticality of his top hat and may have been intended as a visual reminder of the Brahmin elite Whitman was likely to encounter during his stay in Boston. "There is no denying that these Yanks are the first-class race," Whitman wrote his brother Jeff from Boston. "But, without exception, they all somehow allow themselves to be squeezed into the stereotype mould, and wear straight collars and hats, and say 'my respects'—like the rest."[35] Bayard Taylor concurred, asserting: "The general impression which Boston and its environs made upon my friends was that of substantial prosperity and comfort. They also noticed its prim, proper English air, so strongly contrasted with the semi-Parisian vivacity of New York."[36] Several drawings in Whitman's notebook provide visual confirmation of this "semi-Parisian vivacity." In one, Whitman wears a wildly exaggerated top hat whose excessive height and bent crown—together with its overly broad brim, which is pulled down to completely obscure the poet's face—provide a humorous rebuttal to the prim and proper gentleman noted above (Figure 3). Adding to the figure's comic effect are the enlarged buttons of his coat, larger even than those in Mullen's *Vanity Fair* caricature, and his hair, which bristles like the "grass" in McLenan's drawing. Exaggeration and distortion, two of the tools in the caricaturist's arsenal, are here deployed for their full comic effect. The image might well have served as comic accompaniment for an article in the *Saturday Press* titled

3. Caricature of Walt Whitman.
Notebook no. 91, Thomas Biggs Harned Collection of
Walt Whitman, Manuscript Division,
Library of Congress.

"The Bohemian as a Gentleman," which praised the bohemian as "a law unto himself." In contrast to the "snob," who occupies "the little world of fashion, rank, [and] convention," the bohemian, the author noted, meets men in the higher "plain of manhood, truth, and sincerity, which lie behind all artificial distinctions, and are the basis of all that is enduring and invigorating in life."[37]

Three additional images of the poet show him with the darkened nose of an inebriate (Figure 4).[38] Although Whitman was not known as an excessive drinker, alcohol was a staple at Pfaff's, an attribute commonly associated with bohemian behavior and one that Whitman had himself celebrated in the unpublished poem cited above. In a confessional moment recorded in April 1861 in the same notebook as the drawings, Whitman acknowledged a personal tendency to overindulge in both food and drink. From that moment forward, he "resolv'd" to ignore "all drinks (but) water and pure milk—and all fat meats [and] late suppers," a fixture at Pfaff's, in an effort to resume his "great body—a purged, cleansed, spiritualized invigorated body—."[39] Another trait that often accompanied drinking and was cited by contemporary observers as a marker of bohemianism was pipe smoking. Bellew's sign for the Ornithorhyncus Club, a forerunner of Pfaff's that attracted several of the same participants, included the image of an Ornithorhyncus, or duck-billed platypus, "smoking a pipe, while grasping a glass of foaming beer."[40] The most ardent spokesman for the virtues of pipe smoking as a worthy bohemian trait was Henry Clapp Jr. On the pages of the *Saturday Press* he explained: "A clay pipe (not an absurd meerschaum, but an honest clay pipe, made, like ourselves, out of the dust of the earth) is the best conductor of that subtle fluid we call sympathy, in the world. It bridges over the gulf which separates man from man. It is a universal token of fellowship."[41] Behaviors like drinking and smoking, which may have appeared of dubious social value outside the bohemian community, thus symbolized for Whitman and his colleagues the prized bohemian ideal of camaraderie. As if to confirm these sentiments, another drawing in Whitman's notebook shows the profile of a man with a goatee smoking a long-stemmed clay pipe of the type Clapp endorsed.

Humorous images of individuals drinking and smoking appeared frequently in *Vanity Fair*, many of them drawn by Mullen. One in particular, imbued with the full spirit of bohemianism and published on June 30, 1860, a month after Whitman's return from Boston, incorporates several

948

4. Caricature of Walt Whitman.
Notebook no. 91, Thomas Biggs Harned Collection of
Walt Whitman, Manuscript Division,
Library of Congress.

of the themes and visual references prominent in Whitman's notebook (Figure 5). Midway down the page a man in a jester's suit and cap (a frequent theme in Mullen's work) sits comfortably in a chair set off by a curving twig frame. He has the darkened nose of an inebriate and is smoking a curved, long-stemmed pipe, such as the type Clapp advocated and similar to the one in the notebook. Swirls of smoke waft upwards from the pipe, and a cobweb, suggestive of lassitude and inaction, traits commonly associated with bohemians, fills the space immediately below the enclosing twig frame. Below that is a circular pot with writers' pens and artists' brushes crossed behind it, tools of the trade for the contributors to *Vanity Fair* and for the many bohemians at Pfaff's who made their living in the visual and literary arts.

Mullen's design references Whitman directly in its quotations from two of the design elements that set the 1860 *Leaves of Grass* dramatically apart from its predecessors. Whitman took great pride in the freedom granted him by the publishers to work closely with the compositors and to oversee all aspects of the book's design. The wispy tendrils extending outward from the letters of the word "PREFACE" at the top of Mullen's page recall the short, wavy lines that waft outwards from the words "Leaves" and "Grass" on the title page of the 1860 *Leaves*. A second, even more explicit reference to the 1860 *Leaves* evokes Whitman's use of the image of a globe of the Western Hemisphere floating on clouds (Figure 6). The globe was one of three emblematic designs scattered throughout the volume and blind-stamped on the cover. Mullen adapted a simplified version of this design into the smoke wafting from the jester's pipe. Most notable is the image of a figure floating immediately beneath the globe whose presence evokes the profile image of the face (perhaps not intentional, but there nonetheless) in Whitman's cloud. As the jester smokes his pipe, "the universal token of fellowship," his gaze drifts upward toward Whitman's globe, as if to acknowledge what Clapp termed the poet's "sense of unfathomable mystery . . . in which classes, states, worlds, events, are rolled before the mind."[42] Almost unseen at first at the top of the page is a human eye and two fingers, which peak out from a trompe l'oeil tear. With its arched eyebrow, the eye could very well be Whitman's, peering out to reconnect with his bohemian colleagues and the bohemian values of *Vanity Fair* after his extended stay among the Boston Brahmins.

Mullen's hand (no doubt with Whitman's endorsement) seems implicated in yet another celebration of bohemianism, this time in the form

VANITY FAIR, on the 27th day of June, 1860, entered his second *Salon*, in which a number of visitors had assembled to greet him on the attainment of the majority of his Second Volume.

V. F. had been informed by his gentleman's gentleman —a stupendous creature who left his last place because he got Sherry at dinner instead of Madeira, to which latter he had always been accustomed—that a select party of distinguished persons awaited him below stairs in order to congratulate him upon his arrival at man's estate. He instantly dropped his Narghileh, arose from his Indian summer chair, and attired himself in a simple but elegant morning costume. This done, he descended, and found awaiting him with respectful homage, the following persons: Mrs. PUBLIC, with her eldest son, CHER LECTEUR, Alderman BOOLE, Prince SIMMI BOOJSEN NO KAMI, HORACE GREELEY, Hon. H. J. RAYMOND, Col. WEBB, the Editor of the *Saturday Press*, the Editor of the *World*, Mr. AUGUSTUS BELMONT, Count DE GUROWSKI, MORTIMER DOESTICKS, besides a corps of lovely and exquisitely dressed contributors, all of whom carried bouquets in their hands, composed of the choicest exotics of the four seasons.

V. F. floated into—or, we may say, amalgamated with—the select circle of guests that awaited him ; and—but as conversation can never be perfectly given in narrative, let us present this charming scene in a dramatic form :

SCENE.—The Residence of V. F.

5. Edward F. Mullen, Preface, *Vanity Fair*, June 30, 1860.
Courtesy of the Rare Book and Manuscript Library,
University of Illinois at Urbana-Champaign.

Clap the skull on top of the ribs, and clap a crown on top of the skull.

17. You have got your revenge, old buster! The crown is come to its own, and more than its own.

18. Stick your hands in your pockets, Jonathan — you are a made man from this day,
You are mighty cute — and here is one of your bargains.

6. Walt Whitman, *Leaves of Grass*, 1860.
Courtesy of the Walt Whitman Archive.

7. Edward F. Mullen, sketch of a banner for the *Saturday Press*.
Notebook no. 91, Thomas Biggs Harned Collection of Walt Whitman,
Manuscript Division, Library of Congress.

of a proposed new banner for the *Saturday Press* drafted on the pages of
Whitman's notebook (Figure 7). Since its inception, Clapp's newspaper
had assiduously eschewed any indication of its bohemian posture in its
title or physical appearance. The new banner would dramatically change
all that. Emblazoned across it in a typeface consistent with one Mullen
used in *Vanity Fair* are the words "THE BOHEAMIAN"; below it in smaller
type was written "TATE SATURDY PRESS." In contrast to *Harper's Weekly*,
whose banner boldly declared it "A Journal of Civilization," the new banner for the *Saturday Press*, with its flagrant misspellings, sought to align
itself with far messier and less elevated sentiments. Just as the *Boston
Banner of Light* could say of Whitman that "he betrays high culture, even
when he seems almost swinishly to spurn it,"[43] so the proposed new banner seemed intent on celebrating the broadest expanse of American culture by "swinishly" spurning such established markers of civilization as
correct spelling and the classical education that promoted it. At the same
time, Mullen's banner visually confirmed the *Press*'s commitment to the
arts. Flanking the text and appearing to be held in place by slits in the
fabric of the banner are an artist's brush and what resembles a cluster
of writer's pens. Although the *Saturday Press* had no artists on staff and

no ability to showcase their work, it regularly carried articles on art and reviews of art exhibitions. As a vocal supporter of the arts, Whitman no doubt encouraged Mullen's attempt to graphically assert the bohemian sympathy for the arts. What is not known is whether Clapp seriously considered Mullen's banner before the *Press* ceased publication at the end of 1860. Either way, Mullen persisted, and in March 1866, during the paper's short-lived revival, Clapp happily acknowledged Mullen's contribution of "a new top-piece."[44] With no record of this work's appearance, it is impossible to know how it compared with the earlier design. Presumably, though, it too drew attention to the bohemian support for the arts.

References in Whitman's notebook and elsewhere make clear that the poet's interests in art extended well beyond the humorous and often irreverent practices of his *Vanity Fair* colleagues to include the more conventional art practices of his day, such as those favored by Pfaff's more "genteel" bohemians.[45] A member of this group was Launt Thompson, the lone sculptor among the artists at Pfaff's and a close friend of writers Bayard Taylor and Thomas Bailey Aldrich. Following a decade-long apprenticeship in Albany, New York, Thompson, an Irishman, had settled in New York City in the winter of 1858, taking a studio in the prestigious Tenth Street Studio Building just a few blocks north of Pfaff's.[46] The *Saturday Press* acknowledged Thompson's arrival in the city and shortly thereafter praised him as "one of the most talented of all our young sculptors," judging his work "full of character and expression."[47] Thompson, who may have met Whitman in the 1850s during their mutual association with the writers and artists at the Brooklyn studio of sculptor Henry Kirke Brown, devoted most of his career to portraiture, a favorite of Whitman's.

Whitman wrote enthusiastically in his notebook under the heading "To Picture-Makers" about his commitment to such traditional artistic themes as those favoring women and motherhood. "Make a Picture of America as an IMMORTAL MOTHER," he enthused, "surrounded by all her children young and old. . . . Make her picture, painters! And you, her statue, sculptors!" He also urged artists to "Make a 'Picture' of the Indian girl looking at the turtle by an aboriginal American creek."[48] While neither theme was likely to appeal to readers of *Vanity Fair*, the latter was one to which Launt Thompson was devoting considerable effort. Thompson's statue, one of his few ideal works, represented a nude young woman seated on a blanket stroking a turtle, the totem of the Delaware Indians. According to documents at the Metropolitan Museum of Art and the Albany Institute of History and Art, the piece narrates the story of a woman who had been captured years before by the Delaware Indians and, when finally found by her family, had chosen to marry the chief rather than return home to her parents.[49] Thompson's sculpture built on the theme of the captivity narrative popular with his teacher Erastus Dow Palmer, whose *White Captive* had been discussed in the pages of the *Saturday Press*.[50] In his late poem "Yonnondio," written shortly before Frederick Jackson Turner issued his influential frontier thesis, Whitman lamented the disappearance of the American Indian. With "No picture, poem, statement, passing them to the future," he wrote, ". . . unlimn'd they disappear."[51] Although Thompson's female is Euro-American rather than Native American, the work demonstrates sympathy and respect for Native American culture in a format that is succinct and quietly evocative of Whitman's praise for the Indians' unmediated experiences with nature and the land.[52]

In Whitman's notebook, the fluidity and multitudinous nature of bohemian relationships is creatively reinforced by the inclusion of Thompson's caricature drawn, in all probability, by one of Whitman's *Vanity Fair* colleagues (Figure 8). By its presence, this caricature, the notebook's only image of someone other than Whitman thus far identified, underscores Whitman's interest in the thematics and perhaps also the classicizing form of Thompson's work. Like the caricatures of Whitman previously noted, Thompson appears in profile. While the upper part of his torso has been scratched out, still prominent is Thompson's distinctive head, with its conspicuous nose and menacingly long goatee, and the sculptor's mallet he holds in his left hand.[53] Such a mallet provides physical confirmation of Thompson's identity as an artist and links the drawing to the focus on artists' tools in Mullen's previously noted banner and drawing for *Vanity Fair*. Whitman was himself interested in the tools artists used, and while in Boston awaiting completion of the engraved frontispiece for the 1860 edition of *Leaves*, he made reference in his notebook to an artist's "burin—or 'graver,' . . . a sort of composite of gouge, chisel, knife, &c used by engravers."[54] More than a decade later he would celebrate the stunning visual effects of the artist's burin in "Out from Behind This Mask."[55]

In an essay in the *Saturday Press* writer Ada Clare reminded her fellow Pfaffians, "The Bohemian is not, like the creature of society, a victim of rules and customs; he steps over them all with an easy, graceful, joyous unconsciousness."[56] Whitman's relationships with the artists at

8. Caricature of Launt Thompson.
Notebook no. 91, Thomas Biggs Harned Collection of
Walt Whitman, Manuscript Division,
Library of Congress.

Pfaff's followed a similar joyous sidestepping of society's rules and customs. The drawings in Whitman's notebook graphically confirm a level of intimacy and familiarity between the poet and his Pfaffian friends that is remarkable even within the easy give-and-take of the bohemian community. Whitman was particularly drawn to the artists' creative abilities as "Picture-Makers." In the nurturing atmosphere of Pfaff's, the bohemian artists who clustered around Whitman shared the poet's commitment to exploring and extending art's democratizing potential. Especially for those artists associated with *Vanity Fair*, Whitman's longstanding involvement with questions of identity helped strengthen their resolve to celebrate in their work the commonalities, confusions, and ambiguities of their bohemian world. Whether on the pages of Whitman's notebook or in *Vanity Fair*, Whitman modeled and encouraged these artists' pictorial formulations of the bohemian type. The artists who frequented Pfaff's, including those grounded in more conventional artistic practices like Thompson, provide a valuable lens through which to expand our understanding of New York's bohemian culture.

NOTES

1. W[alt] W[hitman], "Something about Art and Brooklyn Artists," New York *Evening Post*, Feb. 1, 1851, rpt. in Whitman, *Uncollected*, 1:236. For a comprehensive overview of Whitman's considerable involvement with the arts, see Bohan, *Looking into Walt Whitman*.

2. *WWC* 3:503.

3. Stansell, "Whitman at Pfaff's," 115.

4. Mott, *History*, 390. On the advantages of wood over steel engraving, see Schrock, "William James Linton," n.p.

5. [Walt Whitman], "Harper's Magazine for June," *BDT*, May 15, 1858.

6. [Walt Whitman], no title, *BDT*, Aug. 16, 1858.

7. *NUPM* 1:248.

8. See Bohan, *Looking into Walt Whitman*, 62.

9. Taylor, *Perceptions and Evocations*, 55.

10. Vedder, *Digressions*, 220, 218–19.

11. *PW* 1:277.

12. Vedder, *Digressions*, 141.

13. *NUPM* 1:468; Vedder, *Digressions*, 193–98.

14. During his stay at 48 Beekman, Vedder began work on two of his most important early works, *The Questioner of the Sphinx* and *The Lair of the Sea-Serpent*. For more on Vedder's art, see Soria, *Elihu Vedder*.

15. Vedder, *Digressions*, 218.

16. Quoted in F.B.S., "A Visit to Walt Whitman," *Brooklyn Eagle*, July 11, 1886.

17. *NUPM* 1:454–55.

18. Stephens, "O'Brien as Journalist and Soldier," lx.

19. Vedder, *Digressions*, 198.

20. See the essays by Robert J. Scholnick and Amanda Gailey in the present volume.

21. Kime, *Fitz-James O'Brien*, 298–99, 371–73.

22. *VF* 1 (Mar. 17, 1860): 183.

23. See Robert J. Scholnick's essay in this volume.

24. In his first counter-jumper cartoon ("Shakespeare for the Counter-jumpers," *VF* 1 [Jan. 28, 1860]: 72), Bellew dressed the counter-jumpers in women's clothing.

25. See, e.g., Karbiener, "Whitman at Pfaff's," 28–30.

26. O'Brien jokingly termed such attire his "banking" suit (Fiske, "O'Brien's Bohemian Days," liv–lviii). A month later Mullen depicted O'Brien, again in plaid pants, this time under the open cage of a woman's hoop skirt and holding a length of printed fabric; see *VF* 1 (Apr. 14, 1860): 243. For additional caricatures of O'Brien, see Kime, *Fitz-James O'Brien*, 21, 22, and 34.

27. *WWC* 3:299.

28. Levin, *Bohemia in America*, 30.

29. *NUPM* 1:431, 453.

30. Levin, *Bohemia in America*, 35.

31. *LG* 32.

32. *Corr.* 1:50.

33. "Leaves of Grass. A volume of poems, just published," *BDT*, Dec. 1, 1856.

34. Notebook #91 in the Thomas Biggs Harned Collection of Walt Whitman in the Manuscript Division at the Library of Congress; *NUPM* 1:431–42.

35. *Corr.* 1:54.

36. Cited in Levin, *Bohemia in America*, 54.

37. D.D., "The Bohemian as a Gentleman," *SP*, June 30, 1860.

38. The other two images are shown in Bohan, *Looking into Walt Whitman*, 35–36.

39. *NUPM* 1:438.

40. Winter, *Old Friends*, 309.

41. "A New Portrait of Paris: Painted from Life," *SP*, Dec. 4, 1858. Drinking and smoking a long-stemmed pipe also figured prominently in Thomas Nast's drawings of Pfaff's published in the *New York Illustrated* (Feb. 6, 1864) and in George Arnold's self-caricature in Arnold, *Poems*, 138–39.

42. [Henry Clapp Jr.], "Walt Whitman and American Art," *SP*, June 30, 1860.

43. Anonymous, "Review of *Leaves of Grass* (1860–61)," *Boston Banner of Light* 7 (June 2, 1860): 4. *WWA*.

44. Figaro, "Dramatic Feuilleton," *SP*, Mar. 3, 1866.

45. See Levin, *Bohemia in America*, 21.

46. Also in residence was the English-born landscape painter and fellow Pfaffian George H. Boughton, whom Thompson had known in Albany. For more on the artists and activities of the Tenth Street Studio Building, see Blaugrund, *Tenth Street Studio*.

47. "Art Items," *SP*, Jan. 1, 1859.

48. *NUPM* 1:435.

49. Elizabeth K. Allen, "Launt Thompson, New York Sculptor," *Magazine Antiques* 162, no. 5 (Nov. 2002): 155–57. The article contains a photograph of Thompson's sculpture, which he called *Unconsciousness*.

50. The *Saturday Press* reviewed the New York showing of Palmer's sculpture, terming it "the most remarkable illustration of [this country's] wealth of material, and its perfect adaptability to the high requirements of Sculpture" ("Palmer's Statue: The White Captive," *SP*, Dec. 12, 1859).

51. *LG* 396.

52. Shortly after the publication of the 1860 *Leaves*, a reviewer in the *Saturday Press* judged the volume "a fitting measure for the first distinctive American bard who speaks for our large scaled nature, for the red men who are gone, for our vigorous young population" (C.P.P., "Walt Whitman's New Volume," *SP*, June 23, 1860).

53. George Arnold, a writer at Pfaff's who had studied art early in his career, produced a similar full-length caricature of Thompson holding a sculptor's tool.

54. *NUPM* 1:426.

55. *LG* 296–97.

56. "Thoughts and Things," *SP*, Feb. 11, 1860.

Adorning Myself to Bestow Myself
Reading *Leaves of Grass* in 1860

LOGAN ESDALE

When Walt Whitman published the third edition of *Leaves of Grass* in 1860, he was again subjected to the charge that his work grossly violated public and poetic decorum. Specifically, the book was condemned for being naked: not only did Whitman depict humanity in its unclothed state, but the language was rudely and perversely antiornamental. Common to the reception of the book in 1855, 1856, and 1860 were not only voices of censure, however; there had also been applause, and by 1860 there was positively a chorus of bravos, led by the bohemian Henry Clapp and his *New York Saturday Press*.[1] The very thing that Whitman's antagonists deplored, the book's nakedness in content and form, was the object of acclaim for the bohemians. In Clapp's words, Whitman, "naked and stalwart," presents "Nature unadorned."[2]

A version of this had been in Charles Dana's review of the 1855 edition: the poet resembles "Adam and Eve in Paradise, before the want of fig-leaves brought no shame."[3] Nakedness, of course, is deeply embedded in the book: the poet of *Leaves of Grass* often goes beyond the rhetorical or figurative to appear wearing nothing but a beard. Figuratively, naked is living outdoors free of convention, and clothed is parlor respectability. Naked is open to experience, diversity, and the unknown; and clothed is closed. Naked is long-running free verse, and clothed is meter and rhyme. And for actual nakedness, this starts with the first page of "Walt Whitman" ("Song of Myself" from 1881 on): "I will go to the bank by the wood, and become undisguised and naked, / I am mad for it to be in contact with me."[4] The poet's often-voiced desire for unmediated contact with people, not just riverbanks, drove the uproar of disapproval; for that, real pants and dresses and everything (maybe not hats) had to be removed.

So when the *Saturday Press* celebrated the Naked Poet, this was a fighting stance, not a critical insight. Whitman appreciated the bohemians' support, but I argue that they incompletely represented his project to depict the naked human figure in a poetic form similarly stripped of common vestments. They rushed too eagerly to his defense—Clapp's phrase "Nature unadorned" goes too far. *Leaves of Grass* in 1860, I suggest, places the concept of *adornment* in opposition to conventional poetic ornament and in tension with nakedness. Adornment mediates the naked-clothed dichotomy that both sides used. With this term we can name Whitman's ability to complicate our false assurance that we know where the body begins and ends. It names the body's extensions and the mode and objects of attachment that Whitman put faith in. Eschewing the language of prohibition—clothes or no clothes—adornment describes an identity made not just by what we reject, but also by what we accept. Through an analysis of adornment, we can then approach the value of clothes without their functioning as disguises. For Whitman, refusing to hide does not necessarily entail a literal nakedness. In exploring the body's possibilities, he associates adornment with positive instances of self-expression. To adorn is to express—and he wanted the body to sing.

EVERY LEAF BUT THE FIG LEAF

Reading *Leaves of Grass* in 1860 begins with an article Whitman published in the *Saturday Press* on January 7 of that year. Writing anonymously, he pretends a skepticism: "Is this man really any artist at all? Or not plainly a sort of naked and hairy savage, come among us, with yelps and howls, disregarding all our lovely metrical laws?"[5] A poem he had recently published, "A Child's Reminiscence," describes the poet's boyhood absorption of his vocation as he listened to the cry of a seabird for its lost mate.[6] Whitman's January article was a response to a review of the poem in a Cincinnati newspaper which had argued that Whitman "has undertaken to be an artist, without learning the first principle of art," namely, that a poem cannot have reason or sense without rhyme or meter; the "unclean cub of the wilderness" needs a bath.[7] Given the poem's inoffensive subject matter, however, the review cannot insist on the "unclean" criticism; instead, the poem is derided for being "inexplicable nonsense." The word "naked" does not appear in the review, so Whitman's epithet "naked and hairy savage" is partly his own invention.

Leaves of Grass was published in mid-May, and later that summer, on August 11, William Dean Howells summarized the position of those who had offered negative reviews, calling Whitman the bull in literature's "china-shop" and concluding:

> You might care to see him, to hear him speak, but you must shrink from his contact. He has told too much. The secrets of the soul may be whispered to the world, but the secrets of the body should be decently hid. Walt Whitman exults to blab them.
>
> Heine, in speaking of the confidences of Sterne, and of Jean Paul, says that the former showed himself to the world naked, while the latter merely had holes in his trousers. Walt Whitman goes through his book, like one in an ill-conditioned dream, perfectly nude, with his clothes over his arm.[8]

Although Howells admixes critique with small concessions—do not touch, though you might care to hear him speak—his conclusion follows what the *New York Times* had offered on May 19: Whitman "rejects the laws of conventionality so completely as to become repulsive; gloats over coarse images with the gusto of a Rabelais, but lacks the genius or the grace of Rabelais to vivify or *adorn* that which, when said at all, should be said as delicately as possible" (my italics).[9] Whitman has no clothes, no adornment, no art. While Howells distinguishes soul from body—only the former's secrets should be spoken (whispered)—Whitman does not. Other poets write of passion but not with passion; their manner is decorous even when the subject is not; euphemism and meter are necessary for the brutes we otherwise would be. Whitman's advocates scorned the bad faith of poets who allude to arousal but displace it onto full moons and blossoms. Whitman directs us to the body's desires. Curiously, the *Times* uses "adorn" to mean "dress up" but also as akin to "vivify," as if adornment can transmute raw existence (what is) into idealized effect (what should be). Art is adornment; without adornment it is not art.

The *Times* probably considered "adorn" and "ornament" as interchangeable terms, but Whitman, I argue, did not. From the beginning to the end of his career he was antiornament: in a self-review of the 1855 edition of *Leaves of Grass* he says that the "theory and practice of poets have hitherto been to select certain ideas or events or personages . . . always with as much ornament as the case allowed. Such are not [my] theory and practice."[10] And in 1891, he asserts that in his poems is "none of the stock ornamentation, or choice plots of love or war, or high, exceptional personages of Old-World song; nothing . . . for beauty's sake—no legend, or myth, or romance, nor euphemism, nor rhyme. But the broadest average of humanity and its identities in the now ripening Nineteenth Century, and especially in each of their countless examples and practical occupations in the United States to-day."[11] Ornamental poetry narrows the vision to "select" or "choice" objects, and Whitman gave to *Leaves of Grass* the endlessly expansive task of describing "the broadest average of humanity."

In the next section I make the case that ornament and adornment are different for Whitman, and the latter is unequivocally positive. Indeed, the terms can be seen as opposites, where ornament is separable and obscures natural form, and adornment is inseparable and expresses natural form. This distinction, however, was observed neither by detractors nor by the book's bohemian readers. The debate between the two sides was over the role of "clothing" in American poetry. Contributors to the *Saturday Press* stated their support for Whitman because he boldly represented a new, naked poetics.

For Moncure Conway, concomitant with the poet's x-ray eyes was his calling things by their unclothed names.[12] In Conway's August review he claimed that to Whitman "the goddess Yoganidra, who veils the world in illusion, surrenders; to [him] there are no walls, nor fences, nor dress-coats, no sheaths of faces and eyes. All are catalogued by names, appraised, and his relentless hammer comes down on the right value of each."[13] Henry Leland's June 16 review likewise depicts Whitman stripping away: the poetic "vine long unpruned has run itself to waste; graceful lines, spiral tendrils, flaunting leaves, but very little fruit. The reformer and the vine-dresser are at hand."[14] With this gardening analogy Leland admits that Whitman's poems may seem like a tree with its branches cut back—exposed and ugly. But for the Tree of Poetry this horticultural necessity, pruning, refreshes the growth cycle.

Thinking of Whitman with shears would seem at odds with the book's largeness, but another analogy bolsters Leland's point. On January 14,

1860, in her "Thoughts and Things" column for the *Saturday Press*, Ada Clare juxtaposed criticism of restrictive women's fashions with praise for Whitman's poetic simplicity. She compares three styles of dress for women: (1) "The attempt to disguise the shape of the women by hanging innumerable heavy skirts about her hips"; (2) the hoop-skirt; and (3) the Bloomer. The hoop-skirt is much lighter than the "innumerable heavy skirts," but it still "entirely indisposes her for outdoor exercise." Clare wishes the Bloomer would come into fashion—it was then facing immense ridicule—because it would "bring with it a freedom for women from conventional lies, from deceit and much uncharitableness, and from their intense desire for money. The dress would be so much less expensive than the present one, and would require taste so much more than extravagance, that one great motive for mercenary marriages were gone. Woman, relieved from the continual burden and fretfulness of an unnatural attire, would grow in good sense and in kindly feeling." Moreover, heavy, disfiguring dresses "devitalize those delicate organs, without which the world could not exist." Clare, like Leland, laments that which impairs new growth: as an unchecked plant can bear little fruit, unchecked clothes might injure the uterus. Clare's article then moves from heavy skirts and Bloomers to two kinds of poems, the first being William Winter's "Orgia: The Song of a Ruined Man," which had recently been published in the *Saturday Press*. Clare mentions having heard this "Song" praised, but for her, its mechanical versifying (rhyming couplets) was much less satisfying than the open form of Whitman's "A Child's Reminiscence." The latter "could only have been written by a poet, and versifying would not help it. I love the poem." Like the Bloomer, Whitman's poetry has been ridiculed for lacking what the "Ruined Man" layers on. As hoop-skirts despise the woman's body, so does versifying despise what *Banner of Light* on June 2 called Whitman's "free habit of expression."[15] But for Clare it was time to reject hoop-skirts and couplets.

In his May 19 review, Henry Clapp anoints Whitman the poet of the "Present Age" because his poems are "ardent and fierce" and "free as the sunshine." The popular poetry, even when it has an "amatory tendency," ignores "the human body"; whether the lyrist is "gay for a feast [or] sorry for a funeral," the language will be "rhymed and measured"; it passes "smoothly over all that is significant in this actual present life." With a keen recognition of poetry's historical moment—the emergence of free verse—Clapp then praises Whitman's refusal "to confine and cripple himself within the laws of what to him is inefficient art. Reverencing the spirit of poetry above the form, he submits that the one shall determine the other. That his volume is poetic in spirit cannot rationally be denied; and, whatever the eccentricities of its form, no critical reader can fail to perceive that the expression seems always the suitable and natural result of the thought."[16] Clapp acknowledges "the eccentricities of its form," but this is not malpractice. This is a naked art, with the thought naturally leading the shape of the form, and the free form expansively receptive to new subject matter.

In the next month Clapp published three reviews by women: Juliette Beach, Mary Chilton, and C. C. P. They cheer Whitman's having abolished poetry's hoop-skirt. Beach says that "Walt scorns the mock delicacy of men and women, and sets at defiance the usual picked words with which most authors clothe truths which might be offensive to their readers. Truth alone, in her own natural dress, whether speaking of body or soul, does he give you." And according to Chilton, the free reader perceives "the unity of all the functions of the human body." One should no more cover the face than any other part of the body. C. C. P. laments the hypocrisy of the popular writers who stimulate "passions we dare not [they say] own"; our "potent physical facts" are "gilded over with poor art." For C. C. P., true virtue comes from owning the undressed facts that the "earnest, sorrowful" Whitman presents.[17]

Building from these reviews and the one by Leland, all appearing between June 9 and 23, Clapp's "Walt Whitman and American Art" on June 30, 1860, opens:

> The staple of all our Art—poetry, picture, sculpture—is effect, ornament, and sentiment. On this solid material continent, we are dying for lack of bread and water of thought. Our literature is whipped-cream. The thing before him, whether it be a horseblock or a revolution, is not fine enough to occupy the writer; he must tag it to something other than itself. Poetry becomes a ruffled-shirt on a bean pole.
>
> The least suggestion of Nature unadorned is felt with instant delight, and greeted with general enthusiasm. . . .
>
> Into the company of poetasters, with their "questionable, infirm paste-pots," paint-pots, varnish-pots, their putty, plaster, rouge, buckram—a miscellaneous theatrical property—walks, naked and stalwart,

Walt Whitman, and all this trumpery seems to shrivel and melt away before his eyes. . . .

He never preaches. He never ornaments. He has made the first extended picture of our life as we live it in America, where thought is not scholastic, where the influence of books is very little, of Nature very great.

Clapp echoes Leland's poet as pruner (trumpery melts away), Beach's natural dress (never ornaments), Chilton's whole body (naked and stalwart), and C. C. P.'s potent facts (the thing before him). Also in this essay Clapp admits Whitman's tendency to "vastness beyond logic" as a "protest against the popular dogmatism, with its monstrous pretension, which bags, explains, defines, and accounts for everything," and then notes that "Whitman is strongest not when he is vague, but when he fastens and defines." Clapp sets up a muddle: dogmatism "defines," and Whitman does too? How are they different? We know that Clapp prefers the bread-and-water poet, not the whipped-cream kind. "Whitman is master of his facts," he insists, even "God's fact"; the poems offer the "solid ground of the actual." Clapp's diction unnecessarily confuses his point, but obviously he felt that poetasters misidentify—they define by what something wears—while Whitman defines by what it is, "Nature unadorned." The act of definition, its accuracy, depends on removing ornamental surface from essential being.

The positive and negative reviews of the 1860 *Leaves of Grass* differ not in conclusion—in form and content the poetry is naked—but in interpretation. Negative reviews behold everyday fact, only that without ornamentation it is not art; indeed, much of it is offensive. Some of the London reviews put an even finer point on this by equating ornament with civilization. One argues that "a naked savage [Whitman] has often a wild grace of movement that a civilized man can hardly possess, but certainly not display."[18] And another casually denounces his lines as "negro shouts."[19] The invocation of race in this way enhances our relief that Whitman had other, more open-minded readers in 1860. However, the Clapp-and-company insistence on the unadorned is its own blinder. Distancing themselves from what Clapp called the vast poet, they focus on the act of separating what one wears from what one is and thereby fail to respond to Whitman's enthusiasm for adornment.

The bohemians celebrated Whitman's peeling away that which cripples the American individual. Removing ("I remove the veil") and exposing ("expose all," he says, "I am for every topic openly") are oft-repeated actions in *Leaves of Grass*.[20] "The hopples fall from your ankles—you find an unfailing sufficiency."[21] The process of building the republic begins with the individual ("Produce great persons, the rest follows"[22]), and he asks that people strip to discover their humanity, equality, and sexuality; naked, they will feel their potential for connection, empathy, and pleasure. Free of externals, the American people are indivisible, and their equality is manifest.

Whitman addresses those who are "demented with the mania of owning things" and takes those things away; what they are left with is who they are.[23] Simply achieving nakedness does not ensure renewal: "To me, all that those persons have arrived at [status and wealth], sinks away from them, except as it results to their bodies and Souls, / So that often to me they appear gaunt and naked" and with a "core" full of the "excrement of maggots."[24] Naked here is a state of disgrace. For some there is "Outside fair costume—within, ashes and filth."[25] When one's ornaments are stripped away, does anything of actual, spiritual value remain? This line of argument invokes paradox—the more you wear, the less you are; the less you wear, the more you are—and ultimately explains why many people keep up their "fair costume." Whitman's strip-and-renew metaphor can thus lose efficacy with those readers most in need of separating essential from inessential. He gives them little enticement to change; "those who corrupt their own bodies [will] conceal themselves"—they are lost to the maintenance of appearance.[26]

Beyond these two representations of nakedness—the first describing a body separable from its clothes, the second a body (and soul) eaten by them—Whitman offers another that avoids their finality, as either free or rotten. This third option goes beyond the inside-outside dichotomy, the game of calling one corrupt and the other pure that both sides were (inversely) playing. This third body represents his intuition that "interiors have their interiors, and exteriors have their exteriors."[27] For this multi-layered body one cannot simply "remove the veil"; clothes are not just on or off. Furthermore, when the poet refers to "the spread of my own body," we connect multilayered with extensive.[28] A stable outline of this body—its spread changing shape—cannot be drawn.

Let's consider two representative examples of Whitman destabilizing the line between what he is and what he puts on. In the first: "my Soul leaning poised on itself—receiving identity through materials, and loving them—observing characters, and absorbing them."[29] Then there is the more explicitly stated metaphor of performance, in which the poet takes on a multitude of American identities: "Agonies are one of my changes of garments, / I do not ask the wounded person how he feels—I myself become the wounded person."[30] This is the poet's creative work, (un)making his identity. These "garments" are living entities, not baubles; they touch and transform. They define him. They come to be more like "blossoms of my blood" than regular clothes.[31] In this case, who you are is what you wear. If the Naked Poet is a white male, the adorned poet can inhabit various identities.

Noah Webster's 1844 edition of the *American Dictionary of the English Language* defines "adorn" as both artificial enhancement and natural extension, but like Whitman, the *Dictionary* emphasizes the latter. Webster lists both "to put on" and "to touch" in the word's etymology, and in the four definitions he offers, three are adornment-as-extension.[32] The first is conventional: "to add to beauty by dress; to deck with external ornaments. 'A bride adorneth herself with jewels' Isaiah 61:10." In contrast, the others define "adorn" as that which reveals and proves the essential excellence or identity of something: "adorn a speech by appropriate action"; adorn "great abilities" by "virtue or affability"; and right living "'adorn[s] the doctrine of God' Titus 2:10." Pushed a bit further, examples of adornment-as-extension can sound almost comically tautological, like saying wheels adorn a car—without adornment it would not be what it is. Crust adorns bread. Emily Dickinson even extends this internally: "a Man / Dainty adorned with Veins and Tissues."[33] Without adornment we might not exist.

Webster's definitions make "adorn" a word for expression. For instance, his "action adorns speech" means that appropriate action expresses one's convictions as effectively as speech. In Whitman's poetry and in free verse generally, form expresses content. This was Clapp's assertion, that "the expression [was the] natural result of the thought." Adornment also means revelation. In 1860 Whitman had critics who acted as if the genitals were like the fig leaf itself, something pinned on, separable. These critics suffered from object impermanence—to clothe the body and not see it made it nonexistent. *Leaves of Grass* reveals its permanence. To present the adorned body (genitals, hair, sweat, veins) is to reveal the body. It is naked, which makes naked and adorned complementary terms, not opposites. Lastly, adornment means inseparability, and Whitman's fear for the national union suggests a political interest in these terms: was the South separable, only an ornament? For the good of poetry, the body, and the nation too, Whitman was drawn to the aesthetics and politics of adornment.

This keyword, adorn, appears five times in *Leaves of Grass* 1860.[34] In "Sleep-Chasings," it verges on the conventional understanding as something separable from the body:

> I am she who adorned herself and folded her hair expectantly,
> My truant lover has come, and it is dark.[35]

Adornment here could be an artificial enhancement, a trick, some face paint or jewel, but there is reason to believe it is native to her, as a beard would be on a man. She did not fold a skirt or bedsheet; she folded a part of herself, her hair. Similarly, she may have adorned herself through arranging her natural attributes. Her own body is what will attract her lover; Whitman's ideal beauty demands no apparel. Perhaps she adorned her body with a smile or laugh or the "smoke of [her] own breath."[36] And it is dark—the ordinary baubles, designed to arouse through the sense of sight, would be irrelevant. And if darkness itself is her lover (on the next page, "darkness and he are one"), then there is a hint of autoeroticism. In almost every way we read this couplet, the adornment object is living and integral to her. Also, the phrase "I am she who adorned herself" suggests that for this poet, gender is an adornment as much as a biological fact. The purely naked body does not always adequately convey an evolving sense of identity. We adorn to express who we are and what we want.

Another instance of adorn, "And the running blackberry would adorn the parlors of heaven," speaks to the place of one's spiritual devotions.[37] The poet conjures a heaven with a place for good souls to visit one another and then wonders what might do for decoration. Ultimately, what best belongs in this place is a wild, running plant winding in through the window. The satirical edge to this line softens as we see that heaven's parlor is actually outdoors among the bushy wilderness. We find heaven's parlor where we find the blackberry; grow your faith there. The terrestrial blackberry expresses heaven.

Adorn also appears twice in "Chants Democratic and Native American 1":

> Others take finish, but the Republic is ever constructive, and ever
>   keeps vista;
> Others adorn the past—but you, O, days of the present, I adorn you!
> O days of the future, I believe in you!
> O America, because you build for mankind, I build for you!
> O well-beloved stone-cutters! I lead them who plan with decision and
>   science,
> I lead the present with friendly hand toward the future.[38]

Whitman's phrase "I adorn [the present]" carries a double meaning: the object of adornment is both the present and the poet. In the first case, to adorn the present, in effect, is to make it a building material for "the future." He is the witness, recording without judgment or exclusion, and also the stonecutter and engineer—the future will be built out of the present, not the past. In the second case, as an adornment of the present, he expresses it.[39] To understand America now, read *Leaves of Grass*. Whitman's repetition of "adorn" is ambiguous, but clearly he is contrasting the "constructive" poet with the ornamental poet who adds "finish" to certain past subjects. A poem should no more memorialize than does the light of day. Also, Webster lists "adorn" in the etymology of "adore." Whitman simply adores the present.

These instances of adorn associate the word with sexual satisfaction, a running spirituality, and the constructive present. The last instance of adorn, in the line "Adorning myself to bestow myself on the first that will take me," brings out themes of circulation and mutuality.[40] Contrast this line with the poet's claim to "have stores plenty and to spare, / And anything I have I bestow."[41] While both passages suggest that others need what the poet can offer, the latter has an air of self-sufficiency ("stores plenty") contradicted by the former—adornment is not extraneous to him; in fact, to have something to bestow, he must adorn himself, and since what he bestows is himself, the act of adornment is necessary for existence and is perpetual. Whitman associates adornment here not only with erotic appeal—others will be drawn to the adorned poet—but with incompleteness. He needs others as much as they need him.[42]

I conclude with excerpts from three poems that further challenge the strip-and-renew theory, the stereotype—built in part by the *Saturday Press*—of Whitman standing for an Adamic nakedness in response to the hoop-skirt hegemony. The first two poems represent a nakedness that necessitates clothing. They depict a world in which people experience uncertainty and vulnerability, and they offer identities other than the white male enjoying his new-world fruits. Stuck on the figure of the Naked Poet, the bohemians did not sufficiently acknowledge the range of speakers in *Leaves of Grass*. And if Clapp had pushed his insight on Whitman's poetic body—that with free verse, form adorns content—he might have distinguished between clothes that hide the body and clothes that express it. The third poem represents a nakedness—a body fully expressing itself—that includes clothing.

In "Leaves of Grass 4," the poet has gone to the ocean to swim and be refreshed, but confronted by a vision of radical organic entropy, the prospect of nakedness arouses fear. Structured by three narrative movements, the forty-eight-line poem opens:

> Something startles me where I thought I was safest,
>
> . . . .
>
> I will not strip the clothes from my body to meet my lover the sea,
> I will not touch my flesh to the earth, as to other flesh, to renew me.[43]

A "compost" of "distempered corpses," the earth is poison to touch. Then in a narrative turn, the poet notices innocent "summer growth" that everywhere flourishes, the marvelous natural "chemistry" at work. Still, he has trouble believing that "when I recline on the grass I do not catch any disease" since "probably every spear of grass rises out of what was once a catching disease." How can the water he drinks be clean? How can the earth grow "such sweet things out of such corruptions"? These contradictions finally paralyze him: "Now I am terrified at the Earth!"[44] Outdoors and exposed, the poet winds down into silence, and the promise of action remains unfulfilled; he will not swim. The earth cannot fully renew itself—the "compost," a diseased past, still directs us—and even with clothes on, the poet feels naked—under threat and unprotected.

"Chants Democratic and Native American 5" puts the reader under threat: the identity and intentions of the speaker are never certain, and we do not know what to trust. Where "Leaves 4" describes environmental toxin (trust nature?), here we meet an unrelenting sarcasm (trust words?). "Chants 5" is a satire on the management discourse of America, its love of brute competition more than love itself. It is also self-parody, a poet disenchanted with the noise and diminishing affect of his exclamatory style. Here are five of the poem's sixty-two lines:

> Let the world never appear to him or her for whom it was all made!
>
> Let every man doubt every woman! and let every woman trick every man!
>
> Let there be wealthy and immense cities—but through any of them, not a single poet, saviour, knower, lover!
>
> Let the theory of America be management, caste, comparison! (Say! what other theory would you?)
>
> Let us all, without missing one, be exposed in public, naked, monthly, at the peril of our lives! Let our bodies be freely handled and examined by whoever chooses![45]

This final line alludes to the slave's body, freely handled by master and auctioneer. The slave's body is naked. To be stripped is to be stripped of one's rights. The naked body is the property of another. "Chants 5," then, countervails the innocent depictions in *Leaves of Grass* of the naked body experiencing the pleasure of contact and a freedom from restrictive clothes and codes. The line between revealed (lover) and stripped (slave master who rapes) is unsettled. Moreover, this poem first appeared in the 1856 edition under the title "Poem Of The Propositions Of Nakedness." As we read these "Naked Propositions," then, exclamation points turn to question marks: "Say! what other theory would you?"[46] This is Whitman free of his own conventions.

Poems such as "Chants 5" and "Leaves 4" imply that when threatened by our poisoned earth or a national disease such as slavery, we should accept the value of clothes. Throughout *Leaves of Grass*, indeed, Whitman plays dressmaker, adorning those who would otherwise be perilously naked. The phrase "renew yourself in sweet clothes," I suggest, is representative and sincere.[47] For every naked swimmer there are, in fact, more working Americans in their "easy costumes."[48] In "Leaf of Faces," for instance, a grandmother with her corona of white hair and cap has been renewed in the sweet clothes of family.[49] The cap is inseparable from the face; it expresses her. She raised children whose children raised the flax; she wears what she has made; the clothes adorn her.

Behold a woman!
She looks out from her quaker cap—her face is clearer and more
    beautiful than the sky.

She sits in an arm-chair, under the shaded porch of the farm-house,
The sun just shines on her old white head.

Her ample gown is of cream-hued linen,
Her grand-sons raised the flax, and her grand-daughters spun it with
    the distaff and the wheel.[50]

The book's opening poem, "Proto-Leaf," offers a pun that echoes this family relation between clothes and body: within the space of a few lines the poet is "clothed in easy and dignified clothes" and then observes "me, well-beloved, close-held."[51] *Close-held* is *clothed*, and vice versa. Whitman asks that we dress him.

Henry Clapp and the *Saturday Press* believed that to support Whitman they needed to defend his reputation as a "naked savage." In their narrative of liberation, however, nakedness becomes a too-static conclusion: self-sufficient, complete, single-voiced. Instead, cognizant of the irony of the new American convention that one must remove the clothes of convention, Whitman asks that we both take things off and try things on—the poet is "costume free" one moment and "Bearded, sunburnt, dressed in [a] free costume" the next.[52] He associates adornment with sexual satisfaction, a running spirituality, the constructive present, and mutual need; in particular, the phrases "I adorn [the present]" and "adorning myself to bestow myself" express the poet's mutability. It's the act of choice that interests us, what you do with your body. It's not enough, in the antiornament spirit, to remind people what they are under their clothes. To read *Leaves of Grass* in 1860 was to try it on.

NOTES
My thanks to Richard Deming for his incisive response to the essay in its early stages.
1. Of the more than thirty reviews, eight were original to the *Press* and two were by Clapp. The *Press* also reprinted five of the other reviews.

2. "Walt Whitman and American Art," *SP*, June 30, 1860.

3. "Leaves of Grass," *New York Daily Tribune*, July 23, 1855, WWA. Emerson's April 1856 note in his journal is a witty footnote to the Dana review: "Whipple said of the author of 'Leaves of Grass,' that he had every leaf but the fig leaf" (*Emerson's Prose and Poetry*, 524).

4. *LG60*, 23. Later, in "A Sun-Bath—Nakedness" (1882), Whitman describes the restorative "Adamic air-bath" (*PW* 1:151). He had been unwell, but after hobbling into the wilderness for "two or three hours of freedom, bathing, no talk, no bonds, no dress, no books, no *manners*," he becomes the essence of nakedness (*PW* 1:150). First the clothes come off and then the clothes of illness. "Nature was naked, and I was also" (*PW* 1:152). The Naked Poet became so well-established that when Ed Folsom saw photographs taken in the 1880s by Thomas Eakins of a naked old man, he quickly gathered the evidence linking the two men. Eakins was about to paint Whitman's portrait, and where Whitman "celebrated the 'purity' of nakedness," Eakins insisted "on the undraped figure as essential for an artist's training" (Folsom, "Whitman Naked?," 201). The two artists were kin. The man in the photographs may or may not be Whitman—but who else could it be? Who else was as naked as nature but Whitman?

5. "All About a Mocking-Bird," *SP*, Jan. 7, 1860.

6. This poem became "A Word Out of the Sea" in the 1860 *Leaves of Grass* (see *LG60* 269–77).

7. "Walt. Whitman's New Poem," *Cincinnati Daily Commercial*, Dec. 28, 1859, WWA.

8. "A Hoosier's Opinion of Walt Whitman," *SP*, Aug. 11, 1860.

9. "New Publications: The New Poets," *New York Times*, May 19, 1860.

10. *LG56*, 372–73.

11. *PW* 2:715. Whitman's 1855 preface contains passages that use "ornament" as if it were "adornment": for example, "that which distorts honest shapes" is a "nuisance and revolt," but "ornaments can be allowed that conform to the perfect facts of the open air and that flow out of the nature of the work" (*LG55*, ix). He revised this passage for "Says 5" in *Leaves* 1860.

12. Two examples of the x-ray poet: "I see through the broadcloth and gingham" (*LG60*, 31) and "dress does not hide him" (*LG60*, 292).

13. "[Review of Leaves of Grass 1860–61]," *The Dial* 1 (August 1860): 517–19. WWA. Reprinted as "Leaves of Grass," *SP*, Dec. 1, 1860, 1. About the book as an object, Conway noted that the poet was "better dressed than we ever expected to see him." Thayer and Eldridge had advertised its high quality (paper, typography, binding), claiming that it would be "an ornament to any book-shelf or table." Conway may have been considering the contents as well: while the twelve poems in the 1855 edition were untitled—a design decision equivalent to nakedness—in 1860 the poems were titled, and many were arranged into thematic clusters.

14. "Walt Whitman," *sp*, June 16, 1860.

15. "Leaves of Grass," *Banner of Light*, June 2, 1860, wwa.

16. "Walt Whitman," *sp*, May 19, 1860.

17. Beach, "Walt Whitman," *sp*, June 23, 1860; Chilton, "Leaves of Grass," *sp*, June 9, 1860; C. C. P., "Walt Whitman's New Volume," *sp*, June 23, 1860.

18. Wathen Mark Wilks Call, "Leaves of Grass," *Westminster Review*, Oct. 1, 1860, wwa.

19. "Verse—and Worse," *London Review and Weekly Journal of Politics, Literature, Art & Society*, Oct. 13, 1860, wwa.

20. *LG60*, 55, 419. The act of stripping away has defined our sense of Whitman's poetics. Sherry Ceniza, for one, has noted that the poems repeatedly turn on the idea of "seeing the world anew (and sexually) once the individual strips off societal frames of reference" ("'Being a Woman,'" 127).

21. *LG60*, 394.

22. *LG60*, 109.

23. *LG60*, 65.

24. *LG60*, 409.

25. *LG60*, 415.

26. *LG60*, 291.

27. *LG60*, 218.

28. *LG60*, 55.

29. *LG60*, 265.

30. *LG60*, 74.

31. *LG60*, 342.

32. The 1844 edition is available online at http://edl.byu.edu/webster.

33. Dickinson, *Poems*, no. 1064.

34. The poems including "adorn" had appeared in the pre-1860 editions. My argument is not that Whitman shifted from being a poet of nakedness in 1855 to one of adornment in 1860, but that reviewers in 1860 failed to complicate, despite the evidence at hand, the simplified figure of the Naked Poet that had been established in 1855.

35. *LG60*, 428.

36. *LG60*, 24.

37. *LG60*, 64.

38. *LG60*, 114–15. This text first appeared as prose in Whitman's 1855 preface: "Let the age and wars of other nations be chanted and their eras and characters be illustrated and that finish the verse. Not so the great psalm of the republic. Here the theme is creative and has vista" (*LG55*, iv). The line with "adorn" was added in 1856 when he transformed the prose into poetry—"Poem of Many in One," which in 1860 was retitled "Chants 1."

39. Behind "adorn the present" may be Emerson's claim that the poet will be a

"teller of news, for he was present and privy to the appearance which he describes"; and "a thought so passionate and alive . . . *adorns* nature with a new thing. The thought and the form are equal in the order of time" (*Emerson's Prose and Poetry*, 185–86; my italics).

40. *LG60*, 39.

41. *LG60*, 84.

42. In a draft poem Whitman rejects the pose of autonomy: "Was it I boasting how complete I was in myself? / O little I counted the comrade indispensable to me!" (Bowers, *Whitman's Manuscripts*, 68).

43. *LG60*, 208.

44. *LG60*, 210.

45. *LG60*, 167–70.

46. In "Leaves of Grass 10," Whitman notes that while ornamental poets praise men of success, for him there is "agitation and conflict"; what they smother he arouses: "unanswerable questions" (*LG60*, 224–25). And from "Song of Myself": "What is known I strip away, / I launch all men and women forward with me into THE UNKNOWN" (*LG60*, 92).

47. *LG60*, 98.

48. *LG60*, 129.

49. As Whitman wrote *Leaves* he told himself to "paint no head without its nimbus of gold-colored light" (*LG60*, 392).

50. *LG60*, 282.

51. *LG60*, 21–22.

52. *LG60*, 141, 77.

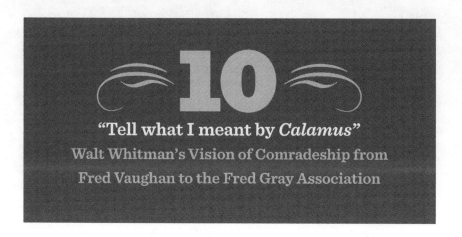

10

"Tell what I meant by *Calamus*"

Walt Whitman's Vision of Comradeship from Fred Vaughan to the Fred Gray Association

STEPHANIE M. BLALOCK

On Christmas Day in 1888, Walt Whitman told his faithful disciple Horace Traubel, "I want you some day to write, to talk about me: to tell what I meant by *Calamus*"—the title Whitman gave to a cluster of forty-five poems on "manly attachment" first published in the 1860 edition of *Leaves of Grass*.[1] It is natural that the aging poet would reminisce about preparing this homoerotic cluster for publication; after all, the late 1850s were the years when Whitman and his lover, a stage driver named Fred Vaughan, drifted apart and when the poet made daily trips to Pfaff's, a popular basement barroom located at 647 Broadway in his native New York. What does prove surprising, however, is that Whitman informed Traubel that an explanation of "Calamus" would require an examination of a series of draft letters the poet had written to Hugo Fritsch, a member of the Fred Gray Association, a rarely studied group of young bachelors the poet met at the beer cellar.[2] In other words, Whitman asserted—at least retrospectively—that "Calamus" was inextricably tied to a circle of friends that he encountered in late 1861 or early 1862, fewer than two years *after* the cluster was published.

At first glance, the men of the Fred Gray Association, several of whom were college graduates and international travelers, seem to have little in common with the poet—a carpenter's son and self-proclaimed "rough" with no formal education beyond the age of eleven. However, after Whitman's estrangement from Fred Vaughan, the Fred Gray members became some of the poet's closest associates. Whereas the association's gatherings at Pfaff's were a welcome, even if only a temporary, extension of rowdy college nights for the association's younger members, they held a long-lasting significance for the poet and his radical "Calamus" vision of a "new City of Friends" founded upon "robust love" between men.[3] This group played a vital role in Whitman's life because they, along with the poet, formed an experimental "Calamus" community: a social circle rooted in the model of comradeship or same-sex attachment that the poet outlined in the "Calamus" cluster. Whitman was not only an active member of the Fred Gray Association during his bohemian years at Pfaff's, but he was also regarded as equal parts mentor and celebrity by the young men who were a part of the group. As such, the theory of "adhesiveness" Whitman put forward in the "Calamus" poems found its initial praxis among the men of the Fred Gray Association.[4]

Like the draft letters to Fritsch that Whitman gave Traubel to help his future biographer "clear up some things which have been misunderstood" about "Calamus," a book the poet read repeatedly in the years before his death provides evidence of his lifelong engagement with the Fred Gray Association.[5] John Frederick Schiller ("Fred") Gray, the medical student and soldier for whom the group was named, gave Whitman a copy of Frederic Hedge's *Prose Writers of Germany* on August 29, 1862, just before Gray left New York to become a Union soldier in the Civil War.[6] Whitman used his copy of *Prose Writers* to create a memory book for his Fred Gray associates by recording the names of some of the group's members as well as an account of his friendship with Gray on the volume's pages. Sometime in the late 1880s, on the book's first blank page, the poet wrote, "Have had this vol. over twenty five years & read it off & on many hours, days & nights."[7] Whitman not only preserved this copy of *Prose Writers*, but in making it clear that he had reread Hedge's collection of excerpts, he implied he had gone over his remembrances of the association too. One of these memoranda is particularly noteworthy because it contains instructions for Whitman and seemingly for future readers: "rem'ber Dr. Russell Charles Chauncey Nat Bloom, Fritschy, the beer garden, the girls 1860 '61."[8] The poet asks readers to recall his participation in two social and intellectual communities: a coterie now recognized as the first American bohemians that included female actresses and journalists and the all-male Fred Gray Association, as represented by Gray and the four other members the poet records here. He also mentions the "beer garden," a likely reference to Pfaff's, which was the preferred meeting place of both groups. In doing so, Whitman suggests that one of his comforts in his old age is returning, even if only in his thoughts, to the summer of 1862, when he drank and caroused with these enthusiastic young twenty-somethings. He explicitly states that the purpose of the Hedge volume is protecting the memory of the association, and while he may not have anticipated that readers would one day be examining his private thoughts about these men, his words appear to encourage our participation in these acts of remembering. The poet's command to "rem'ber" indicates that the lines he penciled on the volume's pages will help to re-member, or piece together, the lives of these companions and the importance of their relationships with him, even if those rememberings will be—as Whitman's fragmentation of the word indicates—fragmentary and incomplete. Here, Whitman calls upon readers to investigate these comrades and implies that, beginning with his personal recollections of his friendships with the association's members, it is possible to reconstruct the narrative of the group's inception and to understand its place in his life.

THE ROOTS OF "CALAMUS":
WALT WHITMAN AND FRED VAUGHAN

In order to describe the social and political project he put forth in "Calamus," Whitman appropriated the phrenological term "adhesiveness," which Michael Moon has defined as "males sticking together, heart, soul, and bodily fluids."[9] When Whitman scholars think of these "adhesive" bonds between men as the poet envisioned them in "Calamus," it is not Whitman's friendships with the members of the Fred Gray Association that come to mind, but rather, his loving comradeship with Fred Vaughan. The seemingly stormy romance that developed between Whitman and Vaughan, a working-class man at least eighteen years younger than the poet, may have inspired Whitman's 1859 sequence of homoerotic love poems titled "Live Oak, with Moss"—poems that became the heart of "Calamus" in 1860.[10] If this was the case, it is easy to see why Vaughan became forever linked to the "Calamus" cluster. Some scholars have also attempted to connect Vaughan to the Fred Gray Association in part because we are only just beginning to identify and understand the social and literary communities Whitman joined at Pfaff's and because Vaughan and the Fred Gray members shared an affinity for the beer cellar and for the poet. However, the absence of Vaughan's name from the list of members that appears in *Prose Writers* and in Whitman's letters to these associates, combined with Vaughan's marriage in 1862, make it unlikely that he was a regular, much less a long-term, member of this circle of bachelors-about-town. Even though Vaughan might reasonably be omitted from the membership roll of the association, his relationship with Whitman was nonetheless a catalyst for the comradeships the poet established with its members.[11]

The emotional distance between Whitman and Vaughan that led to Whitman's participation in the American bohemian community—and his membership in the Fred Gray Association—likely stemmed from two main causes: first, Vaughan's changing attitude about the "adhesiveness" Whitman theorized in "Calamus," and later, the young man's decision to get married. Ironically, the final dissolution of Vaughan and Whitman's comradeship may have begun while the "Calamus" poems, the poet's most poignant verses on "manly attachment," were being printed.[12] While Whitman was in Boston to oversee the publication of the third edition of *Leaves of Grass* in March of 1860, Vaughan remained in New York and attended a lecture in which Ralph Waldo Emerson addressed the significance of friendship between men. In a March 27, 1860, letter to the poet, Vaughan recalled that Emerson had spoken about how men "filled with a . . . not to be shaken by anything Friendship" were worthy of being "worshipped as saint[s]." Vaughan went on to record his reaction, exclaiming, "There Walt . . . what do you think of them setting you & myself and one or two others we know up in some public place with an immense placard on our breast reading Sincere Freinds!!! [*sic*] Good doctrine that but I think the theory preferable to the practice."[13] Vivian Pollak has called Vaughan's distinction between theory and practice "crucial," and indeed, Vaughan's hesitancy to demonstrate affection or to be publicly recognized as a "Sincere Friend" may mark a turning point in his relationship with Whitman.[14] Vaughan's words, far from suggesting that he sees himself as the recipient of others' admiration and praise, instead suggest that the young man envisions himself—or a likeness of him in a public place—wearing a series of symbolic words proclaiming his affection for men across his breast, an image that brings to mind Nathaniel Hawthorne's Hester Prynne, who was forced to wear the titular scarlet letter "A" pinned to her chest as a symbol of her sexual transgressions. Vaughan seems worried about the sense of shame that could result from being labeled a "Sincere Friend"—a term that might be defined here as a man who establishes close relationships with other men that may or may not involve sexual contact. Jonathan Ned Katz has argued that Vaughan's reference to "one or two others that we know" indicates that he and Whitman were part of a "network of such friends [that] was already in place" and that "a self-defined group identity was in the making—or made."[15] Here, Vaughan's remarks suggest not that a group already exists, but rather that the application of the term "Sincere Friends" to certain men will bring such a group into being, thereby setting him, Whitman, and their mutual friends apart as a distinct kind of male community.

By objecting to assigning labels like "Sincere Friends" to men and their relationships, Vaughan gives the impression that he may reject the language of "comrades and lovers" Whitman established in the "Calamus" poems to refer to men's affectionate love for other men as well as the male associations or the "new City of Friends" the poet longed to create.[16] When Whitman published "Calamus," he was offering a new vocabulary that included terms like "manly attachment" and "adhesiveness" to describe relationships between men, since he believed there were "remarkably few words" to name "the friendly sentiments" and men's "most ardent friendships."[17] In doing this, Whitman publicized love between men and emphasized its practice. As Betsy Erkkila explains, "Calamus" "seeks to express, enact, and incite new types of 'manly attachment' and 'athletic love' as the source and ground of a fully realized democratic culture."[18] Vaughan, unlike Whitman, appeared uncomfortable with the possibility that introducing words for men's relationships would encourage the naming or, worse, the public ridicule of individuals to whom such terms might be (mis)applied. Vaughan's thoughts about openly participating in or even publicly celebrating a group of "Calamus" comrades also appear entirely at odds with Whitman's own. After all, in "Calamus 10" Whitman asked his readers to "Publish my name and hang up my picture as that of the tenderest lover," thereby encouraging a public recognition and display of male affection that Vaughan did not endorse.[19] This disagreement with the poet concerning Vaughan's preference for the theory of "adhesiveness" over its practice helps explain why Whitman sought new male acquaintances after the publication of the cluster.

For Whitman, the clearest indicator of a permanent rupture in what had once been a close comradeship with Vaughan came nearly two years later, in May 1862, when the stage driver got married. By this time Whitman and Vaughan had already gone their separate ways: Whitman went to Pfaff's while Vaughan sought work in the city and likely began courting his future bride. Still, the wedding must have come as a shock to the poet, especially if the "Sincere Friendships" between these two men had been part of the inspiration for "Calamus."[20] In what Robert Roper terms an "applecart-overturning note," Vaughan informed Whitman of his impending nuptials one day in advance and begged the poet to attend the private ceremony: "Walt, I am to be marri'd tomorrow . . . I shall have no show! I have invited no company.—I want you to be there."[21] That Vaughan would seemingly deliver this news in a note rather than visiting Whitman to ask him to be the only witness to the vows may suggest how much the two had grown apart even before the poet received the letter.[22] The wedding also set Vaughan apart from the rest of the bachelors who made up the Fred Gray Association. Conversely, when Whitman joined the association, he established relationships with men founded not on the legal, social, and reproductive contract of marriage that Vaughan entered into, but rather on the practice of "Calamus" affection. But because the "Calamus" poems were inseparable from Whitman's feelings for Vaughan, they likely compounded the poet's unhappiness in the aftermath of the wedding by bringing back memories of happier days with the young man. It makes sense, given this emotional crossroads, that Whitman wanted to create new associations—different connections and memories—related to "Calamus." In the following months, he did just that, by spending increasing amounts of time with the Fred Gray Association.

RECONSIDERING THE FRED GRAY ASSOCIATION

Although Whitman turned to the association for companionship after Vaughan's marriage, the group is little known among Whitman scholars. Because Whitman went to Pfaff's with these men, they have often been dismissed as a set of leaners and loafers. Ted Genoways describes the association as "a motley union of young men" with "no loftier goals than drunken bacchanals and the easy camaraderie it inspired," while Christine Stansell writes that Whitman "socialized with a group of young male friends" at the cellar that he would "remember fondly."[23] Vivian Pollak labels the group an "unofficial drinking club" but goes on to make the astute observation that these comrades satisfied Whitman's desire for a social circle of "recognizably elite" middle-class and upper-class friends—a need that could not be met by the American bohemians.[24] While the Fred Gray Association was, indeed, a social club whose members shared a penchant for beer, the personal and professional significance that these comrades held for Whitman and his "Calamus" poems extended beyond the fact that they enjoyed drinking together. Ed Folsom and Ken Price come closest to this view when they describe the group as "a loose confederation of young men who seemed anxious to explore the new possibilities of male-male affection."[25] But only Gary Schmidgall, in his biography *Walt Whitman: A Gay Life*, has pointed out "the homoerotic *Calamus* connection" that the poet made between the cluster and the letters to Fritsch. Yet Schmidgall does not mention the Fred Gray Association by name, and he even attributes Whitman's assertion to an error in chronology—that is, to the poet's misremembering of the fact that the "Calamus" cluster was in print before he attended the group's meetings.[26] Upon closer examination, however, the association appears to be much more than a drinking club, and Whitman's statements to Traubel seem less like errors and more like evidence of how the poet moved on after Fred Vaughan and began searching for men who were not afraid to demonstrate affection with one another; to have those demonstrations, as the poet put it, "always misjudged"; or to be acknowledged as "Sincere Friends."[27] From the moment Whitman found the association, his relationships with these men represented not only an alternative to the institution of heterosexual marriage that Vaughan had chosen, but also a replacement for Whitman's former comradeship with the stage driver.

Until recently, information about the association has been scarce, making it hard not only to identify these men, but also to explain their part in the poet's life and in his interpretation of "Calamus." However, based on newly discovered biographical data, I provide an overview of the association and specific information about individual members. Whitman probably first encountered the members of the group sometime between December 1861 and the late spring of 1862. At that time, nearly all of the association's members were in their twenties, and within a year, at least three of them would enlist in the Union Army. Several members, like Fred Gray, were New York natives and were in the process of attending college or had recently completed their degrees. A few had traveled to Europe; almost all came from middle- or upper-class families; and most were descended from long lines of doctors, judges, merchants, or politicians. The association's members included physicians, merchants, and sportsmen.[28]

The Fred Gray comrades organized their association on the basis of a two-tier structure: an in-crowd, and an extended network of participants and friends. When examined together, the poet's correspondence and the first page of his memory book indicate that members and/or friends of the association included (in addition to the poet) Fred Gray, an aspiring physician; Charles Chauncey, the son of a New York merchant; Hugo Fritsch, then newly arrived in New York as "an attaché of the Austrian Consulate";[29] Benjamin Knower, then a clerk; Nathaniel Bloom, also a merchant; Charles S. Kingsley, a member of the Nassau Boat Club; a man referred to only as "Mullen," who may be the illustrator Edward F. Mullen, who is discussed in Ruth Bohan's essay in this volume (and whose *Vanity Fair* caricature of Whitman, according to Bohan, affirms Calamus-love); and two other men, Samuel M. Raymond ("Raymond"), a first lieutenant in the 131st Infantry of New York volunteers, and Dr. Charles Porter Russell (sometimes spelled "Russel"), a physician and army surgeon.[30] Although the identities of the men Whitman referred to as "Perk" and the "twinkling and temperate Towle" remain uncertain, these and the rest of the associates the poet names made up a network of at least twelve members.[31]

While it is evident that each of the Fred Gray members was engaged in his own educational or professional pursuits, they still had much in common to solidify their friendships: they were seemingly attracted by the literary fame of Pfaff's; they were accomplished men with promising careers ahead of them; they came to the cellar during the Civil War; and they were drawn to Whitman. By the time the association's members visited Pfaff's, its reputation as "the trysting-place" of the American bohemians—"the most careless, witty, and jovial spirits of New York"—had been firmly established.[32] Although some of Clapp's social circle had moved on to other watering holes before the association arrived, Pfaff's reputation as what Whitman termed "the famous habitat of authors" remained.[33] By the time Whitman began going to Pfaff's with the association, one-and-a-half to two years after the publication of the cluster of poems that described "adhesiveness" and that offered a political vision of a nation made up of cities of men, eleven states had seceded from the Union, and Whitman's Northerners as well as his Southerners were embroiled in an escalating Civil War. The war divided the nation and its families, separating men, including some of the Fred Gray members, from their loved ones, but in doing so, it also, as Jonathan Ned Katz puts it, "inspired connections between men" because they "joined others in a mobilization that fostered new kinds of intimacy."[34] Ironically, even as the Civil War produced enmity between men, it also created new sites of intimacy for them. The formation of new male communities—like the association—occurred in part because Pfaff's became the preferred haunt of soldiers, stage drivers, and doctors from the local hospitals, just as it was for artists and actors. Fred Gray seemed to frequent the cellar while he waited for news about the war and its estimated duration before entering military service. The Civil War, therefore, may have brought the Fred Gray circle together before they joined the "mobilization" of Union regiments, even as it also forced the group apart when some of its members enlisted during the fall of 1862. After all, if those first shots had not been fired on Fort Sumter, Gray, then a college student, might have continued studying at the University of Heidelberg in Germany and entered the medical profession immediately instead of putting his education on hold and returning to New York with plans to join the Union cause.[35] But because Gray and his comrades—bachelors of college age and others just beginning their professional lives in the city—were among the men who gathered around Whitman at Pfaff's, the poet had, even if only briefly, a group of men with whom to develop comradeships like those he had written about in "Calamus."

THE FRED GRAY ASSOCIATION AND THE PRACTICE OF "CALAMUS" COMRADESHIP

It was after Whitman had been separated from his Fred Gray comrades for several months—during which time he settled into a routine of visiting wounded soldiers in the Washington hospitals—that he wrote to Hugo Fritsch and revealed how he had come to view his relationships with them. In a July 1863 draft letter, Whitman confided that "it would be happiness for me to be with you all [the Fred Gray members] . . . (so I will for a moment fancy myself,) tumbled upon by you all with all sorts of kindness, smothered with you all in your hasty, thoughtless, magnificent way, overwhelmed with questions, Walt this, Walt that, & Walt every thing."[36] The poet's vision of the association's members showering him with attention highlights how Whitman remembered his interactions with these men in addition to implying that, at a typical meeting of the association, all of the younger men crowded around the poet, hanging on his every word. Even though Whitman named the association after Gray, it is evident that the poet saw himself as the center of their social circle. In doing so, he presents these associates as the key participants in his personal fan club such that each member becomes a Whitman enthusiast who willingly "sign[s] himself a candidate" for the poet's affection.[37]

Whitman's letter may capture the association's appreciation of the poet as a literary figure when it depicts the members as admirers who fall all over one another in their haste to talk with him. Yet it also highlights another aspect of the poet's relationship with them: the physical attraction that Whitman felt for these men. Whitman's use of the phrase "tumbled upon" and the letter's other descriptions of the "love" and the "gayety & electricity" of the men's "precious friendship" reveal the intense emotional bonds Whitman had forged with these associates as well as his physical desire for an evening of playful wrestling with them.[38] In another letter, Whitman confessed that he longed to be "within hands reach" of these comrades, suggesting that he could hardly wait until he was in close physical proximity to these men so that he could touch them and they could return his caresses.[39] For Whitman, the association members were fans of his larger-than-life bohemian personality, but they were also eager to demonstrate the physical and emotional intimacy that characterized the poet's conception of "adhesiveness."

Even though Whitman records his desires to touch and experience the "electricity" of his comradeships with his Fred Gray associates, it is not possible to know definitively whether the poet had sexual relationships with any of them. It is plausible that he did, given his descriptions of the intimate moments the group shared as well as his insistence that the men would remain "in the portrait-gallery of my heart & mind yet and forever."[40] In his October 8, 1863, letter to Fritsch, Whitman confided how much he missed their mutual friend Fred Gray: "my own comrade Fred, how I should like to see him & have a good heart's time with him, & a mild orgie, just for a basis, you know, for talk & interchange of reminiscences & the play of the quiet lambent electricity of real friendship."[41] The deep longing for Gray's companionship Whitman expresses in these lines allows the letter's recipient—not to mention today's readers—to speculate that the poet is looking forward to reuniting with Gray and engaging in activities that might range from accompanying him to Pfaff's for drinks to visiting the young man in his own rooms for a potential romantic encounter. Likewise, in an earlier letter to Fritsch, written after the poet learned of the death of Charles Chauncey, Whitman recalls his comradeship with Chauncey in similar terms, explaining that the two shared many private moments, especially when they took long walks during which the young man related his "experiences, feelings, quite confidential."[42]

Although Whitman is physically attracted to the Fred Gray members, it is important to acknowledge that several of these associates, including Gray, married and started families after the war. Yet, it is also true that knowing that a male friend is lawfully wed hardly designates the limits of his erotic attractions or his sexual desires. While we may never be able to establish precisely whether these men were quintessential examples of nineteenth-century male friends or men who engaged in sexual relations with partners or as a group, what we do know is that Whitman was deeply troubled by the marriage of his former lover Fred Vaughan, and it is likely that he experienced similar emotions when he learned of Fred Gray's wedding. While Gray's marriage does not necessarily mean that he had forgotten what Whitman described as "the need of comrades," it does suggest an increase in marital and familial obligations that changed Gray's relationship with his bachelor friends and, in Whitman's view, likely represented a turn away from the poet's plan for cities founded upon the "institution of the dear love of comrades" instead of the institution of marriage. Whitman admits as much to another lover, Washington streetcar driver Peter Doyle, in a September 2, 1870, letter the poet composed while visiting his family in Brooklyn: "I fall in with a good many of my acquaintances of years ago—the young fellows (now not so young)—that I knew intimately here before the war—some are dead—and some have got married."[43] The acquaintances Whitman refers to likely included his Fred Gray associates, who were among his closest friends before he moved to Washington. The structure of Whitman's phrase nearly equates marriage with death, and rather than seeing death as the beginning of eternal life, he is mourning his dead comrades even as he also appears to be lamenting the changes in, if not the loss of, his comradeships with the married ones. However, the poet did not merely convey his sorrow over the choices made by his male comrades in his letters; instead, in his poetry and in his life, he consistently sought alternatives to marriage by seeking out comrades and participating in male communities—like the association.[44] Regardless of whether the Fred Gray members had sexual relationships with one another, the poet had found a group at Pfaff's whose members seemed willing to participate in an all-male social group, discuss male-male relationships, and experiment with his theories of "adhesiveness."[45]

By June of 1862, approximately six months before Whitman left Pfaff's

for Virginia and then the hospitals of Washington, the poet and the association had already put into practice the model of "adhesiveness" or "men
sticking together" he presented in "Calamus." As Gary Schmidgall has
observed, Whitman's accounts of the association's meetings and supper
parties have much in common with the barroom scene that appears in
"Calamus 29."[46] However, the group's activities did not simply share simi-
larities with the poem; rather, the association consistently, and I would
argue intentionally, re-created those moments of barroom adhesiveness:

> ONE flitting glimpse, caught through an interstice,
> Of a crowd of workmen and drivers in a bar-room, around the stove,
>   late of a winter night—And I unremarked, seated in a corner;
> Of a youth who loves me, and whom I love, silently approaching, and
>   seating himself near, that he may hold me by the hand;
> A long while, amid the noises of coming and going—of drinking and
>   oath and smutty jest,
> There we two, content, happy in being together, speaking little,
>   perhaps not a word.[47]

Since Whitman patronized Pfaff's before the cluster was published, it is
possible that the fictional barroom in "Calamus 29" is based on the beer
cellar. As Karen Karbiener has argued, "the physical details and ambience
of Pfaff's provided a setting that might have encouraged and even enabled
such moments of intimacy and connectivity" as those depicted in "Calamus 29" and like those Whitman would later share with the Fred Gray
members.[48] Although these associates were not laborers or drivers like
Fred Vaughan, this circle of men did stick together, echoing the closeness
and mutual understanding exemplified here by the poetic persona and
the youth who loves him. In his July 1863 draft letter to Fritsch, Whitman
recalled his most memorable times with the association: "I thought over
our meetings together . . . our suppers with Fred and Charley Russell &c.
off by ourselves at some table, at Pfaff's off the other end."[49] Whitman explained that he and the Fred Gray members drank and engaged in boisterous laughter and conversation like the workmen and drivers, even as
they sometimes retired to a backroom at Pfaff's—one that is strikingly
similar to that in which Whitman's poetic persona waits for his comrade
to arrive. Yet, Whitman's letter also revealed that the association's gatherings reenacted the poem's social scene without the domestic stove and
without dividing this social circle into distinguishable couples. As a result,

Whitman experienced the homoerotic affection of "Calamus" with several comrades, who enjoyed the "smutty jests" as much as they did separating themselves from the rest of Pfaff's patrons so they could share a private party. In this light, Whitman's Fred Gray associates seemed to practice the poet's theories of "adhesiveness"—only on a larger scale—in one of the locations he recommended in the poem: the barroom. Because Whitman associated "adhesiveness" with a fictional beer cellar that might have been based on Pfaff's, he linked the cluster with the Fred Gray comrades with whom he developed "Sincere Friendships" on those nights in the barroom. The association, at least during its members' time at Pfaff's, demonstrated and even lived by these "Calamus" tenets.[50] In effect, "Calamus" is Whitman's theory of comradeship—the "good doctrine" Vaughan preferred—while the bonds between the members of the association are the praxis, the basis of a distinct male community that Whitman celebrated but Vaughan could not support.

In addition to reenacting the barroom scene of "Calamus," the association proves ready, as Whitman puts it, "to absorb, to engraft, to develop" into these *élèves*, or students, of the poet's theories of "adhesiveness."[51] Throughout the "Calamus" cluster, the poet calls attention to his search for an *élève*, one who would possess what the poet's persona specified as "blood like mine circl[ing] in his veins," one who "harbor[ed] his friendship silent and endless" and sympathized with the speaker's need for comrades.[52] It is possible that "adhesiveness," or at the very least, this need for comrades and *élèves*, was sexual. This cluster is homoerotic, emphasizing affectionate physical touch among men—like the pair of male comrades who hold hands in the barroom or those whose lips meet in "the comrade's long-dwelling kiss"—without stating one way or the other whether such demonstrations of love between men must remain chaste.[53] The intense affection that Whitman expressed in his letters about the Fred Gray associates, whom he refers to as his "darling, dearest boys" and his "dearest gossips," reinforces the possibility that one or more of these young men were his sexual partners.[54] But his descriptions of these comradeships also illustrate other aspects of "adhesiveness." The poem's persona celebrates relationships based on a mutual and sometimes silent recognition between men. There is, perhaps, no better example of these wordless bonds than those that developed between Whitman and the Fred Gray members, as Whitman's reminiscences about the group's early meetings reveal: "our dear times, when we first got acquainted . . . were so good, so hearty, those friendship-times . . . nothing could be better or quieter & more happy."[55] In his late July letter to Fritsch, the poet remembered "adjusting our friendship . . . although it needed little adjustment—for I believe we all loved each other more than we supposed."[56] The most striking elements in Whitman's reflections are the degree to which these men's lives seem intertwined and his choice of the word "quieter" to signal the strong, silent understanding between them. Although previously unknown to each other, these men recognized one another on sight, and they became close so quickly that they did not worry about a misunderstanding even when there was little verbal communication between them. It was these "adhesive" relationships Whitman forged with his Fred Gray associates, who felt what the poetic persona of "Calamus" called the "like, out of the like feelings" for comrades and recognized those same thoughts and emotions—the very essence of "Calamus"—in Whitman, that caused the poet to insist that the association demonstrated the meaning of the cluster.[57]

THE MAKING OF WALT WHITMAN'S "CITY OF FRIENDS" AT PFAFF'S AND BEYOND

Whitman would come to believe that the Fred Gray Association represented both the extension of "adhesiveness" to a larger group of men and a step toward the "City of Friends" he imagined in the "Calamus" poems.[58] In his "1862 notebook," the poet records the process by which he and these men developed individual and communal comradeships. He reports that he met "Dr. Wm. Lamont Wheeler . . . at Pfaff's, June '62, with Charles Kingsley" and "Pell, young man, American introduced by Chas. Kingsley, at 6th st. lager beer house."[59] These notebook entries reveal that networks of friends formed in beer cellars when one person introduced to others the comrades with whom he felt strong connections. Whitman's notes on his encounters with Kingsley's associates also appear in a broader context of the poet's recordings of names and addresses of New York residents whom he encountered throughout the city. Groups like the association that perhaps began with a single introduction expanded their membership rolls, and each subsequent initiate found himself brought into a new set of relationships with a larger community, or city, of comrades. The organizational structure of the association suggests that Whitman first formed individual friendships with several members and soon became part of the inner circle, which remained a separate unit even as it also served as a building block for the extended network of members and friends. This larger group, in turn, was connected to other individuals on Broadway and beyond by its members' affinities for Pfaff's and their academic and professional lives in the city. When Whitman writes the names of Fred Gray members and explains their connections to one another and to the city in his notebooks, he is not only encouraging readers to make their own associations and links between his comrades, but he is also inviting them to think of the Fred Gray members as the "Calamus" roots of the "City of Friends" he had hoped to cultivate.[60] In this light, "Calamus" is no longer simply a reminiscent work that looks back to the poet's past relationship with Fred Vaughan; the verses are proleptic, representing Whitman's imagining of a society that he actively begins to form with the association *after* the publication of the cluster.

During the final years of the Civil War and those immediately following, Whitman would see his Fred Gray comrades at least twice—once in 1864 in New York and again when he returned to the city in 1867.[61] Whitman's declining health, the geographical distance between the poet and his comrades, and the lives that the Fred Gray members chose for themselves in the aftermath of the war made further reunions unlikely. If Whitman had not lost track of these associates in his later years, however, he would have been impressed with the members' accomplishments even as he would have continued to lament some of his friends' decisions to get married. It is likely that he would have joined the other members in continued remembrance of Charles W. Chauncey, who died on June 29, 1863, following an illness, at the age of twenty-five, and Samuel M. Raymond, who died from "congestive fever" he contracted while marching with his Union Army regiment that same year.[62] Hugo Fritsch, Whitman's frequent correspondent during the war years, advanced to the rank of New York's vice consul of Austria-Hungary.[63] Benjamin Knower listed his profession as "Dry Goods Com. Merchant" in the 1880 U.S. census.[64] After the war, Charles Russell worked for the Metropolitan Board of Health in New York.[65] Whitman's favorite comrade, Fred Gray, resumed his college studies, graduating with medical degrees from New York's College of Physicians and Surgeons and the Medical School at Montpellier, France; he worked as a physician in Europe and the United States.[66]

Like Whitman, the men of the association no doubt looked back fondly on that summer they spent with the poet engaged in discussions of wartime politics and the latest literary publications. For them, those months likely came to represent a carefree interlude between youthful innocence and a Civil War that would take them far away from Pfaff's and their families. For many of the members, those months filled with what Gray called "good old times" were their last chance to enjoy the relative freedom of bachelorhood before getting married and having children or beginning their chosen careers—all of which would require them to settle down and fulfill familial and professional responsibilities.[67] Whereas Whitman's dedication to establishing associations of comrades would continue to be a lifelong love affair, Pfaff's and its social circles appear to have been more akin to one last summertime fling for his Fred Gray comrades. This does not mean that Fred Gray or his associates were less open to exploring "Calamus" affection or that their comradeships with the poet or with one another were less intimate, less homoerotic, or less meaningful in their lives. What it does suggest, however, is that they would come to see the association as a temporary community of friends at a specific time in their lives, whereas for Whitman, who wrote and reminisced about these men long after he had left Pfaff's, they represented the "Calamus" roots of what Whitman called a "City of Friends."[68] Here, a tension emerges between Whitman's understanding of the association as part of a social and sexual experiment that extended well beyond his bohemian years at Pfaff's and the Fred Gray members' seemingly more transitory view of these comradeships as representative of a particular time and place in their youth. This tension has remained pervasive in bohemian movements, which some have viewed as a developmental stage associated with young adulthood and a prelude to a more settled bourgeois existence. For others, including Whitman, bohemia has been a countercultural movement that offers a model for lasting and radical social change.[69]

Even though Whitman may not have been able to maintain contact with the Fred Gray members, he never forgot these comrades. In fact, the poet pasted two card-photographs of Gray in his military uniform inside his copy of *Prose Writers of Germany*. Each time Whitman opened this book, he was taken back to his Pfaffian days, just as he was when Horace Traubel read aloud from the poet's draft letters to Fritsch.[70] On that evening in 1888 when Whitman's eyes filled with tears after listening to Traubel, the poet was no doubt thinking of the late suppers and the barroom conversations he once had with the Fred Gray members. He also may have been thinking of how these men had given him new connections to the medical and literary communities of New York; how some offered him firsthand accounts of life in Germany and Paris, places that he would never visit; and, most importantly, how they participated in his "Calamus" experiment. When Whitman suggested to Traubel that the association was permanently connected to "Calamus," he was implying that he had come to see these poems as an articulation of the theory of adhesiveness and the Fred Gray members' comradeships as the praxis, indeed the embodiment, of that affection. There is still much left to learn about the association and its place in the bohemian space of Pfaff's, but I hope readers can now begin to see these men as I believe Whitman did—as one of the most significant groups he joined and as a set of comrades he would always want to be associated with in the minds of his readers.

NOTES

1. *WWC* 3:385; *LG60*, 341.

2. *WWC* 3:385, and *WWC* 3:367–70, 3:386–88, 3:577–81. For Whitman's draft letters to Hugo Fritsch, see *Corr.* 1:123–24, 1:125–27, 1:158–60.

3. *LG60*, 373.

4. According to Orson Fowler, "adhesiveness" was a phrenological term meaning "friendship; sociability . . . propensity to associate together" (Fowler, "Elemental Phrenology," 322). Michael Lynch argues that Whitman modified the phrenological term "adhesiveness," which meant opposite-sex and same-sex friendships, to refer exclusively to same-sex relationships (Lynch, "'Here is Adhesiveness,'" 90).

5. *WWC* 3:385.

6. For Whitman's friendship with Gray, see Blalock, "'My Dear Comrade.'"

7. From the library of Walt Whitman, with his notes and memorabilia of a former owner, John F. S. Gray. All references to Frederic Hedge's *Prose Writers of Germany* are to Whitman's notes on the early pages of his copy, which is housed in the Special Collections of Canaday Library at Bryn Mawr College. Whitman's notes have been reprinted; see Van Egmond, "Bryn Mawr College."

8. Hedge, *Prose Writers of Germany*.

9. Moon, "Solitude, Singularity, Seriality," 310.

10. For analyses of Vaughan's relationship with Whitman and his potential connections to Whitman's "Live Oak, with Moss" and "Calamus," see Shively, "Fred Vaughan," in *Calamus Lovers*, 36–50; Katz, "Sincere Friends," in *Love Stories*, 123–32; and Schmidgall, *Walt Whitman*.

11. Most of Fred Vaughan's letters to Whitman were written in 1860, and Whitman's wartime correspondence with the association's members indicates that he spent more time with them in June and July of 1862, immediately after Vaughan's wedding in May.

12. *LG60*, 373.

13. Shively, ed., *Calamus Lovers*, 43.

14. Pollak, *Erotic Whitman*, 100.

15. Katz, *Love Stories*, 128.

16. *LG60*, 373.

17. *LG60*, 341; Whitman, *Collected Writings*, 3:740–41.

18. Erkkila, *Walt Whitman's Songs*, 117–18.

19. *LG60*, 356. Betsy Erkkila reads this line from "Calamus 10" (formerly "Live Oak" VII) as evidence of Whitman's "emphasis on publicity and public exhibition" (*Walt Whitman's Songs*, 117–18).

20. Fred Vaughan may have lived with Whitman on Classon Avenue sometime between 1856 and February 1859. By the time Whitman went to Pfaff's in 1859, he and Vaughan may have lived separately. See Morris, *Better Angel*, 28–29; Shively, ed., *Calamus Lovers*, 50.

21. Roper, *Now the Drum of War*, 115; Shively, ed., *Calamus Lovers*, 48.

22. There is no evidence that Whitman attended the ceremony.

23. Genoways, *Walt Whitman and the Civil War*, 145; Stansell, "Whitman at Pfaff's," 107, 118.

24. Pollak, *Erotic Whitman*, xxii.

25. Folsom and Price, *Re-Scripting Walt Whitman*, 62.

26. Schmidgall, *Walt Whitman*, 201–4.

27. *WWC* 3:386.

28. Morris, *Better Angel*, 38.

29. "Consul-General Fritsch," *Buffalo Morning Express*, Jan. 28, 1889.

30. The process of identifying Fred Gray members reveals the extent of their social networks. By placing Whitman's letters to Fred Gray members alongside his copy of *Prose Writers of Germany* and their replies to the poet, the men's identities become clear. Several of my identifications are new discoveries: my identification of Whitman's comrade "Raymond" as Samuel M. Raymond emerges from Whitman's use of his friend's surname in his August 7, 1863, letter to Fritsch and Fred Gray's May 1, 1863, letter to Whitman, which specified that Raymond had died recently from illness during a march from New Orleans with his Union regiment. See *Corr.* 1:127; Shively, ed., *Drum Beats*, 147–49. Civil War records indicate that a "Samuel M. Raymond," a lieutenant in the 131st New York Infantry, died in Louisiana; see Phisterer, *Roll of Honor*, 133. The identification of Dr. Russel (or Russell) comes from Whitman's reference to "Russell" in his August 7, 1863, letter to Fritsch and his entry in his copy of *Prose Writers* to remember "Dr. Russel," and Fred Gray's May 1, 1863, letter to Whitman in which he describes "Charley Russel's" new position in the Union Army. See Shively, ed., *Drum Beats*, 148; *Corr.* 1:127; Carlisle, *Account of Bellevue*, 280. Finally, Whitman described Charles S. Kingsley in a notebook as "upper class" and "fond of training for boat races" (*NUPM* 2:487). There-

fore, it is possible that Kingsley is the man of the same name who helped found the Nassau Boat Club in New York City in 1868; see Janssen, "Nassau Boat Club."

31. *Corr.* 1:85.

32. "Pfaff's," *SP*, Dec. 3, 1859.

33. *WWC* 4:401.

34. Katz, *Love Stories*, 134.

35. "Frances Gray," 1–2. For an account of Gray's Civil War service, see Blalock, "Recently Discovered."

36. *Corr.* 1:124.

37. *LG60*, 345.

38. *Corr.* 1:124.

39. *Corr.* 1:158.

40. *Corr.* 1:159.

41. Ibid.

42. *Corr.* 1:124.

43. *Corr.* 2:109. Peter Doyle's long romantic friendship with the poet is well-established. See Murray, "'Pete the Great,'" 14.

44. *Corr.* 1:11.

45. The Fred Gray associates were not the first Pfaffians to advocate or participate in a radical social and/or sexual experiment. See Lause, *Antebellum Crisis*, 21–43.

46. Schmidgall, *Walt Whitman*, 202.

47. *LG60*, 371.

48. Karbiener, "Whitman at Pfaff's," 2–3.

49. *Corr.* 1:124.

50. Whitman's suggestion that he and the Fred Gray members demonstrated "Calamus" affection may help explain Whitman's August 19, 1890, reply to an August 3, 1890, letter he had received from John Addington Symonds. When Symonds asked whether "Calamus" encouraged "ardent and physical intimacies" between men, Whitman seemed to disavow "the possibility of morbid inferences." Whitman may be, as Jonathan Ned Katz suggests, rejecting the idea that the affection called for by the poems was "morbid." See *Corr.* 5:72n18, 5:72–73. For several possible readings of Whitman's response, see Katz, *Love Stories*, 280–81.

51. *LG60*, 377.

52. *LG60*, 377, 356.

53. *LG60*, 345, 371.

54. *Corr.* 1:84.

55. *Corr.* 1:159.

56. *Corr.* 1:123.

57. *LG60*, 355.

58. *LG60*, 373.

59. Whitman, Notebook LC #94, images 15 and 18.

60. *LG60*, 373.

61. For Whitman's accounts of his reunions with the Fred Gray members, see *Corr.* 1:241, 343.

62. Fowler, "Charles William Chauncey." On the death of Samuel M. Raymond, see Phisterer, *Roll of Honor*, 133.

63. "Funeral of Hugo Fritsch," *New York Times*, Jan. 31, 1889, ProQuest Historical Newspapers.

64. "United States Census, 1880: Individual Record: Benj. Knower, Ossining, Westchester, New York," accessed September 29, 2012, FamilySearch, https://familysearch.org/pal:/MM9.1.1/MZNN-XGZ; "United States Census, 1900: Individual Record: Benj. Knower, ED 102 Ossining Township, Westchester, New York," accessed January 10, 2013, FamilySearch, https://familysearch.org/pal:/MM9.1.1/MSP7-B6F.

65. Henry, "Charles P. Russell."

66. "John Frederic Schiller Gray."

67. Shively, ed., *Drum Beats*, 147–49.

68. *LG60*, 373.

69. See also Joanna Levin's discussion of the "developmental stage" model of bohemianism with regard to the all-male group Bohemian Club of San Francisco (*Bohemia in America*, 214).

70. Shively, ed., *Drum Beats*, 147.

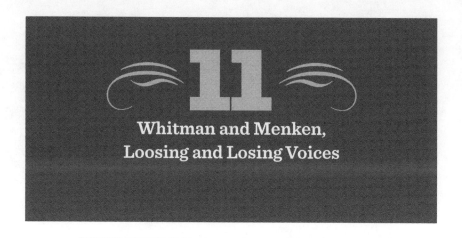

11

Whitman and Menken, Loosing and Losing Voices

ELIZA RICHARDS

Adah Isaacs Menken cultivated celebrity by assuming, performing, claiming, and repudiating multiple, stereotypical, sensational public images, onstage and off. Born in New Orleans of African American, French, Irish, Spanish, and/or Jewish descent; claiming at various times the names Marie Rachel Adelaide de Vere Spenser, Dolores Adios Fuertos, Adelaide McCord, Adah Bertha Theodore, and Rachel Adah Isaacs; married four or five or six times, to a Cuban poet, a boxer who fought in the first world championship, a newspaper editor, a Jewish musician, and a financier; moving from Texas to Cincinnati to New York to California to Paris to London; having scandalous affairs with Alexandre Dumas (père), Algernon Charles Swinburne (whom she reportedly could not persuade that "biting was of no use"), and perhaps George Sand; professing passionate same-sex love for two Mexican women (simultaneously), an Indian woman named Laurelac (when she was being held captive by a tribe in Texas), and a poetess named Hattie Tyng (author of *Apple-Blossoms*), Menken was a woman of many partial, plastic, fabricated, and contradictory identities.[1]

Unlike nineteenth-century Shakespearean actress Charlotte Cushman or Swedish singer Jenny Lind, Menken was not known for her talent, but rather for her frenetic energy, her charismatic presence, and her willingness to expose herself. A "protean comic" early in her brief career, Menken rapidly transformed herself into several (as many as nine) female and male (including black-face minstrel) characters over the course of short, farci-cal plays.[2] As a "breeches" actress, she played a male spy in *The French Sol-dier* and the male lead in a theatrical adaptation of Lord Byron's *Mazeppa*, which made her internationally famous. In that play, a Tartar prince seeks his female lover, only to be captured, stripped naked (this reveals him to be a woman to the audience though he remains a man within the play's fiction), and tied to a wild steed that climbs up an onstage mountain. He then returns in military garb on the now-tamed horse to fight for his people. One of the main draws of her performance was the rare opportu-nity to see a woman's body—in men's clothes or apparently naked—in fre-netic motion. Mark Twain, who saw Menken play *Mazeppa* in San Fran-cisco, offers a devastating description of the "manly young female" whose name was on everyone's tongue:

> in the first act, she rushes on the stage, and goes cavorting around after "Olinska"; she bends herself like a bow; she pitches head foremost at the atmosphere like a battering ram; she works her arms, and her legs, and her whole body like a dancing-jack: her every movement is as quick as thought; in a word, without any apparent reason for it, she carries on like a lunatic from the beginning of the act to the end of it. At other times she "whallops" herself down on stage, and rolls over as does the supportive pack mule after his burden is removed. If this be grace then the Menken is eminently graceful.[3]

Menken's hyperactivity captures Twain's attention not because it is per-suasively motivated by human expression; to the contrary, the whalloping demonstrates what a flexible body is capable of when unconstrained by story or character. Menken's *Mazeppa* offers the spectacle of female ex-posure with no plausible psychological motivation; "every movement is quick as thought," but not informed by thought. Renowned for her "nude" performances in *Mazeppa* (Twain explains that she was actually "dressed from head to feet in flesh-colored 'tights'"), Menken's body was the main attraction.[4] Though a number of reviewers note Menken's raw "genius," they usually mock her acting abilities.

Given Menken's role as a "shape actress" and a shape shifter, how should we read her poetry? If poetry written by women in the mid-nineteenth century was supposed to at least assume the fiction that it wells up from the inmost soul, how would Menken's audience read the work of a woman who prided herself on incoherence, who cast herself as a medium of ex-

9. Adah Isaacs Menken.
Billy Rose Theatre Division, The New York Public Library
for the Performing Arts;
Astor, Lenox, and Tilden Foundations.

posure, and who captivated her audience by acting out their exotic fantasies?[5] For Menken did persistently write poetry during much of her career, first as Alexander Isaacs Menken's devout Jewish wife, publishing in the *Israelite* and the *Jewish Messenger*, then as a Whitman–identified bohemian, publishing in New York's widely circulating newspaper the *Sunday Mercury* and in San Francisco's *Golden Era*. Despite highly mixed reviews, her posthumously published collection of poems, *Infelicia* (1868), remained in print until the early twentieth century and has been republished recently by Broadview Press, in an excellent edition by Gregory Eiselein. Part of a circle of journalists and poets who gathered at Pfaff's in New York City in the early 1860s, Menken knew Whitman, wrote a defense of his poetry, and was an early convert to his signature style of "rhapsody," as a number of contemporary commentators called it ("free verse" was not the term they used). As she was dying of an undiagnosed affliction in Europe, Menken, privileging her Whitmanian verse, selected poems for book publication; a week after her death, *Infelicia* appeared. In these poems, Menken searches for ways that "voices shall be loosed."[6] In doing so, she publicly accepts Whitman's invitation to "loose the stop from your throat," affiliating herself with the mission he proclaims in *Leaves of Grass* to identify and release voices, both the poet's and "the people's."[7] Like Whitman, in the process of finding her tongue, she sought to unblock all unjustly stifled voices—those "strong throats that are choked with their own blood, and cannot cry out the oppressor's wrong."[8] In contradistinction to Whitman, however, the poems protest fatalistically against the impossibility of that resurrection. Only, perhaps, "When God shall lift the frozen seal from struggling voices, then shall we speak!"[9] In Menken's poems, the mute paradoxically speak, only to complain of their voicelessness. And if readers choose to keep reading, they will be repeatedly confronted with the speaker's certainty that they are not listening. Proclaiming "I am dead!," the speaker in "Resurgam" attributes her condition to self-suffocation: "The red mouth closed down the breath that was hard and fierce." Though self-imposed, her silence is unwilling: "Must all lips fall out of sound as the soul dies to be heard?" The lack of a sympathetic audience stifles articulation: "Fainting souls rung out their unuttered messages to the silent clouds."[10] The dilemma of the unresurrected woman who hopelessly cries "Resurgam! Resurgam!" ("I shall rise again!") at the end of this poem is perhaps surprising, given Menken's status as one of the most energetic, riveting, and controversial actresses of the nineteenth century. Though her self-exposure sets other tongues moving, it apparently stills her own. *Infelicia* is a posthumous attempt to exhume a voice that began long before she died (all the poems were published in newspapers and magazines during Menken's lifetime).

This essay explores the ways that speaking for others and speaking for the self are inextricably bound in American ideals of democratic lyrical expression, as well as the ways that gendered cultural identities both enable and prevent reception and transmission of "living and buried speech."[11] My analysis takes its cue from Menken, for she experiments with what it means for a woman—in particular a celebrity actress who is also a "poetess"—to assume the position of democratic bard.[12] Whereas Whitman occasionally finds his throat clogged with an overabundance of suffering voices seeking expression, ultimately he constitutes his "I"—"Walt Whitman, an American, one of the roughs, a kosmos"—from the "many long dumb voices" that find release "through" him.[13] Whitman's representative "voice," in other words, is constituted through the act of speaking for others, not through speaking directly for the self. Menken recognizes that as a hyperembodied actress, she cannot begin to speak for herself until she can legitimately represent others; and yet she cannot speak for others unless she can legitimately speak for herself. Her poetry explores the reasons for this dilemma. Although, and perhaps because, she serves as a focal point for fantasies of emotional nakedness and unreserved female sexual transgression for thousands of nineteenth-century viewers and even for recent critics, that public exposure disables the powers of representative self-expression. Over and over she experiments with ways to release the voices of others—slaves, the Civil War dead, unnamed and unknown sufferers—only to find that her own voice dies with theirs. The long rhythmic lines of Whitman's *Leaves of Grass* have repeatedly been associated with his inclusive mission to speak for the people, particularly those who cannot speak for themselves. Appropriating the model, Menken can find no way to enliven it. Instead, she makes the death of his style at her hands— or more accurately, in her mouth—the subject of her verse. Her poetry therefore provides an occasion to think about whether Whitman's "free growth of metrical laws" universally enables self-expression in the service of democratic representation, or whether the same rules do not apply and even come at the cost of someone like Menken.[14] Indeed, that seems to be exactly what Menken is trying to find out by assuming Whitman's style and its accompanying mission. *Infelicia*, compiled by Menken while she knew she was dying, seeks a way out of a bind; she hopes that her death will give her poetry a new life.

Despite renewed critical interest in Menken's performativity (there has never been a lack of popular interest in the scandalous actress), almost no one has bothered to interpret the poems that were so important to her throughout and particularly at the end of her life; they are glanced over, as if unworthy of the attention lavished on her embodied work. In her cultural biography *Performing Menken*—the best and most reliable study of Menken thus far—Renee Sentilles claims that the poetry was one more act, a public performance of a fabricated private self, devised to market her theatrical career: "her alliance with the bohemians marked the point at which Menken began implying that an intellectual life existed behind the staged Menken. While the flamboyant Menken established herself through action on stage, the private self found expression in poetry and intellectual prose. Performance of a private self was a necessary part of celebrity; there had to be a private self worth knowing, or the public would lose interest."[15] Yet one more mode of manipulating and promoting her public persona, the poems, according to Sentilles, are an empty, cynical marker of introspection.

More recently, Daphne Brooks celebrates Menken's "body in dissent," while neglecting to address her poetic output. Taking the ambiguities of Menken's identity as a subject of analysis rather than as a spur to demystification (she has been reclaimed and disclaimed in African American and Jewish American literary histories), Brooks "min[es] what we might call a politics of opacity that illuminates a way to consider the performances of 'black(ened)' women like Menken who traveled through the trans-Atlantic imaginary." For Brooks even more than for Sentilles, Menken's poetry defines just one more performance of someone who "became . . . whoever a biographer, a culture, a movement, and an epoch needed and wanted her to be": "A tragic female performer punished for her personal and professional choices. An actress who doubted her morals and ethics. A Victorian rebel who actively chose a Bohemian life and subsequently served as an icon for future countercultural revolutions. A struggling poet dedicated to her underrated belles lettres. In her own lifetime and in the years immediately following her death, she has been remembered and dismembered according to the whims of paternalist cultural pundits and legendary feminist icons alike." In a seventy-page chapter, Brooks restricts her reference to Menken's poetry to the single sentence I just quoted. Though Menken "proved herself capable of mixing up, reassembling, and in some cases burning down the boundaries of white supremacist patriarchal forms in her work," this was solely a matter of public performance rather than of poetic expression, according to Brooks.[16]

If we actually read Menken's poetry, rather than dismissing it as a ruse to convince readers of a profound interiority that doesn't exist, we find that she locates the source of her troubles in her embodied performances, which she casts as self-victimizing and depleting rather than liberating, transgressive, or subversive. In "Resurgam," the Menken-identified speaker figures her living body as a deceitful corpse:

> And Death left an old light in my eyes, and old music for my tongue,
>   to deceive the crawling worms that would seek my warm flesh.
> But the purple wine that I quaff sends no thrill of Love and Song
>   through my empty veins.
> Yet my red lips are not pallid and horrified.
> Thy kisses are doubtless sweet that throb out an eternal passion for
>   me![17]

The speaking voice finds expression by repudiating its embodiment. Perversely mimicking the objectifying gaze of her admirers, Menken exposes the death-in-life that results from cultivating an identity based entirely on the desire of others. She suggests that spurring the imaginative identification of others dissociates "the Menken" from her own imagination. Their fantasies displace her sense of reality to the extent that she can no longer assert her existence, except in terms of its absence.

The critical responses to Menken's embodied work underscored and enacted this problem. Though she was repeatedly identified as a representative bohemian, and was frequently mentioned in their voice piece, Henry Clapp's *Saturday Press*, her writings were never published there. Instead, her personal exploits and theatrical performances were the subject of ridicule. In the theater column, the critic Personne (Edward G. P. Wilkins) repeatedly mocked her performance of male roles; in 1859, when Menken performed in New York, he professed fear of reviewing, or even viewing, a performance of the "crinoline warrior," for if he found her lacking, she "could, no doubt, bring a light artillery battery in the field against me, and serve the pieces herself."[18] Later, upon her departure, Personne expressed relief: "Miss Menken, or le Capitaine Menken, has left town, and the *Tribune* office still stands erect."[19] A few years later, Personne mocked the sensation surrounding Menken's doubtful marriage to and separation from the Benicia Boy (John Heenan), suggesting that Menken's acting was less compelling than Heenan's boxing despite the ways that she advertised the scandal to draw an audience to her Bowery performances: "the Girl has had several pitched battles with the old-fashioned melodramas, and a number of friendly contests with changing farces and lightweights of the *Is He Jealous* school."[20] Declining to take a sympathetic viewpoint of her performances, or even to view them firsthand, Personne forged a community of readers at Menken's expense.[21] While she may have been a representative bohemian, then, Menken was never bohemia's representative voice.

It is curious that Menken's poetry is so often ignored or summarily dismissed, since it offers the best way of studying the sustained—if conflicted, perplexing, and perhaps unconvincing—performance of interiority of a woman whose entire life was devoted to self-exposure. The public display of her body in motion, onstage and off, was Menken's primary means of essentially nonverbal expression. Her poems, on the other hand, appeared in newspapers and magazines, and finally in book form, in the United States, France, and England, unaccompanied by her physical voice or body. Nevertheless, the last time Menken's poetry received sustained critical attention was when *Infelicia* appeared, and her contemporaries tried to decide whether it was worth reading. Some, like influential feminist Elizabeth Cady Stanton, believed that the poems belatedly revealed an authentic interiority and the power to express it: "Poor Adah! When she died she left the world a book of poems that reveals an inner life of love for the true, the pure, the beautiful, that none could have imagined possible in the actress, whose public and private life were alike sensual and scandalous."[22] In the introduction to the 1888 London edition of *Infelicia*, Stanton elaborates: "Her poems are as erratic, as impulsive, as faulty, as herself. They may not have the true lyric form. The true lyric cry wails through [the poems] in defiance of form, and goes straight to the reader's heart."[23]

For others, however, the poems were mostly unsalvageable wrecks of mindless mimicry, for which Walt Whitman was often cited as the model. As one reviewer put it: "The strongest [poems], or apparently the strongest, are those in which Whitman's style of rhapsody is copied, and language is thrown about wildly, with here and there a few happy combinations."[24] Menken may have chosen to mimic Whitman in order to express her genuine depths, but in doing so she only aggravated her problem, first because her prototype was suspect, and then because she so clearly identified herself as an imitator. Another reviewer identified the problem:

> The notoriety of the author's life will awaken a degree of interest in this volume to which it is not entitled by any poetical merit. It is little more than an echo of Walt Whitman, Ossian, and other suspicious models, with no assuring proof of originality or even of sincerity . . . she unveils the secrets of her experience as unscrupulously as she went through the displays of the theater, but in both cases, one will detect a morbid love of publicity, inflamed by a passion for admiration and a thirst for gain.[25]

Menken echoes Whitman, who writes after Ossian, whose supposedly third-century Gaelic poems turned out to be the work of eighteenth-century poet James McPherson, who pulled a romantic con game. She is the last and most preposterous in a line of "suspicious models," peddling the "secrets of existence" as if they were any other commodity.

As these reviews indicate, Menken's debt to Whitman is clear; less obvious is why she claimed him as her poetic precursor. Whitman's experiments with channeling voices have long made him the medium through which critics evaluate democratic forms of literary representation in the nineteenth-century United States. Regardless of how he is cast—as the inventor of a revolutionary meter that breaks with the constraints of British tradition; as the promoter of social contract in poetic form; as a writer who grounds his inclusive poetics in transgressive principles of homoerotic desire—Whitman has persistently personified American ideals of ever-expanding and all-inclusive egalitarian promise. F. O. Matthiessen stresses Whitman's desire "to make his voice that of the general bard of democracy." For Kerry Larson, Whitman's "Answerer" is "the living embodiment and medium of indisputable Union," albeit one fraught with the very conflicts and dilemmas his "drama of consensus" seeks to avoid. According to Donald Pease, "Whitman incarnates the voice of *inter*locution," which holds "a neverending conversation" between the lyric "I" and the people's "You." Mark Maslan claims that Whitman authorizes himself by demonstrating the degree to which he invests authority in the people who speak through him. Although Jay Grossman raises fundamental questions about the politics of representation in the American Renaissance, he nevertheless focuses on Ralph Waldo Emerson and Whitman as representatives of the period, precisely because they have held that position since Matthiessen bestowed it upon them, regardless of shifting trends in literary and cultural studies. Most recently, Edward Whitley explores the work of three very different poets who "shared with Whitman an awareness of the symbolic value that came with speaking for the nation from the fringes of national culture" and who "took those aspects of their identities that potentially disqualified them from national citizenship and recast them as their qualifications to speak to and for the nation as American bards."[26]

In *Infelicia*, Menken strenuously and ostentatiously attempts the same project, only to document what she casts as her spectacular failure. Her most insightful contemporary critics identify a conflict between genuine insight and unintelligibility that helps frame her problems with Whitmanian articulations. Perplexed, they formulate a paradoxical equation in which lucid, authentic expression is poised in relation to gibberish: *Infelicia* contains verses that "show much uncultivated pathos in sentiment and senseful love of nature to have existed in the author's mind; also a wilderness of rubbish and affected agonies of yearning after the unspeakable, which achieve the nonsensical."[27] Even though Menken's utterances are marked by self-deception, affectation, incoherence, unintelligibility, and hysteria (and this is just an overview of the ways that critics express irritation and even outrage that there is no clear guiding hand or mind behind Menken's words), passages of "intense beauty" and "genuine pathos" stop several reviewers short before they dismiss the poems entirely.[28] Perhaps this is the reason, after all, for the republication and anthologizing of her verse for decades after her death, long after the sensual, ephemeral pleasures of watching a body in motion on the stage had faded. Consistent with the patterns of reception of her physical performances, her peculiar lover Swinburne told Sir Edmund Gosse "rather drolly" in 1875 that Menken was far better seen than heard: "her only fault was that she would wake up so early in the morning, and insist on reading her poetry to him. She would swing her handsome legs on the edge of the bed, till he thought they would turn into ice in the cold morning air, but the passion of her poetical rhapsody seemed to keep her warm."[29] But while Swinburne stresses Menken's embodiment in order to dismiss her poetry, he nevertheless arranged for his own publisher to bring out *Infelicia*. With nothing at stake, Dante Gabriel Rossetti urged his brother William to include Menken's work in his 1872 collection of American poetry; he said in a letter: "I forgot till this moment that your American selection ought certainly, I think, to contain some specimens of poor Menken. I have her book, which is really remarkable. If there is still time to introduce them, I would mark the copy for extract, and write some short notice to precede them, to save you trouble, as I know the book." Rossetti, like other readers, had a strong urge to separate the wheat from the chaff—"only to print the good stanzas, which make a fine poem enough by themselves."[30] Menken's fragmentary literary remains are further atomized through the selection of "specimens" based on the certainty that the whole is unsalvageable. Apparently in agreement with his brother about the odd mix of rubbish and brilliance in Menken's work, William Michael Rossetti explained in his preface that "the poems contained in her single published volume are mostly unformed rhapsodies—windy and nebulous; perhaps only half intelligible to herself, and certainly more than half unintelligible to the reader. Yet there are touches of genius which place them in a very different category from many so-called poems of more regular construction and more definable deservings."[31] This fascination with the "genius" and "genuine force" of some of her phrasing, the conviction that something compelling peeks through the "wilderness of rubbish," makes Menken's poetry a "literary problem" to be solved, rather than an unfortunate, embarrassing, and mostly failed attempt at convincing readers, too late, that a private Menken exists where there had seemed to be only appearances.[32]

Menken herself recognized the literary problem; she discusses her own bewilderment in "Some Notes of Her Life in Her Own Hand," published in the *New York Times* soon after her death. There she posits a belief in a duality of souls to explain her odd sense of two unrelated existences, one expressed through acting and one expressed through poetry:

> I have always believed myself to be possessed of two souls, one that lives on the surface of life, pleasing and pleased; the other as deep and as unfathomable as the ocean; a mystery to me and all who know me. . . . I have written these wild soul poems in the stillness of midnight, and when waking to the world the next day, they were to me the deepest mystery. I could not understand them; did not know but what I ought to laugh at them: feared to publish them, and often submitted them privately to literary friends to tell me if they could see a meaning in their wild intensity. . . . I have said this much to illustrate, in a poor way, the proof of a *double life.*[33]

Menken does not cast the problem as one of appearances and reality, exteriority and interiority, spectacular performance and genuine expression. It is the difference between an "under life," and an over life, unknown and known, unfathomable and fathomable, unconscious and conscious. She herself makes no claims to understanding what she writes, expresses a willingness to believe that the poems hold no meaning, and offers them to others for interpretation. In doing so, she follows Whitman's lead in asserting that "the proof of a poet is that his country absorbs him as affectionately as he has absorbed it."[34] But she is far less sure than Whitman that anyone might be willing to absorb her, and without that, she has no shot at intelligibility.

That mutual absorption is a stringent and difficult requirement not easily met is made clear in Menken's poems, but here too she finds her precedent in Whitman. Throughout *Leaves of Grass* (I cite here the 1855 edition), Whitman dramatizes the monumental difficulty of absorbing and transmitting "the people" through a single, martyred poetic body via the figure of strangulation. Repeatedly, "Walt" almost chokes on his conception rather than articulating it, because it is so hard to "let it out":

> Speech is the twin of my vision . . . it is unequal to measure itself.
>
> It provokes me forever,
> It says sarcastically, Walt you understand enough . . . why don't you
>   let it out then?
>
> Come now I will not be tantalized . . . you conceive too much of
>   articulation.[35]

Articulating what he has absorbed through vision almost proves too much for Walt; he conceives too much articulation and cannot let it out again. Absorbing and translating the sensory input from "the people" nearly results in a still birth and the death of the author because the enormous task of voicing them throttles the poet: "Steeped amid honeyed morphine . . . my windpipe squeezed in the fakes of death"; "You villain touch! What are you doing? . . . my breath is tight in its throat; / Unclench your floodgates! you are too much for me."[36]

Menken's stylistic echoes both demonstrate an understanding of the complex demands of Whitmanian verse and show how she cannot fulfill them. Through her long, unenjambed lines, her use of anaphora, her unrhymed, self-singing form, Menken shows that she has affectionately absorbed Whitman, but in these echoic forms she registers despair that mutual absorption is an impossibility. Menken's verse is therefore "free" only to express a kind of poetic entombment that cannot conceive of articulation or articulate conception. Most crucially, she cannot command or imagine a responding audience and therefore cannot posit an "I" that emerges from speaking for and merging with others. In the process of a totalizing negation that simulates Whitman's transient moments of creative dissolution or crisis (which in his case resolve into moments of merger), Menken explores and makes evident the stringent limitations and requirements of Whitman's "free growth of metrical laws."[37]

Menken's poem "Resurgam" serves as a singular example of this process. The title echoes Whitman's poem "Resurgemus," published under that title in June 1850 in the *New York Daily Tribune*, then in revised form in the 1855 *Leaves of Grass*, and then under the title "Europe, The 72nd and 73rd Years of these States" in the 1860 edition.[38] Inspired by the year 1848, when there were bloody revolutions across Europe, Whitman's poem imagines the "delicious" pleasure of strangling monarchs: "That brief, tight, glorious grip / Upon the throats of kings."[39] The throttling of kings is the first rendition of the pattern of choking and release in *Leaves of Grass*; "Resurgemus" was the first part of *Leaves of Grass* to be published. Regicide and revolution result in the deaths of many young men and in the birth of the democratic bard who will resurrect those who have fought against oppression by voicing their sacrifice:

> Those corpses of young men,
> Those martyrs that hang from the gibbets,
> Those hearts pierced by the grey lead,
> Cold and motionless they seem,
> Live elsewhere with undying vitality;
> They live in other young men, O, kings,
> They live in brothers, again ready to defy you;
> They were purified by death,
> They were taught and exalted.[40]

The poet's liberating expression resurrects the young men.

The solidarity expressed in Whitman's title "Resurgemus" ("we shall rise again") becomes a solitary and lonely act in Menken's "Resurgam" ("I shall rise again"), the introductory poem of *Infelicia* (it was originally published in the *Golden Era* in 1863). If Whitman speaks both for and through the corpses of young men, enlivening them and giving them presence, Menken's female speaker, an actress who is clearly identified with herself, is left to be both the victim and the savior, in an enclosed and impossible circuit. Still unresurrected at the end of the poem, the helpless woman who repeats the cry "Resurgam! Resurgam!" insists upon the mockery of justice that arises when she tries to repeat Whitman's experiments in mutual absorption and they necessarily collapse into self-absorption: "No woman has died with enough of Christ in her soul to tear the bandage from her glassy eyes and say: / *'Ye crucified me!'* / Resurgam! Resurgam!"[41] In the absence of a response, the cry becomes a bald threat: if the speaker manages to resurrect herself, without help from anyone, she will seek revenge against those who buried her in the first place.

Menken is not simply claiming that she is metaphorically dead onstage because she's acting, and acting is unreal, so she is therefore unable to release her "true" self. Rather, "self" is probably a misnomer, as the poem indicates at every turn, for the speaker's central problem is that she cannot constitute a persuasive identity. There is no self, because there is no one to address and therefore nothing to say: she cannot conceive herself through articulation. She underscores the problem by describing her corpse in precisely the opposite terms from how she actually looked. Menken was olive-skinned and dark-haired; she often wore her hair in short, unkempt curls, like a Byronic boy. She tantalized viewers with the exotic possibilities of otherness, and yet she summons a self-portrait of a blond, white woman who even death refused to kill:

> A lonely, unknown Death.
> A Death that left this dumb, living body as his endless mark.
> And left these golden billows of hair to drown the whiteness of my
>   bosom.
> Left these crimson roses gleaming on my forehead to hide the dust of
>   the grave.
> And Death left an old light in my eyes, and old music for my tongue,
>   to deceive the crawling worms that would seek my warm flesh.[42]

The golden billows of hair that drown a white bosom, the wreath of crimson roses, all suggest that the death is staged, that Menken plays the part of the corpse, and that she is dead in life, or living in death. That woman is so detached from the poem's voice that the corpse is utterly dissociated: it is not her, or it is only figuratively her, or she has no cognizance as to what she actually looks like. "Dead" here is a figure of speech for a state of mind that strands the speaker, divorcing her body from her voice. The speaker is a zombie who appears dead but cannot decay, a sleeping beauty who lies mute and warm, her body simulating and stimulating passionate desire. The alienated body Menken portrays has no ability to speak, which may be why the poem's speaking voice suffers from logorrhea, doomed to repeat the obvious:

> So I am certainly dead.
>> Dead in this beauty!
>> Dead in this velvet and lace!
>> Dead in these jewels of light!
>> Dead in the music!
>> Dead in the dance! [43]

Without access to interiority, the voice describes the body it should be inhabiting from the outside, as a tantalizing visual object that has no ability to explicate itself.

The poem blames Whitman's *Leaves of Grass* for its dubious condition. And before it accuses Whitman, it condemns his poetic progenitor, Emerson, whose "metre-making argument" and call for an American Bard, the "representative man, who speaks not for himself but for the commonwealth," so famously summons Whitman.[44] Recognizing the exclusivity and inaccessibility of this affiliation, Menken launches her complaint against the figure of Emerson's sphinx: "The blazing Sphinx of that far off, echoless promise, shrank into a drowsy shroud that mocks the crying stars of my soul's unuttered song."[45] The sphinx in Emerson's poem by the title is also "drowsy, / Her wings are furled," but she enters into dialogue with the poet before she disappears in a colorful cloud, conceding mastery to him because he had decoded her:

> Through a thousand voices
>> Spoke the universal dame:
> "Who telleth one of my meanings,
>> Is master of all I am."[46]

The master of a thousand voices, Emerson's poet can now serve as a medium for those myriad meanings. His sphinxlike poet appears in Menken's poem to deny the same legacy to her, to "[mock] the crying stars of [her] soul's unuttered song."[47]

Whitman's Answerer doesn't respond either; part IV of "Resurgam" is devoted to charging *Leaves of Grass* with a broken promise. The section begins with a celebratory apostrophe to the shapes and forms of liberty, sailing ships on the open sea, in a recognizably Whitmanian apostrophic address:

> Silver walls of Sea!
> Gold and spice laden barges!
>> White-sailed ships from Indian seas, with costly pearls and
>> tropic wines go by unheeding!
> None pause to lay one token at my feet.
> No mariner lifts his silken banner for my answering hail.
> No messages from the living to the dead.
> Must all lips fall out of sound as the soul dies to be heard?[48]

The section starts out optimistically enough, only to heighten the despair of the undead corpse on the beach that turns out to be speaking: dying to be heard, and dying unheard. Without an answering hail, which is an impossibility from the outset since the living can't hear the dead, there is no hope of poetic resurrection.

Menken goes on in the same section to reproach Whitman for her vacant lines by rewriting his:

> O Rocks! O Chasms! Sink back to your black cradles in the West!
>> Leave me dead in the depths!
>> Leave me dead in the wine!
>> Leave me dead in the dance![49]

Fragmented echoes of Whitman's verse haunt this barren landscape and superfluous plea to be left on the part of one who is already abandoned. An early version of Whitman's "Out of the Cradle Endlessly Rocking" was published in Henry Clapp's *New York Saturday Press* in 1859 (the same time that Menken moved to New York, met Whitman, and started spending time with him and other bohemians at Pfaff's) under the title "A Child's Reminiscence." Instead of the famous title line adopted later, the early version's first line reads "Out of the rocked cradle."[50] While Whitman put the cradle into continuous motion in his revision, in Menken's poem, his adjective becomes an obstructive noun, "rocks," where lives and poems are shattered, guaranteeing that she will never set her measure in motion. That her cradles are black, and that she urges a regressive rather than a future-making motion—she charges the rocks to "sink back to your black cradles in the West!"—underscores her elegy to her own stillborn metrical laws. Instead of sending a child forth to discover the bird's song, she calls for the return of a chasm to its larger vacancy. At the same time, she makes clear that while Whitman's cradles might rock for others, they didn't rock for her, and she rejects them now as a false promise of nurture. As if that weren't enough, Menken concludes the section by reworking Whitman's "frailest leaves of me" from the 1860 "Calamus" sequence (and his leaves of grass more generally) into a plea to "Leave me dead," with the same insistent anaphora that Whitman uses to chant democratic.[51] While Whitman's child becomes a poet by "fus[ing]" the bird's song with the sea's repetitive whisper of the word "Death, Death, Death, Death, Death," Menken enacts her inability to transform Death into the life of the poet's speaking voice and remains, as she was at the start of "Resurgam," "Dead to you! / Dead to the world! / Dead for ever!"[52]

In "Resurgam," Menken takes up Whitman's theme of representative self-constitution, with its accompanying threat of strangulation, in order to suggest that the lack of a sympathetic audience stifles articulation: "Fainting souls rung out their unuttered messages to the silent clouds."[53] By sounding the word "rung" doubly, Menken demonstrates to readers that self-throttling results in a painful, silent singing that goes unheard, or conversely, that lacking listeners throttles speech. This formulation is different from Cheryl Walker's idea that nineteenth-century American women poets are so mired in expectations of mediocrity that they lack the strength to find their voices. It is also different from Virginia Jackson and Yopie Prins's formulation that the generic genre of poetess poetry prevents women from individual self-expression, leaving them to mourn their genericism.[54] It suggests, instead, that no one can speak when no one will listen, and that speaking for others not only entails but also engenders self-expression. Because poetry is fundamentally communicative, it requires as well as cultivates receptive communities.

An unpublished poem by Whitman about the "beautiful young men" at Pfaff's underscores this necessity. In this manuscript, Whitman juxtaposes two vaults beneath a busy street, one where "young men" eat, drink, talk, and hail one another, the other where "the dead in their graves are underfoot hidden." Both are equally dead to the oblivious passersby, "the thick crowds, well dressed—the continual crowds as if they would never end," just as those crowds are dead to the speaker: "You phantoms! oft I pause, yearning to arrest some one of you!"[55] But though Whitman can't "arrest" the attention of the crowds, he can serve as interlocutor (Donald Pease's term) for the beautiful young underground men, commanding them to

"Drink wine—drink beer—raise your voice." His bohemian companions may be outsiders, dead to the crowd on the sidewalk, but they exist to each other, and Whitman speaks for them by encouraging them to speak. Menken may emblematize the bohemians, she may figure their outsider status, but she is not among the "beautiful young men" in the vault, however frequently she played the part of a beautiful young man. She is in the second vault, the one that is "entirely dark," the one analogous to Pfaff's but beyond retrieval. To reject poetry's communicative necessity, Menken shows us, is to locate the literary problem in the person, as her reviewers tended to do.

Menken's poetic problem is representative of women's public performance in the nineteenth century: "as plastic as wax," she only plays parts.[56] So when she stages her own utterance in her poems, she can only convey the emotional cost of inarticulation. The single recognizable sign of authenticity is unintelligibility: "the true lyric cry wails." Menken's *Infelicia* registers a particular "anxiety of reception" that is not rooted in fantasies of posthumous fame, but in a hopeless hope for posthumous expression or communication.[57] In collecting her poems for posthumous publication, she may have hoped that actual death rather than figurative Death would finally be a way to escape embodied problems of identity and to engage in pure communication, in order to gain a listener at last. That is the suggestion, at any rate, in another poem that casts Whitman as an obstacle as well as an inspiration, "Drifts That Bar My Door." In the 1860 version of the poem later titled "As I ebb'd with the ocean of life," Whitman imagines himself and his likeminded comrades ("me and mine!") as "elemental drifts": "We, loose winrows, little corpses, / Froth, snowy white, and bubbles." At the end of the poem he insists that his collectivity is gathered at the feet of the reader: "Whoever you are—we too lie in drifts at your feet."[58] However comforting Whitman's drifts mean to be, they end up blocking Menken's door, and at her death she repeatedly begs the angels to remove them. The poem begins with a plea: "O angels! Will ye never sweep the drifts from my door?" It ends with a more urgent plea, as Menken imagines herself on the brink of death: "O angels! Be quick! Sweep the drifts away,—unbar my door! / O, light! light!"[59] With the drifts of her idol and spokesman swept away, Menken might finally see the light. Associating communication with depersonification, she perhaps hopes that her book will posthumously carry her words to readers, who will then finally constitute a meaning she couldn't discern or assemble while alive.

NOTES

My thanks to Doreen Thierauf for her superb research assistance, and to Gregg Flaxman for his astute comments on a draft of this essay.

1. Gosse, "An Essay," 246 ("biting"). Because Menken was such a sensational figure, rumors abounded, and it is often impossible to confirm their verity or distinguish fact from fiction. In this case, Dante Gabriel Rossetti conveyed Menken's comment about biting to Gosse.

2. Sentilles, *Performing Menken*, 18. I draw much of the information about Menken's life and career from this work.

3. Mark Twain, "The Menken—Written Especially for Gentlemen," *Territorial Enterprise*, Sept. 17, 1863, in Eiselein, *Infelicia*, 198.

4. Ibid., 197.

5. On conventional expectations for women's poetry of the early and mid-nineteenth century, see, for example, Jackson and Prins, "Lyrical Studies"; and Richards, *Gender*. In the 1860s, even more evidently than earlier, women poets explicitly sought ways to revise and challenge these expectations.

6. Menken, "Judith," in Eiselein, *Infelicia*, 51.

7. *LG55*, 15.

8. Menken, "Autograph," in Eiselein, *Infelicia*, 107.

9. Menken, "Myself," in ibid., 70.

10. Menken, "Resurgam," in ibid., 43, 45, 46.

11. *LG55*, 18.

12. When I use the term "poetess" I'm not speaking of Menken's personal identity, but of public understandings of the figure of the female poet that shape and limit the forms of expression available to individual women poets. See Richards, *Gender*, and Jackson and Prins, "Lyrical Studies."

13. *LG55*, 29.

14. *LG55*, v. The preface repeatedly cites "the people" as the proper inspiration for the American bard, e.g., "a bard is to be commensurate with a people" (iv).

15. Sentilles, *Performing Menken*, 140.

16. Brooks, *Bodies in Dissent*, 137, 134, 206.

17. Menken, "Resurgam," in Eiselein, *Infelicia*, 43.

18. "Dramatic Feuilleton," *SP*, Mar. 5, 1859.

19. "Dramatic Feuilleton," *SP*, Mar. 12, 1859.

20. "Dramatic Feuilleton," *SP*, Mar. 24, 1860. On Menken's professional exploitation of the Heenan marriage, see Sentilles, *Performing Menken*, chap. 2.

21. I'm grateful to Ed Whitley for this insight.

22. "Adah Isaacs Menken," *Revolution*, Oct. 1, 1868, in Eiselein, *Infelicia*, 245.

23. Introduction to the 1888 London edition of *Infelicia*, in Eiselein, *Infelicia*, 252.

24. "Miss Menken's Poems," *Every Saturday: A Journal of Choice Reading*, Sept. 12, 1868. American Periodical Series Online.

25. "Adah Isaacs Menken's Poems," *New York Tribune*, Sept. 29, 1868, in Eiselein, *Infelicia*, 244–245.

26. Matthiessen, *American Renaissance*, 547; Larson, *Whitman's Drama*, xxi; Pease, "Walt Whitman's Revisionary Democracy," 160; Maslan, *Whitman Possessed*; Grossman, *Reconstituting the American Renaissance*; Whitley, *American Bards*, 3.

27. "New Poetry," *Athenaeum*, Aug. 29, 1868, in Eiselein, *Infelicia*, 242.

28. Ibid.; "New Publications," *New York Times*, Oct. 21, 1868, in Eiselein, *Infelicia*, 246.

29. Gosse, "An Essay," 246–47.

30. Dante Gabriel Rossetti to William Michael Rossetti, July 3 and July 16, 1871, in Eiselein, *Infelicia*, 250.

31. William Michael Rossetti, "Adah Isaacs Menken," in *American Poems*, ed. William Michael Rossetti (London, 1872), in Eiselein, *Infelicia*, 250.

32. Review in the *Literary World*, in Eiselein, *Infelicia*, 253.

33. "Some Notes of Her Life in Her Own Hand," *New York Times*, Sept. 1868, in Eiselein, *Infelicia*, 199–209, 203.

34. *LG55*, xii.

35. *LG55*, 31.

36. *LG55*, 32–33.

37. *LG55*, v.

38. *LG55*, 87–90; "Resurgemus," *New York Daily Tribune*, June 21, 1850, WWA.

39. "Resurgemus," *New York Daily Tribune* June 21, 1850, WWA.

40. Ibid.

41. Menken, "Resurgam," in Eiselein, *Infelicia*, section 6, 46.

42. Ibid., section 1, 43.

43. Ibid., section 1, 44.

44. "The Poet," *Emerson: Essays and Lectures*, 450. Whitman responds with the assertion that "the United States themselves are essentially the greatest poem" in his preface to the 1855 *Leaves of Grass* (*LG55*, iii); then Emerson validates the younger, obscure poet's work in a letter that begins "I greet you at the beginning of a great career" (*LG56*, 345).

45. Menken, "Resurgam," in Eiselein, *Infelicia*, section 2, 44.

46. Emerson, *Collected Poems*, 5, 8.

47. Menken, "Resurgam," in Eiselein, *Infelicia*, section 2, 44.

48. Ibid., section 4, 45.

49. Ibid.

50. Whitman, "A Child's Reminiscence," WWA.

51. *LG60*, 377.

52. Whitman, "A Child's Reminiscence," wwa; Menken, "Resurgam," in Eiselein, *Infelicia*, 43.

53. Menken, "Resurgam," in Eiselein, *Infelicia*, 46.

54. Walker, *Nightingale's Burden*; Jackson and Prins, "Lyrical Studies."

55. *NUPM* 1:454–55.

56. Anonymous, "Miss Menken's Poems," *Every Saturday: A Journal of Choice Reading*, Sept. 12, 1868. American Periodical Series Online.

57. Newlyn, *Reading, Writing and Romanticism*.

58. *LG60*, 195, 198–99.

59. Menken, "Drifts That Bar My Door," in Eiselein, *Infelicia*, 82–85.

Stedman, Whitman, and the Transatlantic Canonization of American Poetry

MARY LOEFFELHOLZ

Some twenty years after their brief early acquaintance in New York's bohemian circles, the poet, literary journalist, and anthologist Edmund Clarence Stedman produced one of the earliest major critical appraisals of Walt Whitman, published first as an essay in *Scribner's Monthly* (1880) and a few years later, with minor revisions, as a chapter in his *Poets of America* (1885). Stedman's mixed but enduring enthusiasm, and his treatment of Whitman on terms of chapter-length equality with Longfellow and Emerson, Whittier and Bryant, Lowell and Poe, gave Whitman a substantial push toward the center of the emerging canon of American poetry—the canon that Stedman's great turn-of-the-century anthologies of American literature and poetry, along with *Poets of America*, would help bring into being.

Bohemia, in Pierre Bourdieu's influential characterization, arises as a self-conscious "society within a society" when a critical mass of artists, writers, aspirants, and hangers-on converge not only in their shared ambition to make a living by art, but also in their simultaneous invention of a new "art of living," one intended to set bohemia and its inhabitants over and against "all other social categories." Bohemia's precarious, adversarial self-fashioning, Bourdieu mordantly observes, "gives rise to much investigation, first of all among its own members."[1] Stedman's pioneering consideration of Whitman's place in American poetry was just such a retrospective investigation of bohemia by one of its own former habitués: not the first or the last authored by Stedman or other frequenters of Pfaff's, certainly, but one specifically focused on mid-nineteenth-century bohemia as providing the conditions of possibility for Whitman's public emergence as a poet. It was in bohemia, according to Stedman, that Whitman invented an "art of living" inseparable from his invention of a new manner of poetry, and inseparable from his cultivation of an audience. It was in bohemia that (as Christine Stansell puts it) "the particularities of his identity and gifts began to emerge from an urban type":

> No poet, as a person, ever came more speedily within range of view. His age, origin, and habits were made known; he himself, in fastidiously studied and picturesque costume, was to be observed strolling up Broadway, crossing the ferries, mounting the omnibuses, wherever he could see and be seen, make studies and be studied. It was learned that he had been by turns printer, school-master, builder, editor; had written articles and poems of a harmless, customary nature,—until, finding that he could not express himself to any purpose in that wise, he underwent conviction, experienced a change of thought and style, and professed a new departure in verse, dress, and way of life. Henceforward he occupied himself with loafing, thinking, writing, and making disciples and "camerados."[2]

In Stedman's recollection, Whitman's bohemian persona both satisfied the curiosity of New York's "strollers and urban tourists [who] came to expect the streets themselves to provide a spectacle of urban diversities" and played to the bohemians' delight in "provid[ing] for each other a theater of democratic, esthetic camaraderie."[3] As eager as any twentieth-century New Critic to value poetic accomplishment over biography and thematic statement (not "the soundness of [Whitman's] theories" but rather "how poetically he has announced them"), Stedman is forced to see Whitman as having created "not only a poet, but a personage, of a bearing conforming to his ideal. Whether this bearing comes by nature only, or through skillful intent, its possessor certainly carries it bravely, and, as the phrase is, fills the bill."[4]

More than twenty years after coming into view, Whitman's Broadway bearing still evokes in Stedman all the "ambivalent feeling" that stems, Pierre Bourdieu argues, from bohemia's "ambiguous reality"—ambiguous in its class location and in other ways as well.[5] Stedman's sketch of Whitman's "fastidiously studied and picturesque costume" during his bohemian days anticipates Joanna Levin's observation that "the frontispiece of the 1860 edition of *Leaves of Grass*, published during Whitman's period as a Pfaffian, imaged the poet not as the working-class rough of the 1855 edition, but as an elegantly dressed, well coifed, almost dandified presence"—an emblem of bohemian "socioeconomic indecipherability."[6] Reading backward from his acquaintance with the dandified Whitman of 1860, Stedman finds even the famous 1855 frontispiece fastidiously studied in its own way, composed with "an air . . . of him who opposed the gonfalon of a 'rough' conventionalism to the conventionalism of culture. Not that of the man 'too proud to care from whence' he came, but of one very proud of whence he came and what he wore."[7] Stedman's recherché vocabulary—willfully obscure where Whitman's borrowings, like "camerados," are transparent cognates—has the 1855 Whitman marching forward under a medieval Italian heraldic city banner, still another attention-grabbing picturesque costume. Unlikely as it is that Stedman had the opportunity to read Whitman's now well-known manuscript poem on "The Two Vaults," the hypervisibility of Whitman's bohemian sociability in Stedman's essay reverses the darkened working-class ambit of Pfaff's in the notebook poem and, even more so, the silence, stealth, and invisibility attached to the intimacies of the working-class barroom glimpsed "through an interstice" in "Calamus 29." We could say that Stedman's essay on Whitman performs a kind of *outing* of Whitman in bohemia—pulling shadowed persons into the light, replacing indecipherability with brisk assertions of legibility—were it not for Stedman's insistence that this Whitman never was closeted, that he came into being as, and remained, a poet intent on seeing and being seen. Something is being outed in Stedman's essay, the knowingness of his tone leaves little doubt; but what is it?

At the first turn of Stedman's critique, the scandalous object unveiled in "Walt Whitman" is not Whitman himself but the bohemian means of his production, the invisible and anonymous hands serving him. Blessed with "the faculty of exciting and sustaining a discussion in which he has been forced to take little part himself," surrounded by disciples "vying with one another to stay up his hands," Whitman's studied idleness has a marvelous capacity to elicit on his behalf bohemia's occluded industriousness—the unconventional labors of its journalistic and literary "proletaroid intelligentsia."[8] Aware that "Bohemia at large only achieved its fame by inciting bourgeois opposition," Henry Clapp and his circle courted opposition on Whitman's behalf and happily manufactured it whenever supplies ran short.[9] Stedman's essay circles around and around the open secret of bohemia's successful marketing of opposition and its dependence on bourgeois opposition for its coherence and legibility as well as for its material maintenance. Leafing through his piles of press clippings, Stedman ventures that "three fourths of the articles upon Whitman are written by friends who assert that he is neglected by the press."[10] Stedman finds the same oppositional marketing logic at work in the 1876 outbreak of transatlantic commentary, set in motion by Whitman himself, "concerning American neglect and persecution of the poet." Averring (as did many other contemporary American observers) that in fact "Whitman's fellow-countrymen regard him kindly and with pride," Stedman concludes that nevertheless "the outcry . . . was of benefit, in showing that our writers were misunderstood, in stimulating his friends to new offices in his behalf, and especially in promoting the sale of the unique *Centennial Edition* . . . of his collected poems."[11]

This hermeneutic of suspicion, directed at exposing bohemia's economic means of (re)production and their imbrication in the surrounding capitalist economy, is not unique to Stedman but rather endemic to writing on bohemia, including writing by bohemians and former bohemians. Henry Clapp himself turned the circle of this hermeneutic a full 360 degrees in his 1858 sketch of a "little Bohemian" mosquito: like Clapp, the mosquito is a member of "the extensive class of non-producers who, though they have no objection to consuming the productions of the opposite class (without whom, indeed, they might find it difficult to live) have an elegant dislike to witnessing the processes of production"; it interrupts Clapp's nocturnal writing, companionably drinks himself sick on Clapp's claret, and leaves having taught Clapp "many good lessons" in how to evade such bloodsucking parasites as mosquitos, or one's creditors.[12] Clapp's riff on parasites and hosts, deconstructive avant la lettre, exposes bohemia's parasitic means of (re)production but in so doing exposes the parasitism of the moneylenders who finance it, all in the guise of an amusing turn away from exposing or, indeed, practicing the processes of specifically literary production. In Clapp's version of bohemia's economy-within-the-economy, all the actors take their turns as parasites and hosts. By contrast, when Stedman felt torn between his work as a stockbroker and his longing "to follow my natural bent—as a student and a writer," he privately scapegoated "impecunious writers" as parasites on both his critical and his financial enterprises: "Why is it that when a man hasn't brains enough, and pluck enough, to earn his bread—he sets up as an 'author' or 'poet'—and wants me to speculate for him?"[13] Both Stedman's genteel critical irony in "Walt Whitman" and Clapp's mordant little sketch accomplish what Pierre Bourdieu might call a "partial objectification" of bohemian modes of production within the dominant economy—that is, a partial truth-telling, one that narrows the workings of a whole social field to the interests of a single agent or group of agents: here, those of grasping bohemians eager to cash in on their supposed independence of conventional markets. Stedman's portrait of Whitman and his agent-disciples remains partial, silent with respect to Stedman's own self-interested location in the field; perhaps Clapp's satire, narrowing as it does the agency of the whole social field to a mosquito, reflects more self-consciously *on* the partial objectifications so central to the tradition of commentary and polemic on bohemia. Clapp's objectifying recognition of his own economic strategies in those of the parasitic mosquito would be echoed a few decades later by Floyd Dell's disillusioning recognition of his own "haughty and scornful" artistic self in a Greenwich Village hanger-on noted for hawking "psychic candies" to tourists: "Perhaps the imitation, like a malicious caricature, was too close for comfort."[14]

BOHEMIA AND THE CONTRADICTIONS OF AMERICAN LITERARY NATIONALISM

What makes Stedman's objectification of bohemia important is not its originality or penetration, but rather the historical standing of "Walt Whitman" and *Poets of America*, along with Stedman's earlier *Victorian Poets* (1875), as founding documents of professional literary criticism in transatlantic Anglophone letters.[15] "Walt Whitman" makes the urban bohemian poet hypervisible and subdues the person of the professional critic to an urbane voice. Notably, Stedman does not personalize his recollections of Whitman in bohemian New York or narrate or draw quotations from his 1877 visit to Whitman at home in New Jersey, as a journalist (like the younger Stedman) might have or as Stedman would in later essays on English poets.[16] Nor will a reader of "Walt Whitman" learn from the essay that Stedman was an active member of the transatlantic poetic network of friendship, backbiting, and patronage that William Michael Rossetti enlisted in Whitman's support in 1876.[17]

Holding aloof from such bohemian-style personal or parasitic networks of publicity, Stedman tacitly identifies instead with another set of actors or hosts in the literary marketplace, "the magazine-editors, to whom our writers offer their wares" and whose mixed but generally favorable reception of Whitman's work both echoes and enables Stedman's critical appreciation: "Several of them averred that they would rather accept than decline [Whitman's] contributions; they had declined them only when unsuited to their necessities. What magazine-writer has a smoother experience?"[18] Like Stedman the stockbroker, magazine editors bear risk on behalf of ungrateful authors. The editors' brisk, impersonal competence, their uncomplaining acceptance of economic necessity in their roles as agents between authors and audiences, is the closest thing to Arnoldian disinterestedness to be found in "Walt Whitman." Despite or because of his own disillusioning experience in both the literary and the financial markets, Stedman's professional identity as a literary critic takes root in service to an idealized liberal mass marketplace of letters.[19] The mass print marketplace of universal reach, penetration, and impersonal necessity, above the fray of persons and polemics because it is necessarily the sum of all of their interests, reappears sublated in Stedman's aspiration toward "the criticism which, above all, esteems it a cardinal sin to suffer a verdict to be tainted by private dislike or by partisanship and the instinct of battle with an opposing clique or school."[20]

This liberal, mass-market universalism is exactly what Stedman denies Whitman and, behind him, Whitman's bohemia. Not only did the oppositional economy of Whitman's bohemia, and Whitman's later self-marketing strategies, always depend on rousing "the instinct of battle"; in Stedman's view the fundamental appeal of Whitman's poetry is to "the over-refined and the doctrinaires"[21] rather than to the "common people, who know him so well" as a celebrity but who read him so little: "In numberless homes of working-men—and all Americans are workers—the books of other poets are treasured."[22] From the perspective of the increasingly stratified American literary marketplace of the 1870s and 1880s, bohemia's earlier efforts to "protest the widening gap between the literati and the populace" and to "affirm a category of 'literary' writing" not tied to the interests of cultural and economic elites appear to Stedman unrealized, most grievously so in the instance of Whitman.[23]

Though not universal in appeal, Whitman is nevertheless, Stedman agrees, representative—"representative and a personage of mark, if not precisely in the direction of his own choice and assurance."[24] If all Americans are workers and all or most workers treasure the books of other poets than Whitman, then Whitman's claim to be "especially national" makes him representative of the contradictions of American literary nationalism rather than the nation's direct embodiment.[25] At the other pole of what Stedman calls "the perplexing topic of our nationalism"[26] stands John Greenleaf Whittier, a "truer type of the people's poet" as measured by working-men's bookshelves,[27] by the anti-bohemian approbation of "prominent men, . . . active, practical Americans,"[28] and by his choice of ballad forms over Whitman's mannered roughness. As Michael Cohen observes, Stedman, in line with contemporary scholars of balladry like Francis Child, viewed ballads as "the people's genre, the genre that will set in motion the process of creating a national poetry."[29] Yet even Whittier's ballad poetry is "not that of the people at large" for Stedman but that of a section, New England, national only "in being true to a characteristic portion of America" and propelled to national standing by the sections' "superlative divergence" during the Civil War (which Stedman apotropaically avoids naming). Were America's sections ever fully to unite as a nation—and "whether such a faith is well grounded is still an open question," Stedman concedes[30]—Whittier might no longer seem readable as the poet of U.S. national origins. In that case, Whitman's proleptic nationalism, "forcing" into poetic form what has not yet taken political form, yielding "a disjointed series of kaleidoscopic pieces, . . . as unsatisfactory as the ill-assorted elements which he strives to represent,"[31] might still fall into its destined place. Yet the accelerating rhythms of transatlantic print culture, Stedman muses, may by that time have displaced poetry's nation-making authority—"Is a nation changed by literature, or the latter by the former, in times when journalism so swiftly represents the thought and fashion of each day?"—and leveled differences among national literary cultures: "As to the distinctions in form and spirit between the Old-World literature and our own, I have always looked for these to enlarge with time. But with the recent increase of travel and communication, each side of the Atlantic now more than ever seems to affect the other."[32] Between them, Whittier and Whitman define the extremes of a literary nationalism that may disperse before it is fully elaborated.

THE AMERICAN SWINBURNE

Where Whittier points Stedman back to a national literary field splintered by sectionalism, Whitman points forward to an increasingly transnational literary field divided in increasingly complex ways by new forms of capital, including cultural capital. Transnational by virtue of both its cosmopolitan, often immigrant inhabitants and its multilingual cultural tastes (Pfaff's supplied its habitués with the best German, English, and French newspapers), antebellum New York bohemia was a key point of origin for this field in the United States. By the time of Stedman's canon-forming critical works of the 1870s and 1880s on American and British Victorian poetry, the fortunes of bohemia on both sides of the Atlantic were tied in new ways to the rise of cultural elites partly autonomous from economic elites, concerned to distinguish themselves from mass industrial culture, and driven by their own inward-facing autonomous aesthetics of refinement upon and reaction against the burden of artistic tradition. Fronting on mass industrial literature through the labors of its junior, impoverished members, and on middlebrow social literatures of realism and reform at another interface, bohemia at its upper boundary supplied recruits to the more consecrated regions of the avant-garde and their schools of art for art's sake.[33] Joanna Levin observes that post–Civil War American celebrations of "the ideality of 'art-life'" often painted bohemia "as an ideal setting, capable of reconciling or transcending a spectrum of opposing forces."[34] Stedman's critical reading of Whitman, however, roundly rejects his bohemian claims to mediate the stratifications and oppositions of the surrounding late-nineteenth-century cultural field, the field of which the professional critic claims a more disinterested knowledge.

At once hypervisible to and unread by the "common people," Whitman is hyperliterary for those who do read him, Stedman argues, "truly the voice and product of the culture of which he bids us beware. . . . [H]e utters the cry of culture for escape from over-culture, from the weariness, the finical precision, of its own satiety."[35] Like bohemia's oppositional economy-within-the-economy, Whitman's "'rough' conventionalism" requires and refers to "the conventionalism of culture" for its legibility and its appeal to the taste of jaded readers.[36] His "irregular, manneristic chant *is at the other extreme of artificiality*" from a Shakespearean sonnet and, far from breaking with formal expectations, constitutes "formalism of a pronounced kind" (emphasis in original).[37] So far from returning his readers to "Nature without check with original energy," Whitman appears to Stedman as "the poet of a refined period, impossible in any other."[38] Representative, although not in the direction of his own choice, Whitman embodies for Stedman not the American people, but rather the internal logic of a modernizing literary field, written in and on the poet through the agency of poetic form and the medium of transatlantic print culture.

Stedman's hyperliterary, formalist, nearly decadent Whitman is less the American Adam than the American Swinburne. Odd as this homology can seem after a century and more of Adamic Whitman criticism in the United States, it was widely familiar in the 1870s, to the point that 1871 American newspaper reports of Whitman's supposed death in a railway accident blared "Death of the American Swinburne" from Boston to Saint Louis.[39] Knotting together the two poets' shared formal excesses, sexual subject matter, and suspect political enthusiasms, the less sympathetic of the newspaper stories observed of the dead and then marvelously resurrected Whitman, "Like Swinburne he was erratic and erotic, only more so."[40]

It is well-known that Algernon Charles Swinburne himself, from the publication of his poem "To Walt Whitman in America" in *Songs before Sunrise* (1871) through his ambivalent praise for Whitman in *Under the Microscope* (1872) and his slashing later attack on "Whitmania" (1887), did much to incite this homology with Whitman, and then to repudiate it.[41] Less well-appreciated is Stedman's role in closing this transatlantic circuit. Before becoming Whitman's first serious professional American critic, Stedman became Swinburne's, with the 1875 appearance in *Scribner's Monthly* of the articles on "Latter-Day British Poets" that were incorporated into Stedman's *Victorian Poets* (1875). Premised throughout on what he calls, in *Poets of America*, the "transatlantic field" of Anglophone poetry, Stedman's study makes an explicit problem of Swinburne's reception of American poets.[42] Giving credit to Swinburne for his "tribute to Poe" and "just understanding of the merits and defects of Whitman" in *Under the Microscope*, Stedman chastises Swinburne's lack of sympathy with the nationalist mainstream of American poets while borrowing whole Swinburne's diagnosis of "the unconscious formalism" that mars Whitman's poems.[43] Repeated in *Poets of America* ("Swinburne, with his cordial liking for Whitman, is too acute to overlook his formalism"[44]), the charge of "unconscious formalism" becomes "narrow formalism" in a later essay, "Some London Poets" (1882), which recounts Stedman's 1879 meeting with Swinburne and again rehearses Swinburne's quarrels with American poetry. Stedman proposes to Swinburne that "perhaps he too severely tested rhythm by his own brilliant and unprecedented method," in which formal technique threatens to overwhelm "the thought and sentiment beneath it."[45] If "incessant elevated music is sometimes more wearisome than that which has even tame and feeble passages,"[46] Whitman's music at its best shows more "strength" and "command," with "none of the persistent luxury which compels much of Swinburne's unstinted wealth to go unreckoned."[47] Stedman's criticism persistently poses the problem of Whitman's formalism through Swinburne's and the problem of Swinburne's formalism through Whitman's. If Whitman is the American Swinburne, then Swinburne is also something like the English Whitman.

Mobile and contagious, transatlantic "formalism"—the seductions of pure rhythm—links poets who should be diverging, Stedman believes, into distinct national traditions and whom we seldom think to connect today. The contagion did not stop at Whitman and Swinburne, or with Stedman's association of them; competition for Whitman's title of "the American Swinburne" was keen in the 1870s. The buckskinned, swaggering San Francisco bohemian poet Joaquin Miller was accused by the *Atlantic Monthly* of having "caught . . . the mannerisms" of Swinburne, William Morris, and Lord Byron in his strongly rhythmic Western romances and by a *Scribner's* columnist of trying to meet a "slavish" metrical appetite already satiated by "Mr. Swinburne . . . with his superbly resonant and luxuriant, anapestic, alliterative verse"; Miller's American readers, *Scribner's* concluded, have "looked for freshness, aspiration, vigor, and ultimate emancipation from fashions bred in the most sickly and concentrated atmospheres of transatlantic forcing-houses."[48] The Southern poet Sidney Lanier inoculated himself with the virus, transcribing one of Swinburne's poems alongside one of his own in a letter of 1866 to his father (with the comment that his own was clearer), and was rewarded when his contribution to the anonymous 1878 American anthology *A Masque of Poets* met with this tribute from William Dean Howells in the *Atlantic Monthly*: "There is a fine Swinburnian study called The Marshes of Glynn, in which the poet has almost bettered, in some passages, his master's instructions."[49] Swinburne himself, shown some of Lanier's poems by a mutual acquaintance, apparently declined to praise them, but the terms of Swinburne's dismissal—transmitted to Lanier as his preference for Whitman and Joaquin Miller among American poets—only serve to underscore the emergence of this transatlantic Victorian poetic constellation.[50] Twenty years after its heyday, Thomas Wentworth Higginson still recalled that in "literary London" during the 1870s "the younger set of writers . . . read Morris, Swinburne, and for a time, at least, Whitman and even Joaquin Miller."[51]

From the outset, one of the inevitable figures for this constellation was the Atlantic itself. The sea, Yopie Prins observes, was Swinburne's "recurring figure for pure rhythm"; as Lanier wrote in 1868, after the appearance of Swinburne's first volume in the United States, "Swinburne has overheard some sea-conversation which he has translated into good English."[52] Swinburne in his reading of American authors recognized Whitman above all as "a fellow seabird with me . . . I always smelt the sea in that man's books, and never in any Englishman's now alive."[53] In "To Walt Whitman in America," he looks westward for Whitman's "wide-winged word" to arrive, like a seabird, "With the rollers in measureless onset, / With the van of the storming sea, . . . / With the sea-steeds footless and frantic . . . / In the charge of the ruining Atlantic."[54] Stedman himself jumped into the figure early on with his alliterative, dactylic Swinburnian "Surf" (published in an early number of New York's new Whitman-friendly, anti-Bostonian *Galaxy*).[55] By the time of Stedman's late lectures on "The Nature and Elements of Poetry" (delivered at Johns Hopkins University in 1891 and published in 1892), this transatlantic figure, and figure for the transatlantic, was both canonical and canon-making. Naturalizing what previously represented to him the *"extreme of artificiality,"* Stedman pronounces that both Whitman and Lanier (Lanier long dead of the tuberculosis he contracted as a prisoner during the Civil War, Whitman having died just as "The Nature and Elements of Poetry" began to be serialized in the *Century*) "were moving in the same direction; that is, for an escape from conventional trammels to something free, from hackneyed time-beats to an assimilation of nature's larger rhythm, to limitless harmonies suggested by the voices of her winds and the diapason of her ocean billows."[56]

VIRTUAL BOHEMIA: AMERICAN POETRY IN
TRANSATLANTIC PERIODICAL SPACE-TIME

How did the *"extreme of artificiality"* become second nature to Stedman? The repetitive rhythms linking Whitman to Swinburne to Miller to Lanier (with frequent stops as well at Poe, Rossetti, and Tennyson) may owe less to the large diapason of nature than they do to the rhythms of later nineteenth-century transatlantic periodical circulation. With the increasing market for and professionalization of literary criticism, periodicals of established prestige competed with bohemia's endless supply of feisty newcomers for the right to *keep time* for the age—time in Bourdieu's sense, as one of the dimensions of cultural hierarchy and as the measure of distance between positions in the cultural field. "In the space of the artistic field as in social space," Bourdieu observes, "distances between styles or lifestyles are never better measured than in terms of time"; "to bring a new producer, a new product and a new system of tastes on to the market at a given moment is to push the whole set of producers, products and systems of tastes into the past."[57] Or, as the *Scribner's Monthly* columnist for "The Old Cabinet" put it in 1876, "the custom now is to 'mark the time' very distinctly." The columnist was writing of meter in late Victorian poetry, especially that of Swinburne and Tennyson, but Bourdieu himself could not have bettered his description of the nineteenth century's accelerating temporal rhythms of taste: "The tendency toward rhythm, and toward elaborate and experimental forms of verse, may be an outgrowth or a part of the modern artistic self-consciousness . . . A young poet would have to journey far away from the most potent contemporary influences"—including, inescapably, the influences of *Scribner's* own literary columns—"in order to bring back again the free, delicious minstrelsy which seems to have deserted the language."[58] Journey "far away," or, alternatively, stay at home for the canon-forming decade it took Stedman to learn how to dissolve Whitman's formalism back into naturalism.

These developments may help us understand how late Victorian transatlantic periodical space-time generated the Whitman-Swinburne-Miller-Lanier-Poe-Tennyson constellation or rhizome. Its host was the virtual bohemia of the great post–Civil War transatlantic periodicals, triangulating New York, London, and Paris—a transnational literary marketplace that replicated in a new medium the "economy-within-the-economy" of Whitman's antebellum bohemian New York. Like a wave propagating, this body reproduced itself through the "most potent" influences of poetic rhythm, mediated by the strong underlying commercial pulses of periodical circulation. When Swinburne, in "To Walt Whitman in America," figured Whitman "as the rhythmic pump that inhabits and takes possession of Swinburne's song" and, through Swinburne's urgent meter, the body of his readers,[59] he invoked figures of metrical imitation and contagion that the periodicals had already put into circulation about his own verse, and about Whitman's. Their mutual liability to parody, starting with the Whitman parodies circulated in the *Saturday Press*, is another expression of the link between their signature metrical experiments ("The entire body of his work has a sign-metrical by which it is recognized," Stedman noted of Whitman[60]) and the arts of mechanical reproduction—both those of the parodist and those of the press.

Incarnating a transatlantic rather than a national literary field, reproduced without the agency of women, this peculiar composite male body, rather than the individual body of a proto-gay man, may be the queerest object that emerges from Stedman's writings on Whitman, beyond Stedman's better-known objections to the "too anatomical and malodorous" tenor of Whitman's treatment of "the consummate processes of nature, the acts of procreation and reproduction."[61] In the eyes of nineteenth-century readers, the queerness of this composite body apparently owed as much to these poets' relationship to poetic meter as to any biographical heterodoxy of erotic practice or identification. It would be impossible to ascribe a coherent shared sexual identity to Whitman's proto-gay adhesiveness, Swinburne's murky flagellant eroticism, Miller's florid and Lanier's subdued heterosexuality, yet each in his own way instantiated for a transatlantic reading public what Victorianist critic Yopie Prins has said of Swinburne: his "perverse performance of English metrical law," she argues, "materialize[s]" Swinburne's body "as a function of meter."[62] Collectively, the entity of Whitman-Swinburne-Miller-Lanier materializes as function of the rhythmic relationship of male bodies in periodical space-time.

For a remarkable gloss on these associations, almost exactly contemporary with Stedman's essay "Walt Whitman," I turn to Sidney Lanier, whose posthumously published *Poem Outlines* includes the following sequence of prose fragments juxtaposing Swinburne and Whitman, probably written between 1877 and 1881:

[103] It is always the Fourth of July with Mr. Swinburne. It is impossible, in reading this strained laborious matter, not to remember that this case of poetry is precisely that where he who conquers conquers without strain. There was a certain damsel who once came to King Arthur's Court, "'Girt . . . with a sword, for to find a man of such virtue to draw it out of the scabbard.'"—King Arthur, to set example to his Knights, first assayed, and pulled at it eagerly, but the sword would not out. "'Sir,' said the damsel, 'ye need not to pull half so hard, for he that shall pull it out, shall do it with little might.'"

[104] Whitman is poetry's butcher. Huge raw collops slashed from the rump of poetry, and never mind gristle, is what Whitman feeds our souls with.[63]

Fourth of July fireworks that fizzle before the manly deed is accomplished; the sword pulled at, pulled at to release the "strained laborious matter," eagerly at first but then with increasing frustration; Whitman as the slasher of Swinburne's formal and sexual knot? To say no more, Lanier's flight of association offers an astonishing reading not only of Whitman and Swinburne, but also of the transatlantic world of Anglophone poetry. Americans need not travel to Baudelaire's Paris, they need only read by bohemia's gaslight to acquire a taste for the obscene, flagellant rhythmical theater of which Whitman is the master.

How is one to manage this queer collective body in the making of a canonical, pedagogically serviceable American literature? As always, the market was Stedman's universal solvent. Stedman found in Swinburne's American reception a model for the making of a transatlantic audience for avant-garde poetry, eventually including Whitman's. Recalling the furor of interest when Swinburne's *Poems and Ballads* (1866) appeared in the United States, under the racier title *Laus Veneris* (1868), Stedman observes that "the author's reputation . . . now extended to the masses who read from curiosity. Some were content to reprehend, or smack their lips over, the questionable portions of the new book; but many, while perceiving the crudeness of the ruder strains, rejoiced in the lyrical splendor that broke out here and there."[64] On Stedman's redemptive reading of American literary culture, the discerning "many" can be trusted to emerge from within the "masses." In all the world, America's universal mass public of readers is the audience best qualified to recognize the emergence of new poetry as well as the best able to reward new poets: "this is not only the country that affords [the American poet] the most practical return for his thought and song, but one that now is able and willing to open a hospitable market to all men of talent in so far as their productions can add real worth and variety to serial literature."[65]

Awareness of this great mass audience, Stedman hoped, might ultimately bring Whitman (following the practice of his English editor, William Rossetti) to "re-edit his editions in such wise that they would not be counted wholly among those books which are meat for strong men, but would have a chance among those greater books that are the treasures of the simple and the learned, the young and the old."[66] Whitman might then realize his dream to be the national poet of an "America now wholly free and interblending, with not one but a score of civic capitals, each an emulative centre of taste and invention, a focus of energetic life, ceaseless in action, radiant with the glow of beauty and creative power," as Stedman envisions the nation in the closing lines of *Poets of America*.[67] In the end, Stedman's market-based, pedagogical, and canon-forming pre-scription for American literature at the end of the nineteenth century is strikingly consonant with that of the many regional American bohemi-ans who hoped, in Joanna Levin's words, "to resist the centripetal pull of a national culture based in the Northeast," and especially in Manhattan, by promulgating local bohemias in local periodicals.[68] In Stedman's ver-sion of this future, the partial, parasitic, and adversarial urban cosmo-politanism of old New York bohemia, as Stedman saw it, gives way to the productive, decentered urban cosmopolitanism of capital; and in the market's virtuous circle of emulation we might recognize a distant echo of the mimetic desire leaping from body to body in Whitman's "City of my walks and joys!" ("Calamus 18" in the 1860 *Leaves of Grass*)—"O Manhat-tan! your frequent and swift flash of eyes offering me love, / Offering me the response of my own—these repay me, / Lovers, continual lovers, only repay me."[69]

NOTES

1. Bourdieu, *Rules of Art*, 55.

2. Stansell, "Whitman at Pfaff's," 123; Stedman, *Poets of America*, 359. Here-after cited as *PA*.

3. Stansell, "Whitman at Pfaff's," 115.

4. *PA*, 352.

5. Bourdieu, *Rules of Art*, 56.

6. Levin, *Bohemia in America*, 34, 35.

7. *PA*, 357.

8. *PA*, 350. On "proletaroid intelligentsia" in bohemia, see Bourdieu, *Rules of Art*, 55.

9. Levin, *Bohemia in America*, 55. Bohemia's championship of Whitman is now a well-known aspect of Whitman's literary emergence; see also Amanda Gailey's essay in this volume.

10. *PA*, 350.

11. *PA*, 361–62. David S. Reynolds offers a fuller summary of the 1876 brouhaha treated briefly in Stedman's essay in *Walt Whitman's America*, 515–21. Robert Scholnick's "The Selling of the 'Author's Edition'" reprints a number of contempo-rary letters by Stedman and others on the U.S. side of the debate.

12. Henry Clapp Jr., "A Night with a Mosquito," *SP*, Oct. 30, 1858, 4. See also Levin, *Bohemia in America*, 36.

13. Diary entry for July 15, 1882, in Stedman and Gould, *Life and Letters*, 1:576.

14. Quoted in Levin, *Bohemia in America*, 380.

15. On Stedman's professionalizing of American literary criticism, see Cohen, "E. C. Stedman." As Cohen observes, Stedman self-consciously claimed this title in transatlantic space, writing to Moncure Conway that *Victorian Poets* was "professional—not amateur—criticism" (167).

16. Stedman does recount his attendance in the general audience of Whitman's first public lecture in New York on Abraham Lincoln (*PA*, 391). Dated in *Poets of America* to 1878, the lecture was actually scheduled for 1878 but deferred to 1879 by Whitman's illness.

17. For testimony to Stedman's effectiveness in generating an American market for English poets and vice versa, see Cohen, "E. C. Stedman," 169.

18. *PA*, 361.

19. Stedman and Gould, in *Life and Letters*, preserve a record of Stedman's stressful fortunes in the volatile Gilded Age stock market. Like bohemia's impecunious writers, Stedman was no stranger to the economy of debt. While the lows were lower, the gains were greater in the stock market than in the literary: "Made $900. on my stocks," he crows in 1877. "Can now repay the Dodges $2,000. More of my loan, and the interest. . . . I'll bet no other American poet has *made* by his brains and audacity $15,000. the last twelve months—as I have in Wall Street, by careful risks." In the same year he records earning "the pitiful sum of $22.70 from Osgood for six months copyright on *Victorian Poets* and *Collected Poems*. The brokers congratulate me on having 'an income' outside of business!" (1:572).

20. *PA*, 26.

21. *PA*, 386.

22. *PA*, 385.

23. Levin, *Bohemia in America*, 68.

24. *PA*, 21.

25. *PA*, 21.

26. *PA*, 96.

27. *PA*, 385.

28. *PA*, 95.

29. Cohen, "E. C. Stedman," 175.

30. *PA*, 97.

31. *PA*, 21.

32. *PA*, 384.

33. See Bourdieu's classic mapping of the late-nineteenth-century French literary field, *Rules of Art*, 122.

34. Levin, *Bohemia in America*, 130, 135.

35. *PA*, 385.

36. *PA*, 357.

37. *PA*, 387.

38. *LG*, 29; *PA*, 394.

39. On Adamic Whitman criticism, see Morris, *Becoming Canonical*, 3–53. On newspaper coverage of the supposedly dead "American Swinburne," see Richardson, "Walt Whitman's 'Lively Corpse,'" 2.

40. Quoted in Richardson, "Walt Whitman's 'Lively Corpse,'" 10.

41. As Jerome McGann observed, Swinburne's "contradictory attitudes toward Whitman . . . are notorious" (*Swinburne*, 38). Terry L. Meyers argues that "Swinburne's developing coolness may have manifested a defensive homophobia," driven in part by increasing legal repression of dissident sexualities ("Swinburne and Whitman," 2).

42. *PA*, xi.

43. Edmund Clarence Stedman, "Latter-Day British Poets," *Scribner's*, Mar. 1875, 593.

44. *PA*, 386.

45. Edmund Clarence Stedman, "Some London Poets," *Harper's New Monthly Magazine*, May 1882, 881.

46. Ibid., 891.

47. *PA*, 382.

48. "Recent Literature: Joaquin Miller's *The Ship in the Desert*," *Atlantic Monthly*, Feb. 1876, 240; "Culture and Progress," *Scribner's Monthly*, Jan. 1874, 377. Joanna Levin notes Miller's early membership in the Bohemian Club of San Francisco (*Bohemia in America*, 199).

49. Anderson et al., *Centennial Edition*, 7:251; hereafter cited as *CE*. Howells, "Recent Literature," *Atlantic Monthly*, Mar. 1879, 410.

50. *CE* 9:298.

51. Thomas Wentworth Higginson, "Literary London Twenty Years Ago," *Atlantic Monthly*, Dec. 1897, 758–59.

52. Prins, *Victorian Sappho*, 166; Lanier, "Retrospects and Prospects," *CE* 5:286.

53. Lang, *The Swinburne Letters*, 1:208.

54. Swinburne, "To Walt Whitman in America."

55. Stedman, "Surf," *Galaxy*, Nov. 1, 1866, 412. On Whitman's relationship to the *Galaxy*, see Scholnick, "'Culture' or Democracy"; on the connections between the Pfaffians and *Galaxy* editor W. C. Church, see his biographical entry in The Vault at Pfaff's, http://lehigh.edu/pfaffs.

56. Edmund Clarence Stedman, "The Nature and Elements of Poetry: VI. Truth," *Century*, Aug. 1892, 615.

57. Bourdieu, *Field of Cultural Production*, 108.

58. "The Old Cabinet," *Scribner's Monthly*, Apr. 1876, 891.

59. Saville, "Swinburne Contra Whitman," 486.

60. *PA*, 371.

61. *PA*, 366. Like many contemporary American readers, including the 1882 Boston district attorney who scuttled an edition of *Leaves of Grass* on the grounds of obscenity, Stedman abominated Whitman's heterosexual vaunts without bringing into explicit focus male-male eroticism. While David S. Reynolds finds this response evidence of a culture "prudish about heterosexual love but still permissive of same-sex affection" (*Walt Whitman's America*, 540), Robert K. Nelson and Kenneth M. Price discern "veiled defamations" of same-sex love gathering strength over time and through transatlantic association, especially with Oscar Wilde ("Debating Manliness," 504).

62. Prins, *Victorian Sappho*, 151.

63. *CE* 1:260.

64. Stedman, "Latter-Day British Poets," 589.

65. Stedman, "Some London Poets," 881.

66. *PA*, 371. On the American side, Elizabeth Porter Gould's *Gems from Walt Whitman* (1889) entered this marketplace on Whitman's behalf; see Whitley, "Elizabeth Porter Gould."

67. *PA*, 476.

68. On the ways in which such regional bohemias "mediated between the national and the regional," see Levin, *Bohemia in America*, 243–44.

69. *LG60*, 363.

BIBLIOGRAPHY

Ackerman, Alan L., Jr. *The Portable Theater: American Literature and the Nineteenth-Century Stage*. Baltimore: Johns Hopkins University Press, 2002.

Allen, Elizabeth K. "Launt Thompson, New York Sculptor." *Magazine Antiques* 162, no. 5 (November 2002): 155–57.

Allen, Gay Wilson. *The Solitary Singer: A Critical Biography of Walt Whitman*. New York: New York University Press, 1955.

Anderson, Charles R., et al., eds. *The Centennial Edition of the Works of Sidney Lanier*. 10 vols. Baltimore: Johns Hopkins University Press, 1945.

Anderson, Jill. "'Be Up and Doing': Henry Wadsworth Longfellow and Poetic Labor." *Journal of American Studies* 37 (2003): 1–15.

Armstrong, Nancy. *Desire and Domestic Fiction: A Political History of the Novel*. New York: Oxford University Press, 1987.

Arnold, George. *The Poems of George Arnold*. Boston: James A. Osgood, 1880.

Asselineau, Roger. "The Earliest French Review of Whitman (Continued)." *Walt Whitman Quarterly Review* 8, no. 1 (summer 1990): 47–48.

Auclair, Tracy. "The Language of Drug Use in Whitman's 'Calamus' Poems." *Papers on Language and Literature* 40, no. 3 (2004): 227–60.

Batterberry, Michael, and Ariane Batterberry. *On the Town in New York: The Landmark History of Eating, Drinking, and Entertainments*. New York: Routledge, 1999.

Baudelaire, Charles. *The Painter of Modern Life and Other Essays*. Translated by Jonathan Mayne. London: Phaidon, 1995.

Bennett, Paula. "Not Just Filler and Not Just Sentimental: Women's Poetry in American Victorian Periodicals, 1860–1900." In *Periodical Literature in Nineteenth-Century America*, edited by Kenneth M. Price and Susan Belasco Smith, 202–19. Charlottesville: University Press of Virginia, 1995.

Bergman, Herbert. "On Editing Whitman's Journalism." *Walt Whitman Review* 16, no. 4 (December 1970): 104–9.

Berlant, Lauren. *The Female Complaint: The Unfinished Business of Sentimentality in American Culture*. Durham, NC: Duke University Press, 2008.

———. "The Female Woman: Fanny Fern and the Form of Sentiment." *American Literary History* 3, no. 3 (autumn 1991): 429–54.

Blake, David Haven. *Walt Whitman and the Culture of American Celebrity.* New Haven, CT: Yale University Press, 2006.

Blalock, Stephanie M. "'My Dear Comrade Frederickus': Walt Whitman and Fred Gray." *Walt Whitman Quarterly Review* 27, nos. 1/2 (summer/fall 2009): 49–65.

———. "A Recently Discovered Photograph of Fred Gray." *Walt Whitman Quarterly Review* 29 (2012): 99–102.

———. "Walt Whitman at Pfaff's Beer Cellar: America's Bohemian Poet and the Contexts of *Calamus.*" PhD diss., University of Iowa, 2011.

Blaugrund, Annette. *The Tenth Street Studio Building.* Southampton, NY: Parrish Art Museum, 1997.

Bohan, Ruth L. *Looking into Walt Whitman: American Art, 1850–1920.* University Park: Pennsylvania State University Press, 2006.

Bourdieu, Pierre. *The Field of Cultural Production: Essays on Art and Literature.* Edited by Randal Johnson. New York: Columbia University Press, 1994.

———. *The Rules of Art: Genesis and Structure of the Literary Field.* Translated by Susan Emanuel. Stanford, CA: Stanford University Press, 1996.

Bowers, Fredson. *Whitman's Manuscripts: Leaves of Grass (1860), A Parallel Text.* Chicago: University of Chicago Press, 1955.

Brodhead, Richard H. *The School of Hawthorne.* New York: Oxford University Press, 1986.

Brooks, Daphne. *Bodies in Dissent: Spectacular Performances of Race and Freedom, 1850–1910.* Durham, NC: Duke University Press, 2006.

Brooks, Van Wyck. *The Times of Melville and Whitman.* New York: Dutton, 1947.

Butsch, Richard. *The Making of American Audiences: From Stage to Television, 1750–1990.* New York: Cambridge University Press, 2000.

Carlisle, Robert, ed. *An Account of Bellevue Hospital with a Catalogue of the Medical and Surgical Staff from 1736 to 1894.* New York: Society of the Alumni of Bellevue Hospital, 1893.

Ceniza, Sherry. "'Being a Woman . . . I Wish to Give My Own View': Some Nineteenth-Century Women's Responses to the 1860 *Leaves of Grass.*" In *The Cambridge Companion to Walt Whitman*, edited by Ezra Greenspan, 110–34. Cambridge: Cambridge University Press, 1995.

Charters, Ann, ed. *The Portable Beat Reader.* New York: Penguin, 1992.

Charvat, William. *The Profession of Authorship in America, 1800–1870.* Edited by Matthew J. Bruccoli. Columbus: Ohio State University Press, 1968.

"Check List of General Serial Municipal Documents of Brooklyn in the New York Public Library, 31 December 1901." *Bulletin of the New York Public Library* 6 (January–December 1902).

Clapp, Henry, Jr. *The Pioneer: Or, Leaves from an Editor's Portfolio.* Lynn, MA: J. B. Tolman, 1846.

Clark, George Pierce. "'Saerasmid,' an Early Promoter of Walt Whitman." *American Literature* 27, no. 2 (1955): 259–62.

Cohen, Lara Langer. *The Fabrication of American Literature: Fraudulence and Antebellum Print Culture*. Philadelphia: University of Pennsylvania Press, 2012.

Cohen, Michael. "E. C. Stedman and the Invention of Victorian Poetry." *Victorian Poetry* 43, no. 2 (summer 2005): 165–88.

Conway, Moncure. *Autobiography: Memories and Experiences*. Vol. 1. Boston: Houghton Mifflin, 1904.

Cott, Nancy F. "Passionlessness: An Interpretation of Victorian Sexual Ideology, 1790–1850." In *A Heritage of Her Own*, edited by Nancy F. Cott and Elizabeth H. Peck, 162–81. New York: Simon and Schuster, 1979.

Cottom, Daniel. *International Bohemia: Scenes of Nineteenth-Century Life*. Philadelphia: University of Pennsylvania Press, 2013.

Cowley, Malcolm. Introduction to *Walt Whitman's "Leaves of Grass": The First (1855) Edition*. New York: Viking, 1959, vii–xxvii.

Dell, Floyd. *Women as World Builders: Studies in Modern Feminism*. Chicago: Forbes, 1913.

Dickinson, Emily. *The Letters of Emily Dickinson*. Edited by Thomas Herbert Johnson and Theodora Ward. Cambridge, MA: Harvard University Press, 1986.

———. *Poems*. Edited by R. W. Franklin. Cambridge, MA: Belknap, 2005.

Dillon, Elizabeth Maddock. *The Gender of Freedom: Fictions of Liberalism and the Literary Public Sphere*. Stanford, CA: Stanford University Press, 2004.

Dowling, David. *The Business of Literary Circles in Nineteenth-Century America*. New York: Palgrave Macmillan, 2011.

———. *Capital Letters: Authorship in the Antebellum Literary Marketplace*. Iowa City: University of Iowa Press, 2009.

Eastman, Max. *Enjoyment of Living*. New York: Harper and Brothers, 1948.

Eiselein, Gregory, ed. *Infelicia and Other Writings*, Peterborough, ON: Broadview, 2002.

Emerson, Ralph Waldo. *Collected Poems and Translations*. Edited by Harold Bloom and Paul Kane. New York: Library of America, 1994.

———. *Emerson: Essays and Lectures*. New York: Library of America, 1983.

———. *Emerson's Prose and Poetry*. Edited by Joel Porte and Saundra Morris. New York: Norton, 2001.

Erkkila, Betsy, ed. *Walt Whitman's Songs of Male Intimacy and Love*. Iowa City: University of Iowa Press, 2011.

Ferguson, Margaret. "Feminism in Time." *Modern Language Quarterly* 65 (2004): 7–27.

Fineman, Daniel. "The Parodic and Production: Criticism and Labor." *Minnesota Review* 18 (1982): 69–85.

Fiske, Stephen. "O'Brien's Bohemian Days." In *The Poems and Stories of Fitz-James O'Brien*, by Fitz-James O'Brien, liv–lviii. New York: Garrett, 1969.

Folsom, Ed. "Lucifer and Ethiopia: Whitman, Race, and Poetics before the Civil War and After." In *A Historical Guide to Walt Whitman*, edited by David S. Reynolds, 45–95. New York: Oxford University Press, 2000.

———. "Whitman Naked?" *Walt Whitman Quarterly Review* 11, no. 4 (spring 1994): 200–202.

Folsom, Ed, and Kenneth Price. *Re-Scripting Walt Whitman: An Introduction to His Life and Work*. Malden, MA: Blackwell, 2005.

Foucault, Michel. *A History of Sexuality, Vol. 1: An Introduction*. New York: Vintage, 1990.

Fowler, O. S. "Elemental Phrenology." *American Phrenological Journal and Miscellany* 2 (1838–1840): 321–34.

Fowler, William Chauncey. "Charles William Chauncey of New York." In *Memorials of the Chaunceys: Including President Chauncey, His Ancestors and Descendants*, 326–27. Boston: Henry W. Dutton and Son, 1858.

"Frances Gray." *United States Congressional Serial Set*, 58th Congress, 2nd Session, Report No. 474. Washington, DC: U.S. Government Printing Office, 1904.

Fuller, Margaret. *"These Sad but Glorious Days": Dispatches from Europe, 1846–1850*. Edited by Larry J. Reynolds and Susan Belasco Smith. New Haven, CT: Yale University Press, 1991.

Gailey, Amanda. "Walt Whitman and the King of Bohemia: The Poet in the *Saturday Press*." *Walt Whitman Quarterly Review* 25, no. 4 (2008): 143–66.

Gaston, Paul M. *Women of Fair Hope*. Athens: University of Georgia Press, 1984.

Genoways, Ted. *Walt Whitman and the Civil War: America's Poet during the Lost Years of 1860–1862*. Berkeley: University of California Press, 2009.

Goldblatt, Gloria. "Ada Clare, Queen of Bohemia." Unpublished manuscript, 1990.

———. "The Queen of Bohemia Grew up in Charleston." *Carologue* (autumn 1988): 10–11.

Gordon, Adam. "'A Condition To Be Criticized': Edgar Allan Poe and the Vocation of Antebellum Criticism." *Arizona Quarterly* 68, no. 2 (summer 2012): 1–31.

Gosse, Edmund. "An Essay (with Two Notes) on Swinburne." Appendix to *The Swinburne Letters*, edited by Cecil Y Lang. 6 vols. New Haven, CT: Yale University Press, 1959–1962.

Glicksberg, Charles I. "Charles Godfrey Leland and *Vanity Fair*." *Pennsylvania Magazine of History and Biography* 62 (July 1938): 311, 315–16.

Greenslet, Ferris. *The Life of Thomas Bailey Aldrich*. Boston: Houghton Mifflin, 1908.

Greenspan, Ezra. "The Earliest French Review of Walt Whitman." *Walt Whitman Quarterly Review* 6, no. 3 (winter 1989): 109–16.

———. "More Light on the Earliest French Review of Whitman." *Walt Whitman Quarterly Review* 8, no. 1 (summer 1990): 45–46.

———. *Walt Whitman and the American Reader*. New York: Cambridge University Press, 1990.

Grossman, Jay. *Reconstituting the American Renaissance: Emerson, Whitman, and the Politics of Representation*. Durham, NC: Duke University Press, 2003.

Gunn, Thomas Butler. Diaries (1849–1863). Missouri History Museum, St. Louis, MO.

Hahn, Emily. *Romantic Rebels: An Informal History of Bohemianism in America*. Boston: Houghton Mifflin, 1967.

Hamilton, Sinclair. *Early American Book Illustrators and Wood Engravers, 1670–1870*. Princeton, NJ: Princeton University Library, 1958.

Hansen, Bert. "American Physicians' Discovery of Homosexuals, 1880–1900: A New Diagnosis in a Changing Society." In *Sickness and Health in America: Readings in the History of Medicine and Public Health*, edited by Judith Walzer Leavitt and Ronald L. Numbers, 13–31. Madison: University of Wisconsin Press, 1997.

Harper, J. Henry. *The House of Harper: A Century of Publishing in Franklin Square*. New York: Harper and Bros., 1912.

Haynes, John Edward. *Pseudonyms of Authors: Including Anonyms and Initialisms*. New York, 1882.

Hendler, Glenn. *Public Sentiments: Structures of Feeling in Nineteenth-Century American Literature*. Chapel Hill: University of North Carolina Press, 2001.

Henkin, David. *City Reading: Written Words and Public Spaces in Antebellum New York*. New York: Columbia University Press, 1998.

Henry, Guy V. "Charles P. Russell." In *Military Record of Civilian Appointments in the United States Army*, 109. New York, 1873.

Homestead, Melissa J. *American Women Authors and Literary Property, 1822–1869*. Cambridge: Cambridge University Press, 2005.

Hough, Franklin B. *Census of the State of New York for 1865*. Albany, NY: Charles Van Benthuysen and Sons, 1865.

Howells, William Dean. *Literary Friends and Acquaintance: A Personal Retrospect of American Authorship*. New York: Harper and Bros., 1911.

Jackson, Leon. *The Business of Letters: Authorial Economies in Antebellum America*. Stanford, CA: Stanford University Press, 2008.

Jackson, Virginia. *Before Modernism: Nineteenth-Century American Poetry in Public*. Princeton, NJ: Princeton University Press, forthcoming.

Jackson, Virginia, and Yopie Prins. "Lyrical Studies." *Victorian Literature and Culture* 7, no. 2 (2000): 521–29.

Janssen, Frederick William. "Nassau Boat Club: New York City." In *A History of American Amateur Athletics and Aquatics: With the Records*, 222–24. New York, 1888.

"John Frederic Schiller Gray." In *Catalogue of the Sigma Phi with the Thesaurus*, 252–53. Boston, 1891.

Kaplan, Justin. *Walt Whitman: A Life*. New York: Simon and Schuster, 1980.

Karbiener, Karen. "Whitman at Pfaff's: Personal Space, a Public Place, and the Boundary-Breaking Poems of *Leaves of Grass* (1860)." In *Literature of New York*, edited by Sabrina Fuchs-Abrams, 1–38. Newcastle upon Tyne: Cambridge Scholars Publishing, 2009.

Katz, Jonathan Ned. *Love Stories: Sex between Men before Homosexuality*. Chicago: University of Chicago Press, 2001.

Keeling, John. "A Fourierist's Observations of the Antebellum Attakapas." *Louisiana History* 48, no. 1 (winter 2007), 69–82.

Kennedy, J. C. G. *Catalogue of the Newspapers and Periodicals Published in the United States*. New York: John Livingston, 1852.

Kenny, Daniel J. *The American Newspaper Directory and Record of the Press for 1860*. New York: Watson, 1861.

Kime, Wayne R. *Fitz-James O'Brien: Selected Literary Journalism, 1852–1860*. Selinsgrove, PA: Susquehanna University Press, 2003.

Kirwan, Andrew Valentine. *Modern France: Its Journalism, Literature and Society*. London: Jackson, Walford, and Hodder, 1863.

Krieg, Joann. *A Whitman Chronology*. Iowa City: University of Iowa Press, 1998.

Lalor, Gene. "Whitman among the New York Literary Bohemians: 1859–1862." *Walt Whitman Review* 25 (1979): 131–45.

Lang, Cecil Y., ed. *The Swinburne Letters*. 6 vols. New Haven, CT: Yale University Press, 1959–1962.

Larson, Kerry C. *Whitman's Drama of Consensus*. Chicago: University of Chicago Press, 1988.

Lause, Mark. *The Antebellum Crisis and America's First Bohemians*. Kent, OH: Kent State University Press, 2009.

LeMaster, J. R., and Donald D. Kummings, eds. *Walt Whitman: An Encyclopedia*. New York: Garland, 1998.

Levin, Joanna. *Bohemia in America, 1858–1920*. Stanford, CA: Stanford University Press, 2010.

Levine, Lawrence. *Highbrow/Lowbrow: The Emergence of Cultural Hierarchy in America*. Cambridge, MA: Harvard University Press, 1988.

Linton, William J. *The History of Wood-Engraving in America*. Boston: Estes and Lauriat, 1882.

Livingston, E. A. *Brooklyn and the Civil War*. Charleston, SC: History Press, 2012.

Longfellow, Henry Wadsworth. *Longfellow: Poems and Other Writings*. New York: Library of America, 2000.

Loving, Jerome. *Walt Whitman: The Song of Himself*. Berkeley: University of California Press, 1999.

Lynch, Michael. "'Here is Adhesiveness': From Friendship to Homosexuality." *Victorian Studies* 29, no. 1 (autumn 1985): 67–96.

Lynes, Russell. *The Tastemakers: The Shaping of American Popular Taste*. New York: Harper and Row, 1954.

Maher, Paul, Jr. *Kerouac: The Definitive Biography*. New York: Taylor Trade Publishing, 2004.

Maslan, Mark. *Whitman Possessed: Poetry, Sexuality, and Popular Authority*. Baltimore: Johns Hopkins University Press, 2001.

Matthiessen, F. O. *American Renaissance: Art and Expression in the Age of Emerson and Whitman*. London: Oxford University Press, 1941.

McConachie, Bruce A. *Melodramatic Formations: American Theatre and Society, 1820–1870*. Iowa City: University of Iowa Press, 1992.

McCrady, Edward, Sr. Papers. South Carolina Historical Society Manuscript Collection, Charleston.

McElhenney, Ada Agnes. Manuscript Collection. University of South Carolina Library, Columbia.

McGann, Jerome. *Swinburne: An Experiment in Criticism*. Chicago: University of Chicago Press, 1972.

McGill, Meredith L. *American Literature and the Culture of Reprinting, 1834–1853*. Philadelphia: University of Pennsylvania Press, 2003.

———. "Walt Whitman and the Poetics of Reprinting." In *Walt Whitman, Where the Future Becomes Present*, edited by David Haven Blake and Michael Robertson, 37–58. Iowa City: University of Iowa Press, 2010.

Meyers, Terry L. "Swinburne and Whitman: Further Evidence." *Walt Whitman Quarterly Review* 14 (summer 1996): 1–11.

Miller, Matt. *Collage of Myself: Walt Whitman and the Making of Leaves of Grass*. Lincoln: University of Nebraska Press, 2010.

Miller, Perry. *The Raven and the Whale: The War of Words and Wits in the Era of Poe and Melville*. New York: Harcourt, Brace, 1956.

Miller, Tice L. *Bohemians and Critics: American Theatre Criticism in the Nineteenth Century*. Metuchen, NJ: Scarecrow Press, 1981.

Mitchell, Julian. Papers. South Carolina Historical Society Manuscript Collection, Charleston.

Moon, Michael. "Solitude, Singularity, Seriality: Whitman vis-à-vis Fourier." *ELH* 73 (2006): 303–23.

Morris, Roy. *The Better Angel: Walt Whitman in the Civil War*. New York: Oxford University Press, 2000.

Morris, Timothy. *Becoming Canonical in American Poetry*. Urbana: University of Illinois Press, 1995.

Mott, Frank Luther. *American Journalism: A History of Newspapers in the United States*. Vol. 1. New York: Macmillan, 1941.

———. *A History of American Magazines, Vol. 2: 1850–1865*. Cambridge, MA: Harvard University Press, 1938.

Murray, Martin G. "'Pete the Great': A Biography of Peter Doyle." *Walt Whitman Quarterly Review* 12, no. 1 (summer 1994): 1–51.

Myerson, Joel. *Walt Whitman: A Descriptive Bibliography*. Pittsburgh: University of Pittsburgh Press, 1993.

Nelson, Robert K., and Kenneth M. Price. "Debating Manliness: Thomas Wentworth Higginson, William Sloane Kennedy, and the Question of Whitman." *American Literature* 73, no. 3 (September 2001): 496–524.

Newlyn, Lucy. *Reading, Writing and Romanticism: The Anxiety of Reception*. Oxford: Oxford University Press, 2000.

Nord, David Paul. *Faith in Reading: Religious Publishing and the Birth of Mass Media in America*. New York: Oxford University Press, 2004.

North, S. N. D. *History and Present Condition of the Newspaper and Periodical Press of the United States*. Washington, DC: U.S. Government Printing Office, 1884.

Odell, George Clinton. *Annals of the New York Stage*. 15 vols. New York: Columbia University Press, 1927.

Oliver, Charles. *Critical Companion to Walt Whitman*. New York: Facts on File, 2006.

Ostrander, Stephen M. *A History of the City of Brooklyn and Kings County*. Vol. 2. Brooklyn, 1894.

Parry, Albert. *Garrets and Pretenders: A History of Bohemianism in America*. New York: Covici-Friede, 1933.

Pease, Donald. "Walt Whitman's Revisionary Democracy." In *Columbia History of American Poetry*, edited by Jay Parini, 148–71. New York: Columbia University Press, 1993.

Perlman, Jim, Ed Folsom, and Dan Campion, eds. *Walt Whitman: The Measure of His Song*. Duluth, MN: Holy Cow! Press, 1998.

Pfister, Joel. "Glamorizing the Psychological: The Politics of the Performances of Modern Psychological Identities." In *Inventing the Psychological: Toward a Cultural History of Emotional Life in America*, edited by Joel Pfister and Nancy Schnog, 167–213. New Haven, CT: Yale University Press, 1997.

Phisterer, Frederick, ed. *The Roll of Honor, Officers Who Died. New York in the War of the Rebellion, 1861 to 1865*. Albany, NY, 1890.

Pollak, Vivian R. *The Erotic Whitman*. Berkeley: University of California Press, 2000.

Price, Kenneth M. *To Walt Whitman, America*. Chapel Hill: University of North
    Carolina Press, 2004.
Prins, Yopie. "Robert Browning, Transported by Meter." In *The Traffic in Poems*,
    edited by Meredith McGill, 205–30. New Brunswick: Rutgers University
    Press, 2008.
———. *Victorian Sappho*. Princeton, NJ: Princeton University Press, 1999.
Rawson, A. L. "A Bygone Bohemia." *Frank Leslie's Popular Monthly* 41, no. 1
    (1896): 96–107.
Renner, Dennis K. "Brooklyn *Daily Times*." In *Walt Whitman: An Encyclopedia*.
    Edited by J. R. LeMaster and Donald D. Kummings, 164–65. New York:
    Garland, 1998.
Reynolds, David S. *Walt Whitman's America: A Cultural Biography*. New York:
    Knopf, 1995.
———. "Whitman and Popular Culture." In *Walt Whitman: An Encyclopedia*.
    Edited by J. R. LeMaster and Donald D. Kummings, 534–36. New York:
    Garland, 1998.
Richards, Eliza. *Gender and the Poetics of Reception in Poe's Circle*. Cambridge:
    Cambridge University Press, 2004.
Richardson, Todd. "Walt Whitman's 'Lively Corpse' in 1871: The American Press
    on the Rumor of Whitman's Death." *Walt Whitman Quarterly Review* 15,
    no. 1 (summer 1997): 1–22.
Robertson, Michael. *Worshipping Walt: The Whitman Disciples*. Princeton, NJ:
    Princeton University Press, 2008.
Roper, Robert. *Now the Drum of War: Walt Whitman and His Brothers in the
    Civil War*. New York: Walker, 2008.
Russell, Gillian, and Clara Tuite. "Introducing Romantic Sociability." In
    *Romantic Sociability: Social Networks and Literary Culture in Britain, 1770–
    1840*, edited by Gillian Russell and Clara Tuite, 1–23. Cambridge: Cambridge
    University Press, 2002.
Saville, Julia F. "Swinburne Contra Whitman: From Cosmopolitan Republican to
    Parochial English Jingo?" *ELH* 78, no. 2 (summer 2011): 479–505.
Schmidgall, Gary. *Walt Whitman: A Gay Life*. New York: Dutton, 1997.
Scholnick, Robert J. "'Culture' or Democracy: Whitman, Eugene Benson, and
    The Galaxy." *Walt Whitman Quarterly Review* 13, no. 4 (spring 1996): 189–98.
———. "The Selling of the 'Author's Edition': Whitman, O'Connor, and the *West
    Jersey Press Affair*." *Walt Whitman Review* 23, no. 1 (March 1977): 3–23.
———. "'An Unusually Active Market for Calamus': Whitman, *Vanity Fair*, and
    the Fate of Humor in a Time of War, 1860–1863." *Walt Whitman Quarterly
    Review* 19, no. 3/4 (winter/spring 2002): 148–81.
Schrock, Nancy Carlson. "William James Linton and His Victorian History
    of American Wood Engraving." In *American Wood Engraving: A Victorian*

History, n.p. Watkins Glen, NY: American Life Foundation and Study Institute, 1976.

Schroth, Raymond. *The Eagle and Brooklyn: A Community Newspaper, 1841–1955*. Westport, CT: Greenwood Press, 1974.

Seigel, Jerrold. *Bohemian Paris: Culture, Politics, and the Boundaries of Bourgeois Life, 1830–1930*. New York: Penguin, 1986.

Seitz, Don C. *Artemus Ward (Charles Farrar Browne)*. New York: Harper, 1919.

Sentilles, Renee M. *Performing Menken: Adah Isaacs Menken and the Birth of American Celebrity*. Cambridge: Cambridge University Press, 2003.

Shively, Charley. "Vaughan, Frederick B." In *Walt Whitman: An Encyclopedia*. Edited by J. R. LeMaster and Donald D. Kummings, 753–54. New York: Gale, 1998.

———, ed. *Calamus Lovers: Walt Whitman's Working Class Camerados*, 36–50. San Francisco: Gay Sunshine Press, 1987.

———, ed. *Drum Beats: Walt Whitman's Civil War Boy Lovers*. San Francisco: Gay Sunshine Press, 1989.

Skaggs, Carmen Trammell. *Overtones of Opera in American Literature from Whitman to Wharton*. Baton Rouge: Louisiana State University Press, 2010.

Skinner, Charles M. "Walt Whitman as an Editor." *Atlantic Monthly*, 92 (Nov. 1903): 679–86.

Smith, Matthew Hale. *Sunshine and Shadow in New York*. Hartford: J. B. Burr, 1868.

Smith, Stephanie A. "Antebellum Politics and Women's Writing." In *The Cambridge Companion to Nineteenth-Century American Women's Writing*. Edited by Dale M. Bauer and Philip Gould, 69–104. Cambridge: Cambridge University Press, 2001.

Smith, Susan Belasco. Introduction to *Ruth Hall: A Domestic Tale of the Present Time*, by Fanny Fern. New York: Penguin, 1997, xv–xlvi.

Soria, Regina. *Elihu Vedder: American Visionary Artist in Rome (1836–1923)*. Rutherford, NJ: Fairleigh Dickinson University Press, 1970.

Stansell, Christine. "Whitman at Pfaff's: Commercial Culture, Literary Life and New York Bohemia at Mid-Century." *Walt Whitman Quarterly Review* 10, no. 3 (winter 1993): 107–26.

Starr, S. Frederick. *Bamboula!: The Life and Times of Louis Moreau Gottschalk*. New York: Oxford University Press, 1995.

Stedman, Edmund Clarence. *Poets of America*. Boston: Houghton Mifflin, 1885.

Stedman, Laura, and George M. Gould, eds. *Life and Letters of Edmund Clarence Stedman*. 2 vols. New York: Moffat, Yard, 1910.

Stephens, Louis H. "O'Brien as Journalist and Soldier." In *The Poems and Stories of Fitz-James O'Brien*, by Fitz-James O'Brien, lix–lxii. New York: Garrett Press, 1969.

Stiles, Henry Reed. *The Civil, Political, Professional and Ecclesiastical History, and Commercial and Industrial Record of the County of Kings and the City of Brooklyn, N.Y., from 1683 to 1884.* Vol. 2. New York: W. W. Munsell, 1884.

———. *History of the City of Brooklyn.* Vol. 3. Brooklyn, 1870.

Stiles, Henry Reed, and John M. Stearns. *History of the Town of Bushwick . . . and the Town, Village, and City of Williamsburgh.* Brooklyn, 1884.

Stovall, Floyd. *The Foreground of Leaves of Grass.* Charlottesville: University Press of Virginia, 1974.

Swinburne, Algernon C. "To Walt Whitman in America." In *Songs before Sunrise,* 144–45. 1871. Reprint, London: Chatto and Windus, 1880.

Taylor, Bayard. *The Echo Club and Other Literary Diversions.* Boston: James R. Osgood, 1876.

Taylor, Joshua C. *Perceptions and Evocations: The Art of Elihu Vedder.* Washington, DC: Smithsonian Institution Press, 1979.

Terdiman, Richard. *Discourse/Counter-Discourse: The Theory and Practice of Symbolic Resistance in Nineteenth-Century France.* Ithaca, NY: Cornell University Press, 1985.

Theado, Matt, ed. *The Beats: A Literary Reference.* New York: Carroll and Graf, 2001.

Thomas, M. Wynn. *Transatlantic Connections: Whitman U.S., Whitman U.K.* Iowa City: University of Iowa Press, 2005.

Tomsich, John. *A Genteel Endeavor: American Culture and Politics in the Gilded Age.* Stanford, CA: Stanford University Press, 1971.

Van Egmond, Peter. "Bryn Mawr College Library Holdings of Whitman Books." *Walt Whitman Review* 20 (June 1974): 41–50.

Vedder, Elihu. *The Digressions of V.* Boston: Houghton Mifflin, 1910.

Von Frank, Albert J. "The Secret World of Radical Publishers: The Case of Thayer and Eldridge of Boston." In *Boston's Histories,* edited by James M. O'Toole and David Quigley, 52–70. Boston: Northeastern University Press, 2004.

Walker, Cheryl. *The Nightingale's Burden: Women Poets and American Culture before 1900.* Bloomington: Indiana University Press, 1982.

Walker, Nancy A. *A Very Serious Thing: Women's Humor and American Culture.* Minneapolis: University of Minnesota Press, 1988.

Watermeier, Daniel J., ed. *Between Actor and Critic: Selected Letters of Edwin Booth and William Winter.* Princeton, NJ: Princeton University Press, 1971.

Welter, Barbara. *Dimity Convictions: The American Woman in the Nineteenth Century.* Athens: Ohio University Press, 1976.

Whitley, Edward. *American Bards: Walt Whitman and Other Unlikely Candidates for National Poet.* Chapel Hill: University of North Carolina Press, 2010.

———. "Elizabeth Porter Gould, Author of Leaves of Grass: Gender, Editing, and the Nineteenth-Century Literary Marketplace." *ELH* 75, no. 2 (summer 2008): 471–96.

———. "The Queen of Bohemia and The Saturday Press: Ada Clare's Periodical Essays and the Making of Bohemian New York." Paper presented at the Society for the Study of American Women Writers Conference, Washington State University, Pullman, October 2009.

Whitman, Walt. *The Collected Writings of Walt Whitman: Daybooks and Notebooks, Vol. 3.* Edited by William White. New York: New York University Press, 1978.

———. "Democratic Vistas (1871)." In *Complete Poetry and Selected Prose by Walt Whitman*, edited by James E. Miller, Jr., 455–502. Boston: Houghton Mifflin, 1959.

———. *"The Eighteenth Presidency!" A Critical Text*. Edited by Edward Grier. Lawrence: University of Kansas Press, 1956.

———. *The Gathering of the Forces*. Edited by Cleveland Rogers and John Black. 2 vols. New York: Knickerbocker Press, 1920.

———. *I Sit and Look Out: Editorials from the Brooklyn Daily Times*. Edited by Emory Holloway and Vernolian Schwarz. New York: AMS Press, 1966.

———. *The Journalism*. Edited by Herbert Bergman, vol. 1. New York: Peter Lang, 1998.

———. *New York Dissected*. Edited by Emory Holloway and Ralph Adimari. New York: Rufus Rockwell Wilson, 1936.

———. Notebook LC #94 (1862 Notebook), Library of Congress, Thomas Biggs Harned Walt Whitman Collection, http://hdl.loc.gov/loc.mss/whitman.094.

———. *The Uncollected Poetry and Prose of Walt Whitman*. Edited by Emory Holloway, vol. 1. Gloucester, MA: Peter Smith, 1872.

Winter, William. *Old Friends, Being Literary Recollections of Other Days*. New York: Moffat, Yard, 1909.

Worley, Sam. "Principal Influences on Whitman." In *Walt Whitman: An Encyclopedia*. Edited by J. R. LeMaster and Donald D. Kummings, 312–15. New York: Garland, 1998.

Yannella, Donald. "Pfaff's Restaurant." In *Walt Whitman: An Encyclopedia*. Edited by J. R. LeMaster and Donald D. Kummings, 514–15. New York: Garland, 1998.

Young, Robert, Jr. *Frosty but Kindly: A Biography of William Winter, Dramatic Critic*. N.p., 1956. Manuscript held at the Folger Shakespeare Library, Washington, DC.

Zwarg, Christina. *Feminist Conversations: Fuller, Emerson, and the Play of Reading*. Ithaca, NY: Cornell University Press, 1995.

CONTRIBUTORS

STEPHANIE M. BLALOCK is a master's student in the School of Library and Information Science at the University of Iowa. She completed a doctorate in nineteenth-century American literature, also at the University of Iowa, and was a guest lecturer for two years at the Technische Universität Dortmund in Dortmund, Germany. Her work has appeared in the *Walt Whitman Quarterly Review*, and she is a contributing editor for the Walt Whitman Archive and the associate editor of The Vault at Pfaff's.

RUTH L. BOHAN is professor of art history at the University of Missouri–St. Louis and author of *Looking into Walt Whitman: American Art 1850–1920* (Pennsylvania State University Press, 2006). Her articles and essays have appeared in a variety of publications, including the *Walt Whitman Quarterly Review*; the *Mickle Street Review*; *The Société Anonyme: Modernism for America*, ed. Jennifer R. Gross; and *The Cambridge Companion to Walt Whitman*, ed. Ezra Greenspan, among others.

LEIF ECKSTROM is a doctoral candidate at Tufts University. His dissertation provides an historical account of the poetry reading practices that developed out of the periodical circulation of poetry from 1770 to 1866 in the northeastern United States. He has presented papers on antebellum poetics and periodicals at the MLA, NEMLA, ALA, and C19 conferences.

LOGAN ESDALE has edited a workshop edition of Gertrude Stein's *Ida A Novel* (Yale University Press, 2012) and is currently coediting an MLA volume, *Approaches to Teaching Gertrude Stein*. His essay here on Whitman and adornment builds out of work he has done on the epistolary genre and those terms, such as naturalness and the interpersonal, that describe the inseparability of private and public. He teaches poetry and American literature at Chapman University.

AMANDA GAILEY is an assistant professor of English at the University of Nebraska–Lincoln, where she teaches and conducts research on nineteenth-century American literature, editorial theory, and digital humanities. She coedits *Scholarly Editing: The Annual of the Association for Documentary Editing*, and her work has appeared in such publications as the *Emily Dickinson Journal*, the *Walt Whitman Quarterly Review*, and *Textual Cultures*. She is completing a book about the history of American collected editions.

KAREN KARBIENER received her doctorate from Columbia University and teaches at New York University. She edited the Barnes & Noble Classics edition of *Leaves of Grass: First* and *Death-bed Editions* and has contributed to several audio and visual programs, including PBS's *American Experience* documentary on Walt Whitman. As a public scholar, she organizes events such as New York's annual "Song of Myself" marathon (in its eleventh year in 2014) and has curated various exhibitions, including "Whitman and the Promise of America, 1855–2005" (South Street Seaport Museum). She is completing a book titled *Walt Whitman and New York*.

JOANNA LEVIN is associate professor and chair of the English Department at Chapman University, where she teaches American literature and cultural studies. She is the author of *Bohemia in America, 1858–1920* (Stanford University Press, 2010).

MARY LOEFFELHOLZ is professor of English and vice provost for academic affairs at Northeastern University. She is the author of *Dickinson and the Boundaries of Feminist Theory* (University of Illinois Press, 1991) and *From School to Salon: Reading Nineteenth-Century American Women's Poetry* (Princeton University Press, 2004). She is the editor of volume D, 1914–1945, of *The Norton Anthology of American Literature*, and, with Martha Nell Smith, of Blackwell's *A Companion to Emily Dickinson* (2008).

ELIZA RICHARDS is an associate professor in the department of English and comparative literature at the University of North Carolina–Chapel Hill. She teaches and writes about American literature and culture before 1900, with a particular focus on poetry. She is the author of *Gender and the Poetics of Reception in Poe's Circle* (Cambridge University Press, 2004), and the editor of *Emily Dickinson in Context* (Cambridge University Press, 2013). She is currently completing a book on the relationship between poetry and journalism during the U.S. Civil War.

INGRID SATELMAJER has published articles on nineteenth-century poetry and periodicals in *Book History, American Periodicals,* and *Textual Cultures*; her essays also have appeared in Blackwell's *A Companion to Emily Dickinson* (ed. Mary Loeffelholz and Martha Nell Smith) and *Cultural Narratives: Textuality and Performance in the United States to 1900* (ed. Sandra Gustafson and Caroline F. Sloat). She teaches English and humanities courses at the University of Maryland, College Park.

ROBERT J. SCHOLNICK is professor of English and American studies at the College of William and Mary. He has published widely on Walt Whitman and nineteenth-century American periodicals. In addition to the essay included in this collection, he has explored the bohemian magazine *Vanity Fair* in "The Fate of Humor in a Time of Civil and Cold War: *Vanity Fair* and Race," *Studies in American Humor*, 2003.

EDWARD WHITLEY is associate professor of English and director of American Studies at Lehigh University. He is the author of *American Bards: Walt Whitman and Other Unlikely Candidates for National Poet* (University of North Carolina Press, 2010) and the codirector, with Robert Weidman, of The Vault at Pfaff's (http://lehigh.edu/pfaffs).

INDEX

THE IOWA WHITMAN SERIES

47.50